HOCKEY HALL *of* FAME
BOOK OF GOALIES

HOCKEY HALL *of* FAME
BOOK OF GOALIES

PROFILES, MEMORABILIA, ESSAYS AND STATS

EDITED BY STEVE CAMERON

INTRODUCTION BY MICHAEL FARBER

 HOCKEY HALL *of* FAME

FIREFLY BOOKS

A Firefly Book

Published by Firefly Books Ltd. 2010
Copyright © 2010 Firefly Books Ltd.

Text copyright © 2010 Hockey Hall of Fame
Images copyright as listed on page 212

First printing

Publisher Cataloging-in-Publication Data (U.S.)
Cameron, Steve.
Hockey Hall of Fame book of goalies : profiles, memorabilia, essays and stats / Steve Cameron ; introduction by Michael Farber.
[ ] p. : ill., photos. (some col.) ; cm.
Includes index.
Summary: A comprehensive collection of essays about the position of goaltender. Includes photographs and profiles of players who have defined the position.
ISBN-13: 978-1-55407-644-4   ISBN-10: 1-55407-644-7
1. National Hockey League -- Biography. 2. Hockey goalkeepers -- Biography. I. Farber, Michael. II. Title.
796.962/0922 dc22   GV848.5.A1C35 2010

Library and Archives Canada Cataloguing in Publication
Hockey Hall of Fame book of goalies : profiles, memorabilia, essays and stats / Steve Cameron, ed. ; introduction by Michael Farber.
Includes index.
ISBN-13: 978-1-55407-644-4   ISBN-10: 1-55407-644-7
1. Hockey goalkeepers--Miscellanea. 2. Hockey--Goalkeeping--Miscellanea. 3. National Hockey League--Miscellanea.
I. Cameron, Steve, 1981-
GV848.76.H63 2010 796.962'270922 C2010-903992-0

Published in the United States by
Firefly Books (U.S.) Inc.
P.O. Box 1338, Ellicott Station
Buffalo, New York 14205

Published in Canada by
Firefly Books Ltd.
66 Leek Crescent
Richmond Hill, Ontario L4B 1H1

Cover and interior design by Jamie Hodgson/studio34design.ca

Printed in Canada

The publisher gratefully acknowledges the financial support for our publishing program by the Canada Book Fund as administered by the Department of Canadian Heritage.

Page 2: The inside label of Gerry Cheevers Kenesky pads from the 1975–76 AHL season.

Page 5: Johnny Bower's pads that he wore throughout the 1960's with the Toronto Maple Leafs.

Page 7: The toes of Réjean Lemelin's Lowson synthetic pads that he first wore in 1986–87.

CONTENTS

INTRODUCTION

BY MICHAEL FARBER

I N THE 1970s, a lion-masked kook of a goaltender named Gilles Gratton haunted the National Hockey League and World Hockey Association. I've chosen "haunted" because Gratton, better known as "The Count," professed a belief in reincarnation. In one of his previous lives, Gratton insisted, he had been a 16th-century Spanish nobleman.

The Count laid it all out during the 1976–77 season in a joint question-and-answer session with the New York Rangers and New York Knicks at Madison Square Garden for the enlightenment of major corporate sponsors. To the astonishment of emcee Marv Albert and the assorted mucky-mucks, Gratton explained that in the 16th century, while pulling Iberian royalty duty, he amused himself by lining commoners up against a wall and stoning them.

"God has taken his revenge," he told the crowd, in apparent seriousness. "Now I am a goaltender." Alas, Gratton quit after one game in the minors the following season — his abrupt retirement marking the first day of the rest of his lives.

Many of the stereotypes about goalies have changed since The Count's comet briefly arced over the professional hockey landscape. Today's generation of netminders isn't your father's: The modern goalie is no longer the ex-fat kid who was stuck in net because he was not fit enough to play anywhere else; nor is he the guy who practically needed cheese cutters to skate. He also hasn't learned to play the position by thumbing through a dog-eared copy of Jacques Plante's book, *On Goaltending*.

The modern goalie is, instead, a well-conditioned athlete who is often one of the strongest skaters on the team, and certainly one of the most rigorously coached players. In fact, goal is now the most coached position in hockey; and there are, by last check, no left-wing coaches or summer hockey schools dedicated to right wingers.

Gilles Gratton's famous snarling cat mask.

But, as much as the conventional wisdom about the position has evolved in the past 30 years, one thing hasn't. Refracted through the prism of all those "part-timers," (the forwards and defensemen who talk big about "playing 60 minutes" but who spend less than half of the game on the ice), goalies are still regarded with a degree of caution and sometimes amusement. They remain "The Count's sons," at least spiritually. Of course this unenlightened view is tempered with a degree of respect because even fourth-line grinders know goaltending is 70 percent of hockey, unless, of course, your team isn't getting any, in which case it's 100 percent. Says Buffalo Sabre center, Derek Roy, "I definitely will never say anything bad about goalies because mostly they're covering up for our mistakes."

Brian Hayward shared the William M. Jennings Trophy three times as Patrick Roy's partner with the Montreal Canadiens in the late 1980s, which makes him a competent authority on the position and the seeming oddball comportment it propagates. He thinks skaters view goalies suspiciously out of ignorance — the root of most prejudice. Hayward estimates 90 percent of NHL players have zero grasp of the position, which is why a goalie might be screaming about crashing the opposing net or getting in on the forecheck, but no forward will ever offer his goalie even a sliver of advice.

Maybe forwards are better seen than heard, because the goaltending position, dripping with nuance, truly is beyond their grasp. Ex-NHL goalie Glenn Healy, now, like Hayward, a TV analyst, recalls studying videotape of everything from a shooter's angle on tip-ins to the color of tape on the stick knob in case a player had recently changed it (an indication of a slump). "My guess is Tie Domi might have known whether a [goalie caught] right-handed or left-handed," Healy says, "but that's about it."

In a typical 25-save night, a goalie might make 100 distinct movements: preparing for blocked shots, faked shots, shots that miss the net, angled passes that require an explosive burst across the crease, not to mention all the puck-handling and puck-moving responsibilities that come with being the last line of defense. The iconic image of Ken Dryden leaning on his goal stick and gazing godlike

out at the play might have been applicable to the Canadiens of the late 1970s — dynastic teams that provided goalies with their healthy share of Maytag repairman moments — but he was an anomaly in the hyperventilating world of modern hockey. Suggests Sabres' goalie coach Jim Corsi, "There has to be an outlet for all the pent-up energy, for the frenetic nature of the job. Some goalies adopt weird ways. Some are just crazy."

That word, again, in its pejorative splendor. Even a former goaltender like Corsi, deeply embedded in the fraternity, can wallow in the stereotype: goalies are "flakes," or someone "is normal — for a goalie." This is shameless profiling, one rooted in an absolute historical truth.

Tending a net prior to November 1, 1959, when Plante defied Canadiens' coach Toe Blake and wore a crude mask in a game, meant a man had to have been a few strands shy of a comb-over to willingly stand between the pipes. For those seeking a lobotomy, common sense suggested it should have been performed by something other than a streaking vulcanized-rubber disc one inch thick and three inches in diameter.

Glenn Hall, whose brilliant NHL career began in 1952–53, was said to have hated training camp. The reason: training camp is where all the slapshots were.

Crazy? This is the zenith of rationality.

But even the widespread adoption of the mask in the decade following Plante's rebellion, which was supposed to eliminate the fear factor that induced Plante to knit and Hall to toss his lunch before every game, was hardly a panacea for the brave souls who played goal. While Bobby Hull and Stan Mikita were curving the blades of their sticks into missile launchers, the men charged with foiling them were practically naked. St. Louis Blues president John Davidson, who shared the New York goaltending job with The Count, remembers playing back-to-back games, with 50-plus-shots in each, against the Flyers in the late 1970s. After the second match, the Rangers' physician pulled Davidson aside and asked him to report to the medical room at 10 a.m. the next day. The doctor had noticed the deep bruises that had turned Davidson's torso into a painted sunset of purples and yellows and wanted to run tests for leukemia. The goalie bridled. He held up his chest protector and shin guards and said no, he didn't need any blood work, but he sure could use some protective gear that didn't look like prizes out of a Cracker Jack box.

Thirty years on, goalie equipment has caught up and kept pace with the technological revolution in sticks. Now a goalie is as likely to bruise his ego as injure anything else. Sure, perils persist — Al MacInnis slappers got Jocelyn Thibault (broken finger), Chris Osgood (broken hand) and Rich Parent (bruised testicle) in one season — but goalies have lost the terror. They are allowed to be normal now … and not even "normal — for a goalie."

"My cousin Taylor and I are the goalies among a lot of forwards and defensemen in our family, and they still hit us with the obvious clichés," says Buffalo's Ryan Miller, the leading American-born goalie from the distinguished Michigan State University hockey clan. "I realize goalies got the reputation back in the day because they were the ones willing to take a puck off the face " to take some stitches for the team. They probably did have to have a screw loose. But you look around the rinks now, around the dressing rooms, and guys pretty much blend. I don't think they can give us a hard time about being different."

But goalies will always be "different." Even a cursory glance can confirm that. They sport different jerseys, wield a different stick, wear specialized skates and get to tug on a mask that might be a museum-caliber work of art. Everything about the goalie screams look at me. Even dull-witted enforcers can't miss the egocentric nature of the position, which, in 2010, is more likely to attract the kid desirous of attention rather than the one with the poor stride. The inherently negative nature of the job — basically, all a goalie tries to do is say "no" to shooters — is a control issue for Miller, akin to who gets the remote or who makes the final call when the family is debating Chinese takeout or pizza. "I'm obsessive-compulsive in that way," Miller says. "Maybe that relates to some psychosocial thing where, when interacting with a group, you have to have control. At least I get the last word on the defensive side of the puck." Smart, self-aware guy that Miller.

The introspection, not to mention the conspicuous tics, is why Derek Roy says skaters are only too happy to leave goaltenders alone. They can be finicky. Patrick Roy talked to his goal posts early in his Hall of Fame career and never wittingly stepped on the blue or red line. Eddie Belfour's pre-practice routine was so involved that former Dallas Stars' coach Ken Hitchcock had to push back the long-standing start time to accommodate his goalie. Jeff Hackett was paranoid that a teammate might touch his gear in the dressing room. Roman Cechmanek might not have had any of these particular predilections but every match seemed to be Mr. Toad's Wild Ride for the Czech goaltender, including a memorable 2003 playoff game for Philadelphia against Toronto when he ignored the puck to pick up the trapper he had dropped and ceded a goal. A newspaper columnist in the City of Brotherly Love made a snap medical diagnosis and labeled Cechmanek the "bipolar goaler."

"As much as we might like to think that we're viewed as just hockey players, there is something different about guys who know their mistakes are going to end up on the scoreboard," Healy says. "I remember when I was with [the Maple Leafs]. We'd be on the team charter, and [Curtis Joseph] would be studying these horseracing books about breeding and bloodlines. So there's one guy discussing horse semen while the other guy, me, would have an electronic bagpipe chanter, playing and trying to write tunes. At the time I'm thinking there can't be two quirkier goalies in the league.

"But honestly, you can't blame all this on us. Blame our parents. I mean, when we were seven, why did our parents allow us to become a goalie? What were they thinking? They wouldn't let us drive at that age. Why would they let us go in nets? They could have easily persuaded [us] not to play goal if they had promised to take [us] to Dairy Queen. 'I'll buy you a DQ if you agree not to play goal.'" For Healy, his NHL career apparently hinged on soft ice cream — on any given sundae.

So in honor of Gilles "The Count" Gratton and all those before him and since — who persevered beyond the lure of soft serve and the stigma of being a few fries short of a Happy Meal — immerse yourself in the culture, legend and lore of the best goalies the game has ever seen.

Pioneer Puckstoppers

BY CHRIS MCDONELL

EVEN IN THE GAME'S INFANCY, the goalie played a special role, but hockey's goaltending pioneers donned only the most rudimentary equipment to help them do their job. The pioneer goalie's equipment certainly bore little resemblance to the dazzlingly well-armored gladiators who patrol the blue paint today. In team photographs from the first quarter of the 20th century, which player is the goalie is not immediately obvious. Only his beefed-up goal stick and narrow leg pads borrowed from the sport of cricket make him different.

Until 1915 a goalie's gloves were simply the five-fingered variety that the rest of his team wore; the catcher and blocker were still years away from being standard gear. Masks were for bandits, not athletes, and specially reinforced skates, pants, chest and arm protectors came much later. The netminder's stick was his most important tool, and it was generally held with both hands to deflect and sweep pucks away from the net.

A number of rules made goaltending much different from how we now know it today: the goalie could not legally fall to the ice to make a save until the NHL's inaugural 1917–18 season and could not grab the puck and hold it for a faceoff for several decades more. Many of the men from this era have long since faded into history, even for the most passionate of fans. Yet those enshrined in the Hockey Hall of Fame live on there as hockey gods. Georges Vezina is an exception, immortalized before his induction when the award for the NHL's top netminder was named in his honor, but in his day he had peers who were considered his equal, or better. Here are all their stories, testimonies of how the best goalies have always done whatever is necessary — even if it means bending the rules — to keep the puck out of the net.

One of the earliest NHL game-action photographs in the Hockey Hall of Fame collection. This shot captures Chicago's Chuck Gardiner making a diving save during a game against the Detroit Falcons in 1931.

CLINT
BENEDICT

INDUCTED 1965

BENEDICT

A TRUE GOALTENDING PIONEER, Clint Benedict is most frequently remembered today as the answer to a trivia question: "Who was the first netminder to don a face mask?"

Late in his stellar career, during the 1929–30 season, Benedict took a hard shot to the nose from Montreal Canadiens' superstar Howie Morenz. "I saw it at the last, split second and lunged," recalled Benedict. "Wham, I'm out like a light and wake up in the hospital." Accustomed to playing injured, Benedict returned to action with the Montreal Maroons a month later wearing the NHL's first mask. The leather contraption offered no eye protection to speak of, but covered his injured proboscis effectively. Unfortunately, it obscured his vision on low shots and Benedict abandoned the mask after five games. Later that season, barefaced Benedict took another Morenz shot to the throat, effectively ending his NHL career. It would be 30 more years before another NHL goalie donned a mask, when the Canadiens' Jacques Plante gave the protective equipment an improved design, and the mask arrived to stay.

Benedict's more lasting contribution to the game was his role in changing the rule restricting goalies to a standing position at all times. His effective strategy of "accidentally" falling to the ice in order to make a save or smother the puck led to his famous nickname, "Praying Benny." His tumbling act also led the NHL to change the game's rule halfway through the league's inaugural 1917–18 season. Previously, a goalie was assessed a penalty for dropping to the ice. "You had to do something," said Benedict. "Quite a few of the players could put a curving drop on a shot, and the equipment wasn't exactly the greatest in those days." With the new rule in place, Benedict took to the ice at will.

Benedict, an Ottawa native, got an early start in the game and showed steady and rapid improvement. At age 15, he moved into senior hockey and at 20 joined the Ottawa Senators of the National Hockey Association (the forerunner of the NHL). In 1915, he was with the Senators when they lost the Stanley Cup final to the Vancouver Millionaires, but he stuck with the Ottawa club through the formation of the NHL and Stanley Cup victories in 1920, 1921 and 1923. Sold to the NHL's new entry, the Montreal Maroons, on October 20, 1924, he led his club to Stanley Cup victory in the 1925–26 season with four playoff shutouts and a sterling 1.00 goals-against average — the first goalie to backstop two different Cup-winning NHL teams.

In 1919–20, Benedict's 2.66 goals-against average was more than two goals less than the league average, a difference that has never been bettered. In six of seven NHL seasons with Ottawa, he led the league in wins, with the lowest goals-against average in five of those campaigns. He also posted the NHL's lowest goals-against average with the Maroons in 1926–27.

Clint Benedict retired with 58 NHL career shutouts and played one final pro season (1930–31) with the Windsor Bulldogs in the IAHL before retiring for good.

CONNELL

ALEX
CONNELL
INDUCTED 1958

IT'S SAID THAT Alex Connell played goal for the first time while stationed at Kingston during World War I. Since he could not skate, he had no option but to be the team's goaltender. True or not, Connell was an all-round athlete who excelled at baseball, lacrosse and football as well as hockey. He joined the Kingston Frontenacs Juniors of the Ontario Hockey Association in 1917 before moving to the Ottawa City League in 1919. After five years in the Canadian capital, "The Ottawa Fireman" (he was secretary of the city's fire department) made his NHL debut with the Ottawa Senators in 1924–25 as a free agent and he showed enough promise that Ottawa sold superstar goalie Clint Benedict to the Montreal Maroons. Connell did not disappoint, establishing himself as the league's premier goalie over the next decade. His career 1.91 goals-against average remains tied with his contemporary George Hainsworth's as the lowest ever in NHL history.

Connell was among the first NHL goalies to get a set of Emil "Pop" Kenesky's new style of leg pads — squared at the edges, wider and thicker than the more rounded cricket-style pads previously worn — and he led the league with seven shutouts in his first season. In 1925–26, Connell led the league with a goals-against average of 1.49 and 15 shutouts in the 36-game schedule. The following campaign, he posted 13 shutouts in 44 games and backstopped the Senators to a Stanley Cup victory. He notched 15 more shutouts in 1927–28, including a record six in a row. His record 446:09 minutes of shutout hockey remains untouched and is unlikely to ever be bested.

When the Ottawa Senators suspended operations for a year due to the Great Depression, Connell joined the Detroit Falcons for 1931–32. He played every match of the 48-game season, notching a 2.12 goals-against average, second best in the league. The following year, he was back with Ottawa in what proved to be the Senators' final NHL campaign (the team transferred to St. Louis for a year, then folded) until the franchise was re-established in 1992. Connell was hobbled by injuries, however, and played only 15 games. In 1933–34, the New York Americans borrowed him for one game when their star Roy Worters was injured, and announced his retirement afterward.

When Clint Benedict also decided to retire, the Montreal Maroons convinced Connell to come back for another hurrah in 1934–35. Connell once again led the league in shutouts, with nine, and more important, led

his new team to a Stanley Cup victory. Connell shut out Chicago completely in the quarterfinal before vanquishing the New York Rangers and then sweeping the Toronto Maple Leafs in the final. The Maroons' manager and coach, Tommy Gorman, called Connell's performance in the 1935 playoffs the "greatest goalkeeping performance in the history of hockey." Yet Connell sat out the next season when the Maroons went with Lorne Chabot in goal. He returned to Montreal for the 1936–37 campaign, and it was his last. Connell was elected to the Hall of Fame in 1958. He died two weeks later.

CHUCK GARDINER

INDUCTED 1945

CHUCK GARDINER PLAYED every second of every game from his first game in the autumn of 1927, when he joined the lowly Chicago Black Hawks, to the Hawks' Stanley Cup victory in the spring of 1934. Along the way, he distinguished himself as one of the game's preeminent goaltenders of all time, entering the Hall of Fame as a charter member in 1945.

Born in Scotland in 1904, Gardiner immigrated with his family to Winnipeg at age seven. He rose through the local hockey ranks, eventually turning pro with the Winnipeg Maroons in 1925. His success at the minor pro level was noted by the newly formed NHL team in Chicago, who bought his contract and put him between the pipes for the Black Hawks' second season, in 1927–28. The team was bad, but Gardiner was a standout, and his affable nature served him well and helped make him a crowd

GARDINER

on his head, defying the Leafs to knock it off for the rest of the game. He wore it off the ice too." After winning only 13 games over two poor seasons, the Hawks made the playoffs in 1929–30, but everything really started to come together in the following season's campaign.

Gardiner made the NHL's inaugural All-Star Team in 1930–31, leading the league with a personal-best 12 shutouts. He posted a 1.73 goals-against average, good for second in the league, and backstopped his club all the way to the Stanley Cup playoffs. Despite his sparkling 1.32 goals-against playoff average, the Hawks failed to score in the deciding fifth game and the Montreal Canadiens triumphed.

Gardiner won his first Vezina Trophy in 1931–32, a feat he replicated two seasons later. He repeated as First All-Star Team goalie, made the Second Team in 1932–33, and made the First Team again the following season. Gardiner also received the honor of being named team captain in the 1933–34 season, in what turned out to be his final campaign. On February 14, 1934, he played in the NHL's first All-Star Game, a benefit for injured Toronto player Ace Bailey. After leading the league in the regular season

favorite. He yelled frequent encouragement to his teammates, teased his opponents and exchanged barbs with hecklers. *Toronto Daily Star* reporter Lou Marsh recorded one of his many joking exchanges with the fans: "Late in the last period, an overenthusiastic fan threw his iron lid [a derby hat] out on the ice. Gardiner, as cool as a cucumber, skated over and picked up the Christy stiff and stuck it

with 10 shutouts, Gardiner capped an excellent year with a shutout in double overtime in the deciding fourth game of the playoffs. Chicago had its first Stanley Cup victory. Sadly, Gardiner died shortly after the Hawks' Cup win. He suffered a brain hemorrhage in the days following the victory and died two months later. Chicago played the next season without a team captain.

GEORGE
HAINSWORTH

INDUCTED 1961

HAINSWORTH

GEORGE HAINSWORTH COMBINED an unflappable approach with exceptional puck-stopping ability to create a legacy as one of hockey's dominant goaltenders of the 1920s and '30s. While demonstrating plenty of quickness and exceptional

positioning, he also seemed rather nonchalant and inappropriately laid back much of the time. Contrasted with the acrobatic goaltenders who dominated the position at the time, diving and sliding to make saves, Hainsworth's style was dull and lackluster. As he himself said, apologizing for his colorless approach after backstopping the Montreal Canadiens to a Stanley Cup victory on April 14, 1931, with a shutout, "I'm sorry I can't put on a show like some of the other goaltenders. I can't look excited because I'm not. I can't shout at other players because that's not my style. I can't dive on easy shots and make them look hard. I guess all I can do is stop pucks."

And stop pucks he did.

Born in 1895, Hainsworth enjoyed a successful junior and amateur career in Kitchener, Ontario, before heading out west in 1923 to play professionally for Saskatoon in the Western Canada Hockey League. When the league folded after the 1925–26 season, he joined the Montreal Canadiens. Montreal netminder Georges Vezina had died that year and Hainsworth quickly established himself as a worthy successor, notching a league-leading 14 shutouts in 1926–27 and winning the inaugural Vezina Trophy (then awarded to the goaltender with the best goals-against average — in honor of Georges Vezina) with a 1.47 goals-against average. "Little George," as he was known for his diminutive stature (5-foot-6 and 150 pounds), won the Vezina in both of the following two seasons as well.

Hainsworth's 1928–29 campaign remains one for the ages. Over the 44-game season, he posted 22 shutouts, which remains a league record. Although league scoring was at a historic low (that season's scoring champion, Toronto Maple Leaf Ace Bailey, tallied 22 goals and 10 assists), Hainsworth allowed only 43 goals, and when overtime is factored in, his goals-against dropped to an incredible 0.92 average per 60-minute game. Unfortunately, come playoff time, his team could only muster two goals over three games and were swept by the Boston Bruins.

League scoring was up in 1929–30 with the introduction of the rule allowing forward passes in all zones, but Hainsworth still notched a league-leading four shutouts and a 2.15 goals-against average. The Canadiens marched undefeated through the playoffs and Hainsworth claimed his first Stanley Cup. The following season, the Canadiens successfully defended their Stanley Cup championship with Hainsworth recording a 2–0 shutout in the final match.

In a blockbuster move, Montreal traded Hainsworth to the Toronto Maple Leafs for goaltender Lorne Chabot on October 1, 1933. Hainsworth's steady play over the next three seasons backstopped the Leafs to two trips to the Stanley Cup playoffs. Unfortunately, Toronto did not come away with a championship. Hainsworth alternated games in the Leaf net with Turk Broda to start the 1936–37 season, but retired after three starts. However, the Canadiens came calling later that season, and Haisnworth played four more games before retiring for good at age 41.

When he posted his 64th NHL shutout in the 1931–32 season, Hainsworth passed Alex Connell to become the league's all-time shutout leader. He didn't relinquish that lead until Terry Sawchuk passed him in the 1963–64 season. To this day, only Sawchuk and Martin Brodeur have tallied more than Hainsworth's 94 career shutouts, and his 1.91 goals-against average remains tied (with Alex Connell) as the all-time best career total.

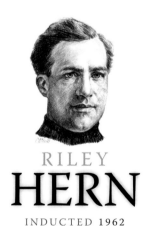

RILEY HERN

INDUCTED 1962

SINCE HE NEVER played in the National Hockey League, Riley Hern remains one of the more obscure members of the goaltending fraternity in the Hockey Hall of Fame. A standout in the game at the turn of the 20th century, he has the distinction of being the first professional goalie to backstop a team to a Stanley Cup victory. Hern joined the Montreal Wanderers of the Eastern Canadian Amateur Hockey Association (ECAHA) for the 1906–07 season. He posted a 10–0 win-loss record before helping defeat the defending champions from Ottawa for the Cup, 12–10, in a two-game, total goals final for the Stanley Cup. However, life for the Stanley Cup winner was a little more complicated during Hern's career than it is now.

In those days, the Cup was a challenge trophy, and Hern and the Wanderers participated in eight official challenges. They were successful seven times, surrendering the Cup to the Kenora Thistles in January 1907 before winning it back two months later. Hern's personal statistics don't stack up favorably compared to those of goaltenders from other eras, such as his 5.43 goals-against average in his final season in 1910–11, but in his day, he was a superstar.

Hern's hockey career began at an early age while playing for the local school teams in St. Marys and Stratford, in southwestern Ontario. He played as a forward for some of his formative years in the game, but he truly shone as a netminder. Hern turned pro with the Pittsburgh Keystones of the Western Pennsylvania Hockey League (WPHL) in the 1901–02 season. He led the league with nine victories in 14 games as the Keystones took the WPHL title, and Hern was selected to the league's First All-Star Team. He left Pittsburgh, a pro hockey haven at the time, after receiving a more lucrative offer from the Houghton-Portage Lakes team of the International Professional Hockey League in the fall of 1903. Hern led the team to two successive league titles and earned a First Team All-Star selection in 1905 and a Second Team All-Star selection in 1906.

The Montreal Wanderers came calling for the 1906–07 season, after the ECAHA voted to permit pro players. In 1909, the Wanderers were instrumental in the formation of the National Hockey Association, the immediate predecessor of the NHL, and therefore two of Hern's Stanley Cup wins came as a result of the Wanderers being ECAHA champions, and two as NHA champs. Hern later served as an NHL referee and a goal judge.

HOLMES

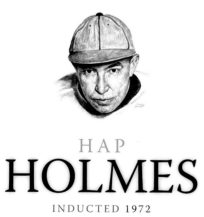

HAP
HOLMES

INDUCTED 1972

HARRY HOLMES' NICKNAME, "Hap," was a joking reference to his steely demeanor. "Hap" or "Happy" Holmes rarely cracked a smile at the rink, and was described as "nerveless" by one scribe. Yet he had plenty of reason to be pleased with his

work. Holmes excelled in all five of the top pro hockey leagues from 1912 to 1928. He made an impact in the National Hockey Association (NHA), Pacific Coast Hockey Association (PCHA), Western Canada Hockey League (WCHL), Western Hockey League (WHL) and NHL. A sterling playoff performer, Holmes backstopped two Stanley Cup wins in Toronto and one each in Seattle and Victoria. He was the leading goalie six times in the PCHA/WCHL, competing against rivals such as Hugh Lehman and George Hainsworth. In Stanley Cup action, he out-dueled such legends as Georges Vezina and Clint Benedict.

Before turning pro, Holmes, a native of Aurora, Ontario, played with the Toronto Canoe Club, Parkdale Canoe Club and Toronto Tecumsehs. He made his debut in the NHA with the Toronto Blueshirts in 1912–13 and enjoyed an outstanding sophomore year by leading the league in wins and helping the club become the first

Toronto team to win the Stanley Cup. The victory over captain Lester Patrick and his Victoria Aristocrats made a strong impression. Early in the 1915–16 campaign, Patrick came calling after he and his brother Frank decided to form a new team in Seattle. Holmes joined the Seattle Metropolitans with former Toronto mates Jack Walker and Frank Foyston. Once again, Holmes was a part of history when he backstopped the Metropolitans to the first Stanley Cup won by a U.S.-based outfit. Holmes continued his knack of being in the right place at the right time when he was loaned to the Toronto Arenas in January 1918, where he helped the club win the Stanley Cup at the conclusion of the inaugural NHL season.

Holmes returned to Seattle for 1918–19 and remained there for more than five years. In his first year back, the Metropolitans met the Canadiens in an infamous Stanley Cup series that was called off due to the global influenza epidemic and the death of Montreal's Joe Hall. The fourth game of the series was arguably Holmes' finest performance. Following a scoreless 60 minutes of regulation time and 20 minutes of overtime, referee Mickey Ion declared the game a draw.

Holmes traveled east with Seattle in 1920 to challenge Ottawa for the Stanley Cup. Despite his brilliant play, the westerners lost a close series to the powerhouse Senators. He led the PCHA in shutouts four times and in wins on two occasions. He enjoyed two successful years with the Victoria Cougars from 1924 to 1926, leading the WCHL/WHL in goals-against average.

In 1924–25, Holmes' brilliance led Victoria to the Stanley Cup championship match with the Montreal Canadiens, in which he starred. Victoria became the last non-NHL team to win the Stanley Cup, and Holmes became the first goalie to win the Cup with four different franchises.

The WHL disbanded in 1926, and an NHL expansion team, the Detroit Cougars, picked up the rights to Holmes. He recorded 17 shutouts in two seasons with the Cougars and retired. He died in 1940, but was not forgotten. Since 1948, the Harry "Hap" Holmes Memorial Award has been presented to the American Hockey League's goalie with the lowest goals-against average.

BOUSE
HUTTON

INDUCTED 1962

THE MULTI-SPORT athlete is not uncommon, but John "Bouse" Hutton hit rare heights as one of Canada's top all-around athletes early in the 20th century. He was primarily known as the goaltender for the famous Ottawa Silver Seven club, a team he joined in 1899–1900 when it was known only as the Ottawa Hockey Club. (The flashy septet — three forwards, two defensemen, one goalie and one rover — picked up its sterling moniker after each received a silver nugget from the team director Bob Shillington after a Stanley Cup win over the Montreal Victorias in March 1903.) But Hutton was also a lacrosse goalie for the Ottawa Capitals, who won the first Minto Cup national championship in 1901, and repeated in 1906. In a dramatically different role, Hutton also starred as a fullback for the Canadian Football League's Ottawa Rough Riders.

Hutton and the newly christened Silver Seven successfully defended a Cup challenge from the Rat Portage Thistles a few days after winning their first Stanley Cup as the 1902–03 Canadian Amateur Hockey League (CAHL) champions over Montreal. Although double-digit scores were not uncommon in this era, Hutton limited the Thistles to two goals a game as Ottawa won the two-game total goals series, 10–4. In January 1904, the Winnipeg Rowing Club was unsuccessful in its Stanley Cup challenge versus the Silver Seven, a game in which Hutton posted a rare shutout in the deciding third game. That series marked the first time that goal lines were drawn between the posts.

In February 1904, Hutton's team bested the Toronto Marlboros 6–3 and 11–2 in a challenge for the Cup. Hutton and the Silver Seven defended the Cup a third time, beating the Brandon Hockey Club 15–6 in a two-game total goals series in March of the same year. The Montreal Wanderers had also challenged for the Cup, but a refusal to play games in Ottawa led Montreal to forfeit. Hutton then decided that he was done with hockey, and retired from the game.

After his second Minto Cup lacrosse win in 1904, Hutton toured England with the Ottawa team, winning 23 of 24 games. When he returned to Canada, he moved to Brantford, Ontario, to pursue his lacrosse career.

The Silver Seven defended their Stanley Cup crown four times without him before Hutton returned to Ottawa in 1907. With Percy LeSueur entrenched as the Silver Seven's goalie, Hutton joined the newly formed Ottawa Senators in the Federal Amateur Hockey League — a team dominated by former Silver Seven players — in December 1908. After five games, with a shutout and a respectable 5.20 goals-against average, Hutton retired for good. He was inducted into the Hockey Hall of Fame in 1962 and died later that year.

HUGH
LEHMAN

INDUCTED 1958

HE PICKED UP the nickname "Old Eagle Eyes," but Hugh Lehman's success came from more than good vision. Lehman was an aggressive and adventurous goaltender who frequently wandered from the goal area, corralling loose pucks and passing to his teammates. The story goes that he even scored a goal in the Ontario Professional Hockey League (OPHL) after a rush up the ice, in the days when a goalie was not restricted to his half of center ice. While that may be folklore, what can be confirmed is that he was wonderfully adept at stopping the puck.

Lehman was born in Pembroke, Ontario, a hockey hotbed, in 1885 and played his first games for the Pembroke Lumber Kings in the Ottawa Valley Hockey League as a teenager. He joined the OPHL's Berlin (now Kitchener) Professionals for the 1908–09 campaign. After three OPHL seasons, he struck out for the west. It was in the Pacific Coast Hockey Association (PCHA) that Lehman truly left his mark. In his 13-year PCHA career, Lehman led the league in goals-against average five times, recording his best season in 1922–23 with a 2.33 average and five shutouts. He was named as a league All-Star in 10 of those 13 seasons. Unfortunately for Lehman, personal success did not always translate into team success.

"Hughie" Lehman competed in the Stanley Cup playoffs a total of eight times in his career, but won only once. After unsuccessful bids for the cup with the Galt Professionals and the Berlin Professionals (both in 1909–10), Lehman joined the PCHA's New Westminster Royals in 1911–12. After three seasons with the Royals and no Cup challenges, Lehman signed with the PCHA's Vancouver Millionaires in 1914–15. With a 13–4 record and a league-best 4.08 goals-against average, he backstopped the Millionaires to the league title and a date with the Stanley Cup, as the Millionaires defeated the NHA's Ottawa Senators in three straight games in a best-of-five series. Lehman's name and those of his teammates and manager was engraved on the inside of the Cup bowl, before the tradition of engraving names on the outside rings of the Cup was established.

Five more Cup appearances (1918, 1921, 1922, 1923, 1924) found Lehman and his mates on the losing end each time. When the Western Hockey League disbanded at the end of the 1925–26 season, Lehman went to Chicago to play for the NHL's Black Hawks. At 41 years of age, he

LEHMAN

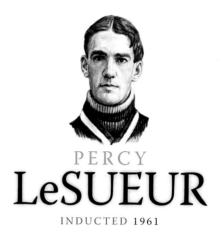

PERCY
LeSUEUR

INDUCTED 1961

A **STUDENT OF HOCKEY,** Percy LeSueur made numerous contributions to the game. In 1909 he penned an influential handbook, *How to Play Hockey*. In 1912, he designed the first net with a crossbar and webbing to trap rising shots. He created an improved gauntlet for goalies, affording them a little more protection on their forearms.

When LeSueur returned from military service after World War I, he did some refereeing, and then coached at the amateur, minor pro and NHL level. He managed hockey teams and arenas (including the famous Detroit Olympia when it first opened). As a *Hamilton Spectator* hockey columnist, he introduced the "shots on goal" statistic to game summaries. LeSueur was also a popular "Hot Stove League" commentator in the early radio broadcasts of Hockey Night in Canada. But playing hockey was still the highlight of his multi-faceted career.

Percy LeSueur played right wing originally, and accredited himself well enough to play for the Quebec Seniors in Quebec City. Not long after, he transferred to the Smiths Falls (Ontario) Seniors in 1904, where he donned the rudimentary goalie equipment of the day when the team's regular goaltender suddenly took ill. LeSueur never looked back.

Strong at clearing the puck, he also was a quick study. In March of 1906, his Smiths Falls team earned the right to challenge the Ottawa Silver Seven for the Stanley Cup. Although his team was swept in the best-of-three series, 6–5 and 8–2, LeSueur impressed the Stanley Cup champs.

appeared in all 44 games for the 1926–27 Hawks, a league-leading mark, but played only four times the following year. Lehman handed the goaltending chores to up-and-comer Chuck Gardiner and took over the coaching duties. Hugh Lehman was inducted into the Hockey Hall of Fame in 1958.

When Ottawa was hammered 9–1 by the Montreal Wanderers in another Cup challenge a week later, they called on LeSueur to help them out. Three days later, with the ink barely dry on his contract, LeSueur started the second of the two-game total goals series. Needing to win by at least eight goals, Ottawa fell short, winning 9–3. But LeSueur had a new home.

LeSUEUR

"Peerless Percy" spent the following eight seasons in the Ottawa goal. He backstopped the Ottawa Senators (formerly the Silver Seven) to league and Stanley Cup victories in 1908–09, and helped defend the team's crown against Cup challenges in January 1910 from the Galt Professionals (winning the two-game total goals series 15–4) and the Edmonton Eskimos (a 21–11 single-elimination game victory). Ottawa had to relinquish the Cup to the Montreal Wanderers at season's end, as the newly formed National Hockey Association declared that the winner of league play was to be awarded the Cup.

In 1910–11, LeSueur and the Senators won the NHA title and reclaimed the Stanley Cup. In single game challenges in March 1911, they defended the Cup with a 7–4 victory over Galt and a 14–4 drubbing of the Port Arthur Bearcats. LeSueur served as team captain for his last three seasons in Ottawa

LaSueur's stick from his time with Ottawa and Smith Falls, used between 1904–09. LeSueur carved the dates of his Stanley Cup wins on the shaft and paddle.

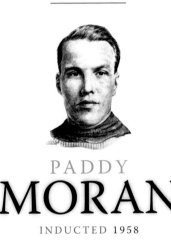

before being traded to the Toronto Shamrocks for the 1914–15 campaign. He played one last NHA season for the renamed Toronto Blueshirts the following year, and then enlisted during World War I, serving overseas with the 48th Highlanders. His return to the game as a referee, coach and commentator sealed his path to the Hall of Fame.

PADDY
MORAN

INDUCTED 1958

WHILE ALMOST EVERY piece of goalie equipment has changed dramatically since the early years of the twentieth century, the oversized sweater has a long history. Paddy Moran frequently wore an oversized cardigan in net, claiming that it kept him from getting a chill. But he usually kept it unbuttoned, so that it was useful for catching pucks.

Considered hefty in his day, the 5-foot-11, 180-pound Moran was also a feisty netminder. He played in the days before a goal crease was marked on the ice, so he frequently took matters into his own hands when it came to protecting the space around his goal. Moran was aggressive and his quick stick was used for more than deflecting shots. It's said he once chased sharpshooter Newsy Lalonde the length of the ice because of a transgression. He was also a tobacco chewer, and not above spitting at a foe. Opposition teams respected Moran's "crease."

Moran started playing hockey at age 15 and by the age of 19 was tending goal for Quebec City's Crescent Intermediates. He graduated to the Quebec Athletics for the 1901–02 season, where he played until 1905–06, when he

MORAN

Comets and the All-Montreal squad in the Canadian Hockey Association (CHA).

Back with the Bulldogs, who entered the NHA in 1910–11, Moran led the league with 10 wins in 1911–12 and 16 victories in 1912–13. More important, he established himself as a clutch performer with stellar performances in Stanley Cup competition. The Bulldogs claimed their first Cup by winning the NHA league championship in 1911–12, and then defended the Cup from a challenge by the Moncton Victorias of the Maritime Professional Hockey League, winning the best-of-three series 2–0 with an 8–0 victory in Game 2 — Moran's first pro shutout.

The Bulldogs retained the Cup by winning the NHA league title in 1912–13, and in March 1913 faced the MPHL's Sydney Millionaires challenge, winning 14–3 and 6–2. Moran played four more seasons, but his team finished second or third in the standings and never got their hands on the Cup again. Moran retired after playing seven games in 1916–17, at age 39, and was proud to say that he'd built his $4,000 house, a considerable sum then, entirely from his hockey earnings. He entered the Hall of Fame in 1958 and died in 1966.

TINY
THOMPSON
INDUCTED 1959

SIGHT UNSEEN, ONE would assume Tiny Thompson was yet another of the many short men who populated the NHL goalie ranks for so many years. But Cecil Thompson picked up his nickname as the biggest boy on his midget team. At 5-foot-10 and 180

made his big-league debut with the Quebec Bulldogs of the Eastern Canada Amateur Hockey Association (ECAHA).

With the rules of the day placing considerable restrictions on a goalie's movements considered essential today — no falling to the ice, no holding the puck — and the spartan equipment available, Moran routinely posted a high goals-against average, peaking at 9.61 for the 1906–07 season. It can also be said that he generally played for weak teams. But there were some great moments along the way, and personal and team successes. Moran stuck with the Bulldogs for the rest of his professional career, save the 1909–10 campaign when his team was denied entry into the National Hockey Association (NHA). Moran then tended goal for both the NHA's Haileybury

THOMPSON

and the only time Thompson would have his name engraved on the Cup.

With forward passing rules relaxed for the 1929–30 season, scoring went up, but Thompson led the league with a 2.19 goals-against average and earned his first of four Vezina Trophies. The Bruins enjoyed a season for the ages, with 38 wins, five losses and a tie, but were upset 2–0 in a best-of-three playoff series against Montreal (prompting the NHL to mandate best-of-five series the following season).

The NHL began handing out All-Star nominations for its best players in 1930–31, and Thompson played his way to a Second Team All-Star selection, an award he would be honored with three more times — twice a First Team selection.

On April 3, 1933, in what was dubbed "the Ken Doraty Derby," Thompson made history, tending goal in the then-longest NHL playoff game (it remains the second longest in NHL history). Unfortunately for him and the Bruins, he was on the losing side. In the fifth and deciding game of Boston's semifinal series with Toronto, both teams were held scoreless throughout regulation time. Thompson and his opposite number, Lorne Chabot, were perfect through five overtime periods and into their sixth — the deadlock held through 164

pounds, he was actually large for goalies in his day.

Thompson made an auspicious debut with the Boston Bruins in 1928–29. He posted a dozen shutouts and a stingy 1.15 goals-against average. Keep in mind, however, that this was the low point in NHL scoring, with a league-wide average of less than three goals scored per game. Nonetheless, Thompson sparkled. He outdueled Montreal's George Hainsworth in the playoffs with shutouts in the first two games against the Canadiens, sealing the best-of-five series with a 3–2 victory in Game 3. Thompson then blanked the New York Rangers in the first game of the best-of-three final, and allowed only a single goal in the second game to win the Stanley Cup. It was the Bruins first championship

"TINY" THOMPSON

Thompson's hockey card from the 1933 Ice Kings collection produced by the Montreal World Wide Gum Company.

minutes and 46 seconds — before the Leafs' Doraty beat an exhausted Thompson. The Bruins were out. He entered the NHL record book again in 1935–36 when his pass to defenseman Babe Siebert led directly to a goal, making Thompson the first goalie ever to earn an NHL assist.

Thompson sat out two games at the start of the 1938–39 season because his eyes were bothering him. Rookie Frank Brimsek stepped in and played so well that on November 16, 1938, Thompson was traded to Detroit for netminder Norman Smith (who never reported) and $15,000. Thompson played two seasons for the Red Wings before retiring. He later played one game with the Buffalo Bisons of the American league in 1940–41 and a handful of contests for the Calgary RCAF Mustangs during World War II. He was elected to the Hockey Hall of Fame in 1959.

GEORGES
VEZINA
INDUCTED 1945

GEORGES VEZINA'S NAME was immortalized when the NHL began presenting its top goaltending award in his memory the year after Vezina passed away. A key figure in the early history of the Montreal Canadiens, Vezina's life was steeped in both tragedy and glory. In 1909–10, starring for his hometown Chicoutimi Sagueneens, Vezina shut out the Montreal Canadiens in an exhibition match. The Canadiens, a new team in their first season in the National Hockey Association, were duly impressed and signed the man, who became known as the "Chicoutimi Cucumber" for his calm demeanor, for the 1910–11 campaign.

VEZINA

Vezina then began an epic run with the Canadiens, leading the NHA with a 3.03 goals-against average in his rookie season, and playing the first of a remarkable 367 consecutive games — including 39 playoff contests — over 15 seasons. Vezina led the Canadiens to their first Stanley Cup by claiming the 1915–16 NHA league title and defeating the first ever American Cup challenger, the Portland Rosebuds, 3–2 in the best-of-five series. Vezina posted a 2.60 goals-against average over the five games.

The Canadiens would vie for the Cup two more times over the next three seasons, each time battling the Seattle Metropolitans, who got the best of Vezina and the Canadiens in 1916–17: a 3–1, best-of-five blowout. In 1918–19 Vezina backstopped the Canadiens to a series tie with the Metropolitans in the fifth game, but the Cup was never

The final pair of skates Vezina wore before leaving his 325th consecutive game after only 20 minutes, and retiring immediately thereafter due to tuberculosis.

claimed, as five members of the Canadiens fell ill with the Spanish Influenza and the series was never completed.

Vezina didn't taste Stanley Cup action again until 1924. After leading the NHL with a 1.97 goals-against average and three shutouts, he won four consecutive games, defeating the Vancouver Maroons 2–0 in a best-of-three semifinal and the Calgary Tigers 2–0 in the best-of-three final to win his second Stanley Cup.

Frank Boucher, a star Maroons centerman described Vezina in 1924 as "the coolest man I ever saw, absolutely imperturbable ... He stood upright in the net and scarcely ever left his feet; he simply played all his shots in a standing position. Vezina was a pale, narrow-featured fellow, almost frail-looking, yet remarkably good with his stick. He'd pick off more shots with it than he did with his glove."

Vezina's "frail-looking" appearance was due to un-diagnosed tuberculosis, but the disease didn't have the best of him yet. In 1924–25, he led the NHL again with a 1.81 goals-against average and a career-best five shut-outs. In the playoffs, he shut out the Toronto St. Patricks in the second game, taking Montreal to the Stanley Cup final with a 5–2 win in the two-game total goals series. The Canadiens lost to the Victoria Cougars, though, and Vezina's career was almost over.

In the second period of the 1925–26 season home opener, Vezina collapsed on the ice, coughing up blood.

He was rushed to hospital and never played another game. He died later that spring and the Montreal ownership immediately established the Vezina Trophy for the league's top goalie. Until 1981–82, the award went annually to the goalkeeper(s) with the lowest goals-against average. Since then, it has gone to "the goaltender adjudged to be the best at his position," selected by the league's general managers. Georges Vezina was a charter member of the Hockey Hall of Fame in 1945.

ROY
WORTERS
INDUCTED 1969

AT 5-FOOT-3 AND 130 pounds, it isn't hard to imagine how Roy Worters became dubbed, "Shrimp." What might be harder to fathom is that despite playing most of his career with sad-sack teams, Worters tallied a sensational 66 shutouts over 12 NHL campaigns. More remarkable, he won the Hart Memorial Trophy as the league's MVP in 1929 (the first of only five goaltenders to ever do so), and in 1931 he earned the Vezina Trophy for the lowest goals-against average, despite playing every minute of the season for a team that didn't even make the playoffs.

After junior success in Toronto and stints with clubs in northern Ontario, Worters joined the ostensibly amateur Pittsburgh Yellowjackets in 1923–24. His club won the United States Amateur Hockey Association (USAHA) championship two years in a row. Worters posted 17 shutouts in 39 games in 1924–25, prompting the team to transfer to the NHL in 1925–26. Renamed the Pittsburgh Pirates, the team fared surprisingly well with essentially the same lineup, and Worters enjoyed a modicum of success for three seasons. He set a record (since broken) by stopping 70 of 73 shots in one game. And although he routinely saw a lot of rubber with the Pirates, he liked Pittsburgh. When he was sold to the New York Americans on November 1, 1928, Worters at first refused to report.

Suspended by NHL President Frank Calder, Worters eventually joined the Americans, where he spent the rest of his career. He immediately carried the team on his shoulders and into the playoffs for the first time with a career-low 1.15 goals-against average and 13 shutouts, winning the prestigious Hart Trophy. Unfortunately, his team failed to score in the playoffs. Facing their hometown rivals, the New York Rangers, in a two-game, total goals series, Worters posted a shutout in a 0–0 draw. In the second game, he again blanked the Rangers in regulation time before losing 1–0 in the second overtime period.

Worters won the 1930–31 Vezina Trophy with an amazing 1.61 goals-against average, allowing only 74 goals over the season. On offense, however, his team only mustered 76 goals, and finished fourth out of the five teams in their division. His achievement earned Worters a monster contract: a three-year deal worth $25,500 in U.S. funds.

The Americans didn't make the playoffs again until 1935–36, and Worters stole the show posting a

WORTERS

shutout in Game 1 on the way to a two-game, total-goals series victory over the Chicago Black Hawks. Facing the defending Cup champion Toronto Maple Leafs in the second round, Worters did all he could to keep the Americans in it, posting one shutout, but New York only scored twice, losing the best-of-three series 2–1.

Gritty to the end, Worters retired after the 1936–37 season, playing his last few games even though he was suffering from a painful hernia. He died of throat cancer in 1957 and was elected posthumously to the Hall of Fame in 1969.

HARDWARE HEROES

BY BRIAN COSTELLO

GEORGES VEZINA, whose name is inscribed on the trophy belonging to the best goalie in the NHL, was an unassuming, soft-spoken goaltender who earned the nickname "Chicoutimi Cucumber" because of his cool play under pressure.

William Jennings, whose name is honored with a trophy for the NHL goaltender(s) with the fewest goals scored against, was a Princeton and Yale-educated lawyer who helped spearhead the growth of hockey in the United States.

The two men never met — Jennings was just a five-year-old boy with no interest in hockey living in New York City when Vezina died of tuberculosis at age 39 in 1926 — but they share trophy space on the mantels of some of the best goaltenders in the history of the game.

Turk Broda in 1948 with the Vezina Trophy, his second. Broda played 60 games in 1947–48, posting a 32–15–13 record with five shutouts, allowing 143 goals for a 2.38 goals-against average.

Vezina's 1910–11 rookie card. The 24-year-old goalie is shown in a sweater that was worn by the Canadians for only that season.

THE VEZINA TROPHY

The Vezina Trophy was created by Montreal Canadiens' owners Léo Dandurand, Louis Letourneau and Joe Cattarinich during the 1926–27 NHL season as a tribute to their fallen comrade. Vezina was the NHL's first superstar between the pipes and also the only goalie the Canadiens needed between 1910 and 1925. The Chicoutimi Cucumber played every minute of every game until the fateful season of 1925–26.

At 38, the durable Vezina began sweating profusely in training camp and dropped 35 pounds during a six-week stretch leading up to the season opener. The Canadiens opened November 28 against the Pittsburgh Pirates. Not telling anyone about his ailment and looking as frail as a skeleton, Vezina started that game, but collapsed in the net with a high fever in the second period. Coughing up blood, he was given medical attention and a few days later was diagnosed with late-stage tuberculosis.

The news was devastating.

Five days after that game, Vezina returned to the Montreal Forum for his public retirement announcement and a final goodbye to his teammates. After telling them he was sick and could no longer be their goalie, Vezina grabbed his sweater, slumped into his stall and cried inconsolably.

Less than four months later, at his home in Chicoutimi with his wife and children nearby, Vezina, 10 months shy of his 40th birthday, succumbed to the disease.

The Canadiens' ownership group graciously paid Vezina's wife Marie the goaltender's $6,000 annual salary for 1925–26, even though he played just 20 minutes that season. And then came the ultimate tribute: In memory of Georges Vezina, the Vezina Trophy would be given to the NHL's goalkeeper(s) of the team allowing the fewest goals during the regular season.

The interesting thing about Vezina's amazing 15-year run with Montreal is that he would have won the award bearing his name just four times. For him, it was about performance and winning. It was never about shutouts and goals-against average. In fact, his 15 shutouts in 367 games is remarkably low for a goalie with his credentials.

The Canadiens of the early 1920s were transitioning from the stalwart veterans of Newsy Lalonde, Didier Pitre and the Cleghorn brothers, Odie and Sprague, to young stars and future Hall of Famers such as Howie Morenz, Aurel Joliat and Sylvio Mantha. Yet it was Vezina who was the leader in 1923–24, the season of Montreal's first Stanley Cup win as a member of the NHL. With almost the same crew the next year, Montreal won the NHL title in 1924–25, then lost the Stanley Cup to the Western Canadian Hockey League's Victoria Cougars.

But without Vezina in 1925–26, the two-time defending NHL-champion Canadiens were unable to defend their title and fell to last place overall — even with a 23-year-old Morenz just hitting his prime. The goaltending duties that season were handled by 25-year-old rookie Herb Rheaume, who previously played senior hockey in the United States Amateur Hockey Association, and 27-year-old Alphonse Lacroix, who had played for the 1924 U.S. Olympic team. Both never played in the NHL again after that dreadful season.

Dandurand said this about Vezina following his forced retirement: "I doubt if hockey will ever know his like again. He has been a credit to professional sport. A great athlete and gentleman. Quiet to taciturnity, he lets his deeds speak for him."

THE ORIGINAL WINNER

As fate would have it, the first winner of the Vezina Trophy was the man who replaced Vezina as a fixture between the Montreal pipes. George Hainsworth starred for the Saskatoon Sheiks in the Western Canadian Hockey League (WCHL), a professional league on par with the NHL. He was a relatively ancient 31 when Montreal came calling — on the recommendation of former Canadien-turned-scout Newsy Lalonde — and the Vezina Trophy was his for the next three seasons.

Hainsworth joined the Canadiens in 1926 and for as much as he dominated in the same quiet, unassuming way that Vezina had, he did so in a dimension that was also awe-inspiring from a statistical standpoint. Just 5-foot-6, 150 pounds, Hainsworth must have had invisible pads that were just as big. He helped the Canadiens rebound from 23 points in 1925–26 to 58 the next season and 59 in the following two.

In addition to his three Vezina wins in those first three seasons, Hainsworth set single-season records for shutouts (22) and goals-against average (0.92) that remain to this day. But that wasn't enough to win over the fickle fans of Montreal in the early years. Because he spoke no French, knew no one in the city and played a stand-up, nonchalant style, Hainsworth was often booed during Montreal losses, even in his 22-shutout season.

"He didn't get a lot of credit because he wasn't acrobatic," hockey historian Bob Duff told *The Hockey News* in 2008. "He was very unspectacular, a real technician. In that era, goalies tended to be very athletic and were sprawling around making spectacular saves. And he was a guy who always just seemed to be in the right spot."

Eventually, Hainsworth won over the fans — winning back-to-back Stanley Cups (1930 and 1931) will do that. One local businessman even manufactured mini-statuettes of Hainsworth and they immediately sold out.

Sadly though, the Vezinas never followed Hainsworth beyond those first three seasons. The year after he recorded his 22 shutouts, the league altered the rules to allow forward passing and he finished 1929–30 with just four shutouts and his goals-against average rose from 0.92 to 2.42.

TRAGIC HERO

If Vezina was the NHL's first marquee goaltender, Charlie Gardiner had the makings of becoming the best ever. Tragically, he never lived to see his 30th birthday and only the most ardent hockey fans of today are aware of the legend of this ill-fated superstar.

Born in Edinburgh, Scotland, and raised in Winnipeg, Gardiner wore his emotions like a wristwatch, which is to say right at his sleeve. He was the ultimate competitor because he was driven to play every game and every practice as though it were his last. When he lost big games, he'd cry. When he was booed, he thought about quitting. When he stopped an opponent on a breakaway, he had the nerve to puff his chest and say "tough luck, try again sometime."

Gardiner was called the greatest goalkeeper in the world by many observers. Even the legendary Howie Morenz once said, "He was the hardest netman I ever tried to outguess."

So, why don't we rate this Hall of Famer among the best ever, or mention him in the same breath as legends such as Vezina or Terry Sawchuk or Glenn Hall or Jacques Plante?

Could be because Gardiner broke in with the moribund Chicago Black Hawks in 1927 and won just 13 of 84 games his first two seasons. Only three times in Gardiner's seven seasons did Chicago have a winning record and make the playoffs. Yet in that time, he won the Vezina twice and was a First-Team All-Star three times, while posting a career goals-against average of 1.43 in Stanley Cup play.

Gardiner's Black Hawks lost the 1931 Cup final to Hainsworth's Canadiens, but when the Black Hawks made it back in 1934, the goaltender effectively sacrificed his life to win it all. Ignoring a painful tonsil infection that spread through his body that spring, Gardiner led Chicago to a championship victory over Detroit. He paid the ultimate price a few days later when he collapsed and was rushed to hospital. In a coma, he died June 13, 1934, at age 29 from a brain hemorrhage, originating from the tonsillar infection.

Like many goalies of his era, Gardiner easily could have played another 10 years at a top performance level in the NHL. He won his Vezinas at age 27 and 29, so we could conservatively prorate his Vezina wins from two

Lorne Chabot in the Leaf net. Chabot played five seasons with the Leafs, from 1928–29 to 1932–33. He played every game for the Leafs in both his first and last seasons in Toronto.

to five, especially considering there wasn't a dominant stopper post-Gardiner. (Eight different goalies won the award over the next 10 seasons.) Had he won five or more Vezinas, Gardiner would have been in the same company as Ken Dryden (5), Dominik Hasek (6), Bill Durnan (6) and Jacques Plante (7) among all-time hardware leaders.

UNDER THE RADAR

The death of Charlie Gardiner hit the Black Hawks hard in 1934. As defending Stanley Cup champions, Chicago had to recover quickly. They bent, but did not break. Enter Lorne Chabot, generally regarded as the best goaltender not inducted in the Hockey Hall of Fame — and also one of the most traveled.

The Montreal-born Chabot was 33 and a two-time Cup winner when he arrived in Chicago. It was the fourth of six stops in the all-too-short 10-year career of the NHL's first vagabond goaltender. Chabot was 26 when he broke in with the expansion New York Rangers in 1926 and led them to the division title. The next season, Chabot guided the Rangers all the way to the Stanley Cup final, but couldn't finish the deed because of an eye injury when hit with a puck in Game 2. Remarkably, coach Lester Patrick grabbed Chabot's equipment — bloody jersey and all — went into the crease and the Rangers beat the Montreal Maroons 2–1 to tie the series 1–1. The Rangers used the New York Americans' goalie Joe Miller in the final three games and captured the Cup.

"They win the Stanley Cup, then wouldn't you know it, Patrick calls my grandfather and tells him he's going to trade him because he was concerned the eye injury would make him puck shy," said Donny Chabot, grandson of Lorne Chabot.

Chabot was shipped to Toronto, where he had an impressive five-year stint that culminated in the Maple Leafs winning the 1932 Stanley Cup. Chabot was in his glory in the final as the Leafs swept the Rangers. In the off-season, Chabot made the mistake of asking GM Conn Smythe for a raise based on performance and results.

"My grandfather entered the league making $6,500 per year and after six years and two Cups, thought he should ask for a $1,000 raise," Donny Chabot said. "He threatened to retire and go back to his first career of being a police officer, and in the end Smythe had to give him what he wanted. It was all verbal agreements back then and as they shook hands, Smythe, in spite, vowed this would be Chabot's last season in Toronto, regardless of how the team did."

Chabot led the Leafs to the Cup final the next season, but this time the Rangers won. Before the start of the next season, Smythe, true to his word, traded Chabot, in his prime at 32, to Montreal for 38-year-old George Hainsworth. The Leafs and the Canadiens finished one-two in the Canadian Division with their new goalies, but the Habs were close to bankrupt and in a move to shed salary, traded Chabot and Howie Morenz to Chicago. The Hawks, of course, were in need of a stopper after Gardiner's tragic death.

It turned out to be the best season of Chabot's career as he won the Vezina Trophy, posting eight shutouts and a 1.80 goals-against average in 48 games. In April 1935, the red-hot Chabot became the first hockey player to appear on the cover of *Time* magazine. Unfortunately, in the playoffs, the defending Cup champion Hawks lost a two-game, total goal series 1–0 and team owner Tommy Gorman was steaming mad.

Sadly, for the second great Chicago goalie in consecutive years, it was the beginning of the end. Chabot developed leg problems — it was later learned it was the onset of Bright's Disease (an old classification for what are now many different types of kidney disease) — and the Hawks decided to go with a predominately American-born lineup, including stopper Mike Karakas. Chabot was traded back to the Canadiens in February of 1936, then to the Montreal Maroons a week later.

"My grandfather was badly broken down," Donny Chabot said. "He only played 16 games with the Maroons that year, then another six with the New York Americans the next year. But he wasn't the same person. The game had taken a toll on him and the disease was starting to surface."

Chabot retired to his Peterborough dairy farm and was soon restricted to getting around with the aid of forearm crutches. Five days after celebrating his 46th birthday, Chabot died of Bright's Disease.

Donny Chabot has spent the past 20 years campaigning the Hall of Fame's selection committee to induct his grandfather, and he even has a website to register signatures.

"My grandfather is 10th on the list of all-time shutouts [73 in just 411 games], has the lowest goals-against average of any goaltender to play at least 10 seasons, won the Vezina and two Stanley Cups," Donny Chabot said.

FAT BOY MAKES GOOD

Hainsworth played three more NHL seasons with Toronto after the trade from Montreal involving Chabot. And the Maple Leafs were satisfied with the aging puckstopper. With 38-year-old Hainsworth holding the fort, Toronto posted a league-best 26–13–9 record in 1933–34, then again the following season with a 30–14–4 mark. But the Leafs slipped to 23–19–6 in 1935–36 and late that season GM Conn Smythe knew he would soon have to find a replacement for Hainsworth, who was turning 41 that summer.

The cagey GM was told about an impressive 24-year-old goalie by the name of Earl Robertson, playing with the Windsor Bulldogs in the International League (IHL). The IHL in those days was an eight-team professional league a tier below the NHL. So Smythe went on a scouting trip

Broda in 1950–51, tipping the Toledo at 194 ¾ pounds.

to watch Robertson and the Bulldogs face the league's top team, the Detroit Olympics. Robertson was all right, but Smythe walked away from that game more impressed with Detroit goalie Turk Broda, a plump 21-year-old kid from Brandon, Manitoba. The GM knew he'd found his man.

Broda spent the next seven years as the mainstay in the Toronto crease, missing just 4 games out of 338. He won the Vezina as the league's top goalie in his fifth season, 1940–41, and guided the Leafs to the Stanley Cup the next season. A jovial and happy-go-lucky soul, Broda spent his entire career in a constant battle with weight gain. If he'd played well, nobody would say a word. If he struggled, people pointed to his excess weight as the reason. A couple poor performances in a row and all of a sudden "Fat Boy" was eating his way out of the NHL, critics would claim.

Prior to the start of 1950–51, Smythe had an addendum written into Broda's contract. It included a dollar-per-pound bonus clause. Turk was listed at 5-foot-9, 165 pounds, but his playing weight was considerably more, often up to 40 pounds over that weight, not including

equipment. Broda had to step on the scales every payday and if it registered under 190 pounds — a reasonable compromise Smythe thought — there would be a bonus added to his cheque. If Broda's weight exceeded the maximum on Thursday, Smythe could cull some dollars off his stipend.

It's a stunt that wouldn't fly for a second in today's unionized league, but it made for great headlines at the time.

Broda's first trip to the Toledo scale touched 194 ¾ pounds, but he took it in stride. "I work out at the West End Y every day and I don't expect any trouble shedding those few pounds," he said in *The Hockey News*. "I got rid of more than that last year [when he was reported to have played at 200-plus pounds]."

Broda was known to spend time in a steam chamber prior to the weigh-in to get closer to 190. On the ice, Broda often looked slow and unorthodox, yet he had an amazing sense of positioning and was at his best in clutch situations. He left the NHL for three seasons in the mid-1940s to serve in the Canadian military during World War II. Upon his return, he led the team to three straight Stanley Cups — the first goalie in NHL history to do so — and won his second Vezina in 1948.

Typically, Broda didn't take himself too seriously. He ate when he felt like it, smoked in the washroom stalls between periods and loved his beer. Case in point is the story of him drinking the night away with an American GI during an NHL exhibition series in Los Angeles after the 1942–43 season. The story goes that in the wee hours of the morning, an MP searching for missing soldiers found Broda's drinking partner passed out in the orchestra pit at a famous Hollywood nightclub. Where was Broda? He was seated at the piano, playing a duet with that night's headliner, legendary jazz pianist Hoagy Carmichael.

Later that same day, Broda blanked the Montreal Canadiens 1–0 in the final game of that series. He was on Toronto's 1951 Cup-winning team, his fifth NHL championship, and retired after one game the next season, happily overweight. A heart attack claimed Broda at age 58 in 1972.

PLANTE'S DOMINATION

The debate is always heated when the topic of best goaltender of all-time comes up. Between Jacques Plante, Terry Sawchuk and Glenn Hall of the Original Six era and Patrick Roy, Dominik Hasek and Martin Brodeur of the modern era, discussion can last for hours.

While Brodeur will retire with a firm grasp on the wins and shutouts records, Plante goes down as the most innovative goaltender in the history of the game. As the pioneer of the goalie mask and the first stopper to venture from the crease to play the puck, Jake the Snake was a trailblazer. He also goes down as the goalkeeper with the most Vezina Trophy wins — seven.

Plante won the Vezina in each season during Montreal's five consecutive Stanley Cup victories from 1956 to 1960. He was the beneficiary of a dynastic squad of forwards and, quite frankly, was the last line in a defense that few opponents could penetrate. Montreal allowed 17 fewer goals than its nearest competitor in 1955–56, two fewer the following season, a remarkable 30 fewer goals in 1957–58, an astounding 43 fewer the next season and two fewer in 1959–60. After a one-year break in 1961–62, Plante won the Vezina again for the league-leading Habs in 1961–62.

In short, Jacques was a terrific goalie playing on a fabulous well-rounded team. It was an aberration when he didn't win the Vezina. So it goes without saying that Plante's most memorable and unlikely Vezina title came in 1968–69 when at age 40, following a three-year retirement from the game (during which he cared for his ailing wife), he blew the field away for the two-year-old team out of St. Louis. With the Blues, Plante and platoon-mate Glenn Hall allowed just 157 goals in 76 games. The next closest team was the New York Rangers at 196 goals allowed. The Cup champion Canadiens gave up 202 goals.

"I keep telling myself that all this can't be happening," Plante said on the evening of the Vezina Trophy presentation. "It really is hard to believe, isn't it? I mean it when I say I never played this well before. During the three seasons I missed, I had a chance to study hockey as I never could before. I looked carefully at each man in the NHL

and the moves he made and now I am playing with this knowledge in the back of my head."

It was hardly a swan song for Plante. The following season Plante and Ernie Wakely finished runners-up for the Vezina, just nine more goals allowed than Chicago's spectacular rookie Tony Esposito. Then, during a season in which he turned 42, Plante trumped his previous statement about playing the best hockey of his life.

The Toronto Maple Leafs acquired Plante in a three-way deal involving Tim Horton and the New York Rangers. The Maple Leafs finished that season (1970–71) sixth out of 14 teams and Toronto's goals-against average was fifth. But Plante could have easily won another Vezina had it been put to a vote. He allowed 73 goals in 40 games (a league-leading 1.88 GAA), while Toronto's other goalies Bruce Gamble, Bernie Parent and Murray McLachlan gave up 133 goals in 39 games (3.39 GAA).

"I'm playing the best goal of my life," Plante said on his 42nd birthday. His final professional season was with the World Hockey Association's Edmonton Oilers in 1974–75 during which he turned 46.

THE SPARK FOR A CHANGE

In the early years of hockey, and for virtually the entire Original Six era, teams remarkably had just one goaltender. He was the man, game in, game out. He played hurt much of the time and heck, he didn't even need a mask.

So reliable, so durable was the goaltender through the first half of the 20th century, that the most untouchable of all long-standing sports records belongs to a goaltender. Glenn Hall played 502 consecutive games for Detroit and Chicago from 1955 through 1962. It's a number that has become symbolic to Hall almost half a century later. Today, it would be the cover story in *The Hockey News* if a goalie made it to 50 straight games, let alone 502.

Gradually, the number of games in an NHL season rose from 50 in the Original Six years to 60 to 70 to 74 and beyond. The slapshot was invented, the curved stick was created, players got bigger and brasher. Emergency backup goalies became team regulars and the vocation mushroomed.

Bunny Larocque, dressed as the backup, skates in warm-ups as Denis Herron prepares to take the net.

In time, the Vezina Trophy became a watered down version of its former self. It still went to the goalkeeper(s) of the team that allowed the fewest goals, but in the process it went to some less accomplished goalies as well. In the first 38 years of the Vezina, it went to just one goalie per season. Then, for a stretch of 17 years beginning in 1965 and ending with the re-definition of the Vezina Trophy in 1981, it was shared by two or more goalies in 13 of those seasons.

When Michel "Bunny" Larocque won his fourth "shared" Vezina in 1981, the league discreetly said enough is enough.

"I don't want this to sound disparaging to the man, but there is some logic to that statement," former Boston Bruins coach/GM Harry Sinden said about Larocque's run of Vezinas. "He won the Vezina what, four times? I think

a lot of people in the league had the feeling the Vezina should be given to the best goalie in the league, not necessarily all the goalies for the team with the best [goals-against average]."

Larocque happened to be the beneficiary of being the backup goalie to Ken Dryden on the Montreal Canadiens dynasty teams of the late 1970s. The Hull, Quebec, native played more games than most backup goalies, and he played on a team that allowed few shots and scant scoring opportunities. It's not surprising to see 10 players from those Montreal teams of four straight Stanley Cups now in the Hockey Hall of Fame.

Larocque spent eight years as the backup in Montreal, never playing more than 39 games in a season. A requirement to being eligible to share the Vezina was having played at least 25 regular season games, and Larocque did that in all four of his trophy winning seasons. Had he played three more games in 1975–76, Larocque would have shared his fifth Vezina. Instead, Dryden won it alone that year.

Should Dryden have won all five Vezinas alone? A goalie purist would say yes, but technically, Larocque did play the 25 games minimum, as did other less accomplished Vezina-winning backups such as Denis DeJordy with Glenn Hall in 1967, Gilles Villemure with Ed Giacomin in 1971 and Gary Smith with Tony Esposito in 1972. And let's not forget about the controversial 1980–81 season, which led to a change in Vezina governing.

Firewagon hockey was approaching its zenith in 1980–81. Wayne Gretzky was just about to embark upon an unprecedented scoring domination that would change the game. It was all about offense and as for the goalies, well, God bless them.

Scoring rose from a modern day low of 4.8 goals per game (both teams combined) in 1952–53 when Terry Sawchuk won his first of four Vezinas, to 6.0 in 1961–62 when Jacques Plante won his sixth Vezina in seven years, to 6.5 in 1972–73 when Ken Dryden was beginning his five-Vezina run. In 1980–81, scoring was at 7.7 goals per game (on its way to the all-time high of 8.025 the following season, 1981–82).

Richard Sevigny in the Montreal net against the Boston Bruins.

Dryden retired at the conclusion of the 1978–79 season, and Larocque was given the No.1 spot by the Habs. In 1980–81, Montreal got off to a good start with Larocque shouldering most of the load. When Denis Herron (the Habs backup whose share of ice time was only slightly below that of Larocque) broke a collarbone and Larocque suffered a sliced hand, the Canadiens turned to third stringer Richard Sevigny and the 23-year-old was brilliant. Even Rick Wamsley, the fourth goalie on the depth chart, proved special with a 1.90 GAA in five games.

Larocque returned from injury and wasn't about to sit quietly as he slid down into a backup's role. He openly complained, was moved into coach Claude Ruel's doghouse and was a healthy scratch for more than a month. Larocque demanded a trade and was moved to the struggling Toronto Maple Leafs in March.

The Canadiens continued to surge behind Sevigny and moved into the lead in the league goals-against depart-

ment. Problem was, with 16 games remaining, Larocque was the only Habs goalie who had played the required 25 minimum games to win the Vezina and he was now a Maple Leaf. What happened next is pure manipulation. Let the facts show the Canadiens flip-flopped Sevigny and Herron down the stretch so they would both have enough appearances to get to 25 games. In those final 16 games, Sevigny played 14 times and Herron 9. That meant there were seven games in which one was pulled and replaced with the other. One might not blink at this fact had the Montreal goalkeepers been struggling, but the Canadiens went 9–4–3 in those 16 games and the team GAA fell to a league low 2.90.

Georges Vezina and goaltending purists would not be impressed with this type of manipulation, clearly done to get the names of the active Montreal goalies on the Vezina. The award that season went to three goalies for the first time: Larocque, Sevigny and Herron — and that was enough to cause change.

Billy Smith, recipient of the first GM-voted Vezina Trophy.

THE EDICT IS DELIVERED

The NHL, plain and simple, wanted to ensure the game's best goalie was recognized with an award. And that hadn't always been the case. *The Hockey News* asked St. Louis Blues president and general manager Emile Francis to explain the league's rationale, and this is what he wrote in the October 2, 1981, edition of the magazine.

"The best goalkeeper hasn't always had a chance to win the Vezina Trophy, or any major award for that matter, because unless you're on the best team, there's no way that you could win the Vezina, since the award was always attributed to the goal-against record.

"I think that it's more appropriate that one player be chosen to win the Vezina Trophy as the best goaltender, just as Georges Vezina, for whom the trophy was named, was an outstanding goalkeeper in his time. By the same token, there will be a trophy given for the team with the least goals allowed, which is fine. As it stands now, they don't give out a trophy for the team that scores the most goals, but that's about what we were doing in reverse. We were giving a trophy to the team which allowed the least goals, but the trophy wasn't really going to the team, but only to the goaltenders on the team.

"I feel it's good for the league to go about awarding the Vezina the way they are planning. Now a goalkeeper will get the proper recognition, the same as a defenseman or the best checking forward, the leading scorer and so on.

"When you're selecting the Vezina winner, I think it should be given to the best goalkeeper or the most outstanding goalkeeper in the league. It might bring about a situation where statistics aren't as important as they were before. Previously, in order to win, you had to have the lowest goals-against average. Period. But this way, the player selected will be chosen like they do for the other major award winners. He'll simply be the most outstanding goaltender, and he could be on a last-place club and still win it."

The NHL made it official. Starting in 1981–82, the league's GMs would vote to select the Vezina Trophy winner. The team with the best goals-against average would be given another award. But what should they call it?

THE JENNINGS TROPHY

With the NHL adopting a new goaltending award and re-defining the criteria behind the Vezina winner, the next question was what to name the hardware given to the stopper with the best goals-against average. Twenty years had passed since Jacques Plante revolutionized the game by creating a goalie mask and in 1981 he was six years retired from the crease. What better way to honor this living legend than to name a goaltending award after Plante.

But over the years, the NHL had a propensity for taking care of its old boys first when it came to naming trophies. The award for league MVP is named after a former coach-manager, Cecil Hart, who never played in the league. The award for top scorer is named after another former coach-manager, Art Ross, who scored plenty of goals, but just one in the NHL. The awards

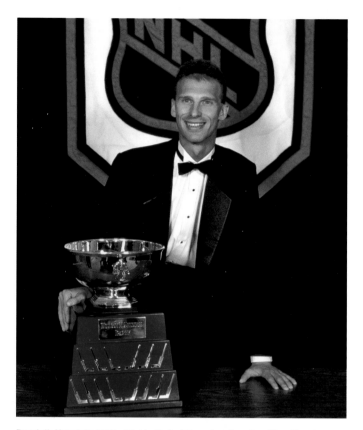

Dominik Hasek in 1994 with his first of three Jennings trophies. Hasek played 58 games in 1993–94, posting a 1.95 goals-against average. He shared his win with Grant Fuhr.

for top rookie, defenseman, playoff MVP and defensive forward are all named after league builders. The Vezina Trophy is one of the exceptions.

That leads us to William Jennings, the unlikely Ivy League-trained lawyer who would have his name linked to many of the game's great masked men. Born in New York City, Jennings never played hockey and admittedly didn't even convert to the game until he was an adult. A partner at the law firm of Simpson Thacher and Bartlett in Manhattan, Jennings became indoctrinated into the world of the NHL at age 38 when the Graham Paige Company bought Madison Square Garden from James Norris and Arthur Wirtz in 1959. The young lawyer handled the transaction.

When New York Rangers' president, General John Reed Kilpatrick, died in 1960, Admiral John J. Bergen took over and enlisted Jennings to become more active with the team, not just the facility. After the 1961–62 season,

the Garden Corp. made a change in the superstructure of the team, electing Bergen to chairman of the board and naming Jennings, just 41, president.

Prior to Jennings coming aboard, the flagging Rangers had missed the playoffs 13 of the previous 19 seasons, a sorry fact made even worse when you consider four of the six teams in the NHL at the time made the post-season. Jennings brought former goalie-turned-coach Emile Francis on board in 1964 and fortunes started to turn. The Rangers became relevant in New York again. Their winning record in 1966–67 was their first in nine seasons.

"I never went for that bunk that the Rangers had a small hardcore clientele," Jennings, then 46, told *The Hockey News* in 1967. "Hockey is and has been very popular around New York for a long time. Now that we are not finishing fifth and sixth, the fans are more vocal. Heck, I have been a rooter for 22 years — and think that hockey is the best spectator sport of all."

Jennings had arrived as a builder, but what he had accomplished with the Rangers was nothing compared to what he would do with the league over the next few years. The energetic New York lawyer was the point guard behind the league's expansion in 1967. Jennings, with the help of the NHL's expansion committee and then president Clarence Campbell, engineered the first expansion of the league from 6 to 12 teams. His motives were simple, wrote Norman MacLean in *The Hockey News*. "He wanted hockey to be truly major in scope — and to get in on some of the television money which football was lapping up. He talked his [NHL] lodge brothers into expansion."

Jennings helped spearhead hockey's first U.S. TV deal with CBS and was also behind the contract with NBC that decade. He was responsible for the league opening up an office in New York and hiring a public relations director in the U.S. He was also chairman of the NHL's board of governors from 1968 to 1970, was awarded the Lester Patrick Trophy in 1971 for outstanding contribution to hockey in the U.S. and inducted into the Hockey Hall of Fame in 1972.

By the time Jennings, a voracious smoker, died of throat cancer at 60 in 1981, the number of U.S.-based NHL teams had grown from 4 to 14. The Ivy League lawyer died a hockey man through and through.

"I don't think he knew the first thing about hockey when the Rangers thing fell in his lap," Emile Francis said in 2010. "But it wasn't long before he was pulling a lot of strings behind the scenes in the league. He was the driving force behind expansion. He was very ambitious and very driven."

"It made sense to honor his many contributions to the game by naming the new trophy after him," Harry Sinden said. "And that's what we did."

THE VEZINA PROCESS

With the Jennings Trophy being awarded for statistical achievement, the Vezina Trophy became much like the Hart and other merit-based trophies — it is all about the gut feel.

The race for the Jennings Trophy can be monitored daily on hockey websites during the season by looking at the stats links. It goes to the goalies on the team with the fewest goals allowed. A goalie must have appeared in 25 games for that team to be eligible. In the 28-year history of the Jennings, a team tandem has won it 16 times and an individual 11 times. Three goalies won it in 2003 after New Jersey and Philadelphia tied for fewest goals allowed — Martin Brodeur for the Devils and Roman Cechmanek and Robert Esche for the Flyers.

Patrick Roy and Brodeur are the all-time Jennings leaders with five apiece, while Ed Belfour, Dominik Hasek and Brian Hayward each have three.

So, while the statistician does all the work for the Jennings, it's the NHL general managers who vote for the Vezina. Each GM gets a ballot at the conclusion of the regular season (playoff performance is not factored in) and lists his top three candidates in order. The weighted system gives five points for first place, three for second and one for third.

One of the closest battles in recent seasons was when Montreal's Jose Theodore and Colorado's Patrick Roy tied with 105 voting points in 2001–02. Theodore won the Vezina because he had more first-place votes (15) from NHL GMs compared to Roy (12). Roy had 15 second-place votes compared to Theodore's nine votes for second

and three for third. What's interesting about that season is that Theodore also won the Hart Trophy as the league's MVP (voted on by the Professional Hockey Writers' Association) in a tiebreaker with Calgary winger Jarome Iginla. They had the same number of voting points, but Theodore had three more first-place ballots. Capping things off in that most unusual year is the fact Hart and Vezina Trophy winner Theodore was just a Second-Team All-Star. That's because Roy made it to the First All-Star Team based on the voting results from a different group of observers — the Professional Hockey Writers' Association.

Another interesting season in Vezina balloting was 1998–99. Dallas goalie Ed Belfour won the Jennings for top goals-against average, but finished a distant seventh in Vezina voting. Toronto's Curtis Joseph had the most first-place votes (10) ahead of Buffalo's Dominik Hasek and Boston's Byron Dafoe (eight apiece). But Hasek made up the ground in second-place votes and outdistanced Joseph and Dafoe in total voting points, 73–64–58.

In voting for the Vezina, GMs look at a number of different factors.

"The first thing I do is look at the statistics and see which goalies dominated in each of the categories [wins, goals-against average, save percentage, shutouts]," said former Boston GM Harry Sinden. "Then I look at what each goalie meant to his team. Was he on a top team with an excellent defense? Did he have a young defense? Or maybe the team played a wide-open system. So statistics don't tell you everything, but they are a starting point. Then I think the most important thing you ask is how vital was that goalie to the success of the team? If the team is in first place, is it because of the goalie? If the team barely made the playoffs, is it because of the goalie? It's never an easy decision, but in a lot of years, you can narrow it down to two or three guys."

Another former GM said he rarely looked at statistics when determining his Vezina vote.

"I think for the Vezina, it's more of a gut thing," said Emile Francis, former New York Rangers GM. "I'll put the statistics aside and base it more on my assessment of how they played that season. It was a lot easier when there were

Jose Theodore in the Montreal net. Theodore won both the Vezina and
Hart trophy for his performance in the 2001–02 season.

only six teams in the league and we saw each other play many times. But you had to base it on how they played that season, not the season before or what kind of a career they had. And that sometimes made it tough because there weren't many games on TV. You had to go by the games you saw live — and that was mostly your own team — and listen to reports from other people you trusted."

Since the inception of the Jennings Trophy in 1982, nine times a goalie has won both the Vezina and the Jennings in the same season, including Patrick Roy (1989 and 1992), Ed Belfour (1991 and 1993), Dominik Hasek (1994 and 2001), Martin Brodeur (2003 and 2004) and Miikka Kiprusoff (2006).

"[The rare combination of a goalie winning the Jennings and the Vezina] goes to show you the best defensive team doesn't always have the best goalie," Sinden said. "In fact, in most cases [the GMs] will give the Vezina to the goalie who has to battle the hardest without the benefit of the best defense in the league. That's the way I looked at it anyway."

Sinden's hypothesis could be one reason why Brodeur, the winningest goalie of all time, didn't capture his first Vezina until 2003 when he was 31, had 10 years in the league and three Stanley Cup titles. His New Jersey Devils were renowned for a tight, defensive system. Maybe the thought among GMs was, "Brodeur is good, but other goalies have to work harder with less help to accomplish a fraction as much." No worries though. Brodeur won his fourth Vezina in 2007–08 at the age of 36.

1995–96 Vezina trophy winner Jim Carey in net in 1996–97. He was traded to Boston on March 1, 1997.

FALLING STAR

In the 28 years since the Vezina mandate was changed, 13 goaltenders have been one-time winners. Throughout the history of the trophy, 25 goalies have taken home the hardware just once in their career. And of this select group of goalies, it is safe to say none has had a career trajectory like 1996 winner Jim Carey. If ever there was an analogy to describe the career of Carey, it's the one about the star that burns the brightest just before it's about to implode.

Carey burst onto the NHL scene in 1994 as a precocious 20-year-old stopper from Dorchester, Massachusetts. Within two years, he had finished runner-up for the Calder Trophy as top rookie and won the Vezina. Yet like that burning star falling from the sky, Carey was out of hockey for good before he even turned 25 — Jim Carey, we hardly knew ye.

The Washington Capitals surprised a lot of hockey experts when they selected Carey 32nd overall in 1992. Not because they were going after a battle-green goalie from Catholic Memorial High School in West Roxbury, Massachusetts. It was because the Capitals used a relatively early selection to choose a goalie — another goalie. Just three years earlier in the 1989 draft, Washington had picked Olaf Kolzig in the first round and Byron Dafoe in the second round and looked set in the crease for the next 10–15 years.

As it turned out, both Kolzig and Dafoe did have distinguished careers and during the lockout-shortened season of 1994–95 were supposed to be ready for prime time in Washington. Don Beaupre and Rick Tabaracci were Washington's goalies in 1993–94, but management wanted to make a change and Kolzig and Dafoe were ready. Carey, meanwhile, had finished his second year at the University of Wisconsin in 1993–94, but left school early to turn pro.

While the NHL and the Players' Association dithered over a collective bargaining agreement until January, Carey was a rising star with the Portland Pirates, leading the American League with six shutouts. When the 48-game NHL season began, the Capitals declared Carey the No. 1 man between the pipes and Kolzig and Dafoe would fight it out for the backup's job. Carey didn't disappoint, compiling an 18–6–3 record, while Kolzig and Dafoe combined to be 3–9–3. Only Peter Forsberg's exploits in Quebec were enough to take the Calder away from Carey.

Carey took it up a notch as a 21-year-old his second season. He was a workhorse, playing 71 games, and led the NHL with nine shutouts, was second with 35 wins and third with a 2.26 GAA. In Vezina Trophy balloting by GMs that spring, Carey was a narrow winner over Detroit's Chris Osgood by a 52–46 point-system vote.

"He stepped in the year before and gave Washington a chance to win every game and he did it even better the next season," Boston GM Harry Sinden said. "He was just a kid and he was the best goalie in the league."

Sinden truly was impressed. With Boston falling from a 40–31–11 record in 1995–96 to the worst record in the league the next season, he made a blockbuster six-player trade with Washington on March 1, 1997. Carey was the key figure, arriving in Boston with Anson Carter and Jason Allison in exchange for Adam Oates, Bill Ranford and Rick Tocchet. The Bruins would finally have their next great stopper, right?

Shockingly, Carey left his "A" game in Washington. Or so it seemed. There was no other logical explanation. His goals-against average ballooned to 3.82 the remainder of 1996–97. It didn't help that Boston's offense lost future Hall of Famer Cam Neely to retirement (Neely had scored 229 goals in his final 307 games with the Bruins before his body broke down for good at age 30) and 24-goal man Shawn McEachern to Ottawa and 23-goal man Dave Reid to Dallas. Moreover, Ray Bourque missed 20 games that season with injuries and the blueline felt his loss. But still, goalies Bill Ranford (3.49) and Rob Tallas (3.33) had much better numbers than Carey.

Sinden had no choice but to secure a capable backup during the 1997 off-season in case Carey continued to struggle the following year. So he acquired Dafoe from Los Angeles, the same Byron Dafoe that Carey forced out of NHL work in Washington.

Dafoe was a savior for the Bruins in 1997–98 and Carey, he played just 10 NHL games and wound up on the farm team in Providence. It was strictly AHL action in 1998–99 as well until the Bruins let him go, and the St. Louis Blues decided to give him a chance. After all, how often do you see a 24-year-old former Vezina Trophy winner free for the taking? In just four games with the Blues, Carey had a meager .829 save percentage and 3.86 GAA.

The fallen star was completely washed up. He didn't play another game professionally.

"I don't know how to explain that," Sinden said in 2010. "How does a goalie go from being the best to one of the worst in a couple of years? It's just one of those things that happens, and you don't have an answer for it so you don't ask. I remember when Gilles Gilbert was 24, he carried us to the Stanley Cup final in 1973–74, I turned to [assistant GM] Tom Johnson and said we're set in goal for the next decade. Sometimes things just don't turn out the way you thought they would."

ROOKIE SENSATIONS, PLAYOFF HEROES AND LEAGUE MVPS

The Vezina and Jennings were created specifically for the puckstoppers, but many brilliant goalies have won numerous other awards.

Sixteen goaltenders in the 77-year history of the Calder Memorial Trophy have been named the NHL's top rookie. That's about a one-in-five ratio, which seems appropriate given the breakdown of players by position. But when you consider goaltending is the most important job in the game, it's a credit to those 16 individuals who were able to move from a lower development league to the big top in one fell swoop and still get named best freshmen ahead of any skaters.

None of those 16 Calder-winning stoppers have as captivating a tale to tell as Tom Barrasso, who at the age of 18 in 1983, advanced from tiny Acton-Boxborough

Tom Barrasso in 1984–85. Barrasso followed up his 1983–84 Vezina by earning the 1984–85 Jennings Trophy with a 2.66 goals-against average in 54 games played. He shared the trophy with Bob Sauve.

High School in suburban Massachusetts all the way to the NHL — facing the game's top marksmen without missing a beat. He's one of just four goalies to win both the Calder and Vezina in the same season. The other three are Boston's Frank Brimsek (1938–39), Chicago's Tony Esposito (1969–70) and Chicago's Ed Belfour (1990–91).

The Buffalo Sabres had three picks in the first 11 selections in the 1983 NHL draft, so they felt they could take a gamble on one of them. They drafted forwards Normand Lacombe 10th and Adam Creighton 11th, but the flyer they took was in the fifth spot when they gambled and selected an American high school goalie.

"There's no way you could evaluate a goalie playing 20 games a year at a level so far less than major junior," said Boston GM Harry Sinden. "We'd go there to scout him and he'd only face a few shots, there would be nothing we learned. But the Sabres had all those picks and took the chance. I never would have done that with a pick so early."

Barrasso had fabulous stats at Acton-Boxborough (0.99 goals-against average), but he surely needed some seasoning in college or with the 1984 U.S. Olympic team. That was the plan. The Sabres were already set with 27-year-old Bob Sauve and 22-year-old Jacques Cloutier (the tandem finished sixth out of 21 teams in goals-against average the previous season). Barrasso had different ideas.

The tall, lanky netminder from Stow, Massachusetts, beat Cloutier out of a job in training camp, then ended up playing more games than Sauve, the proven starter — and

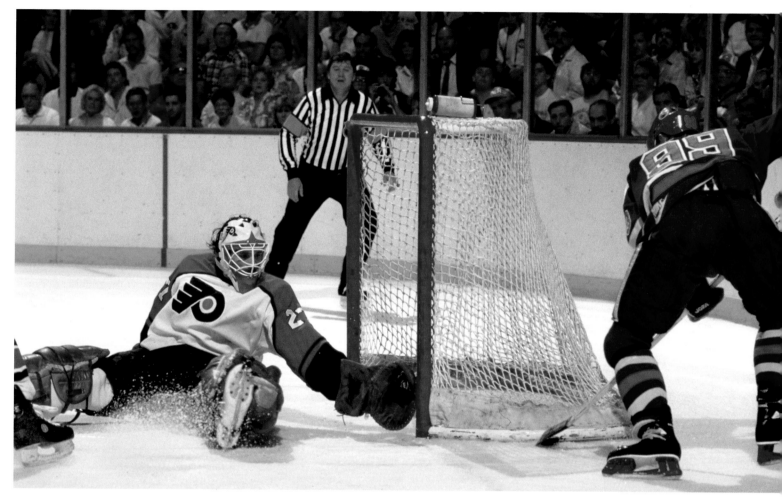

Ron Hextall vs. Wayne Gretzky in 1987 Stanly Cup action. Hextall took home the Conn Smythe in a losing effort, and was later awarded the Vezina – all in his rookie season.

his numbers were far superior. Barrasso played 42 games with a 2.84 GAA and .893 save percentage; Sauve had a 3.49 GAA and .869 save percentage in 40 games. The Sabres finished runner-up to the Washington Capitals for the Jennings Trophy for team GAA, and as for the Vezina, Barrasso won it over Calgary's Réjean Lemelin.

"Let me tell you, that was an unbelievable story," Sinden said. "It's been 25 years since that happened and it gets more remarkable the more you think about it ... an 18-year-old from high school stepping in and becoming the best goalie in the NHL. Think about that for a second."

During the awards ceremony to honor Barrasso, Washington's Rod Langway, winner of the Norris Trophy

as top defenceman, called Barrasso the best goalie in the world — and hockey people weren't arguing with him.

"I knew he was good, but the degree of his excellence still sort of shocks you," Minnesota North Stars GM Lou Nanne told *The Hockey News*. "I'm just sorry I didn't draft him last year. I'm happy with Brian Lawton [first overall in 1983], but a goaltender like Barrasso, well they just don't come along that often."

Barrasso played 20 seasons in the NHL and won two Stanley Cups with the Pittsburgh Penguins in the 1990s. But other than a second All-Star Team honor in 1992–93, that was it for individual accomplishments. That's probably one reason why Barrasso has eluded Hall of Fame induction since first becoming eligible in 2006.

Other goalies to win the Calder are: Chicago's Mike Karakas (1935–36), Toronto's Frank McCool (1944–45),

Boston's Jack Gelineau (1949–50), Detroit's Terry Sawchuk (1950–51), New York Rangers' Gump Worsley (1952–53), Detroit's Glenn Hall (1955–56), Detroit's Roger Crozier (1964–65), Montreal's Ken Dryden (1971–72), New Jersey's Martin Brodeur (1993–94), San Jose's Evgeni Nabokov (2000–01), Boston's Andrew Raycroft (2003–04) and Steve Mason of Columbus (2008–09).

The Conn Smythe Trophy for playoff MVP is weighted favorably in the goaltender's position. Fourteen stoppers in 44 seasons since the award's inception in 1966 have been given the honor. That's a 32-percent ratio.

What's notable about the Smythe is that just five times in its 44-year history has it been given to a player not on the Stanley Cup winning team — and four of the five were goalies.

In the first few seasons after the Smythe Trophy was created in 1965–66, the Montreal Canadiens must have thought they were banned from winning the award. The Habs won the Stanley Cup in 1966, but the Smythe went to second-year Detroit goalie Roger Crozier, who was fabulous in a losing effort. Montreal rallied from a 2–0 series deficit to win 4–2, finally able to crack the wall that was 24-year-old Crozier.

Montreal won the Cup again in 1968, but the Smythe went to future Hall of Famer Glenn Hall in the St. Louis Blues net. It was the first year in the NHL for St. Louis and the Blues had a losing record (27–31–16), but they won the division and made it to the final. Montreal was in the midst of a six-Cup-in-nine-year surge and beat St. Louis 4–0 in the final series that season, but each of the wins

Vezina Winners

Season	Winner
1926–27	George Hainsworth, Montreal
1927–28	George Hainsworth, Montreal
1928–29	George Hainsworth, Montreal
1929–30	Tiny Thompson, Boston
1930–31	Roy Worters, N.Y. Americans
1931–32	Charlie Gardiner, Chicago
1932–33	Tiny Thompson, Boston
1933–34	Charlie Gardiner, Chicago
1934–35	Lorne Chabot, Chicago
1935–36	Tiny Thompson, Boston
1936–37	Normie Smith, Detroit
1937–38	Tiny Thompson, Boston
1938–39	Frank Brimsek, Boston
1939–40	David Kerr, N.Y. Rangers
1940–41	Turk Broda, Toronto
1941–42	Frank Brimsek, Boston
1942–43	Johnny Mowers, Detroit
1943–44	Bill Durnan, Montreal
1944–45	Bill Durnan, Montreal
1945–46	Bill Durnan, Montreal
1946–47	Bill Durnan, Montreal
1947–48	Turk Broda, Toronto
1948–49	Bill Durnan, Montreal
1949–50	Bill Durnan, Montreal
1950–51	Al Rollins, Toronto
1951–52	Terry Sawchuk, Detroit
1952–53	Terry Sawchuk, Detroit
1953–54	Harry Lumley, Toronto
1954–55	Terry Sawchuk, Detroit
1955–56	Jacques Plante, Montreal
1956–57	Jacques Plante, Montreal
1957–58	Jacques Plante, Montreal
1958–59	Jacques Plante, Montreal
1959–60	Jacques Plante, Montreal
1960–61	Johnny Bower, Toronto
1961–62	Jacques Plante, Montreal
1962–63	Glenn Hall, Chicago
1963–64	Charlie Hodge, Montreal
1964–65	Johnny Bower, Terry Sawchuk, Toronto
1965–66	Gump Worsley, Charlie Hodge, Montreal
1966–67	Glenn Hall, Denis DeJordy, Chicago
1967–68	Gump Worsley, Rogatien Vachon, Montreal
1968–69	Glenn Hall, Jacques Plante, St. Louis
1969–70	Tony Esposito, Chicago
1970–71	Eddie Giacomin, Gilles Villemure, N.Y. Rangers
1971–72	Tony Esposito, Gary Smith, Chicago
1972–73	Ken Dryden, Montreal
1973–74	Tony Esposito, Chicago
1973–74	Bernie Parent, Philadelphia
1974–75	Bernie Parent, Philadelphia
1975–76	Ken Dryden, Montreal
1976–77	Ken Dryden, Michel Larocque, Montreal
1977–78	Ken Dryden, Michel Larocque, Montreal
1978–79	Ken Dryden, Michel Larocque, Montreal
1979–80	Don Edwards, Bob Sauve, Buffalo
1980–81	D. Herron, M. Larocque, R. Sevigny, Montreal
1981–82	Billy Smith, N.Y. Islanders
1982–83	Pete Peeters, Boston
1983–84	Tom Barrasso, Buffalo
1984–85	Pelle Lindbergh, Philadelphia
1985–86	John Vanbiesbrouck, N.Y. Rangers
1986–87	Ron Hextall, Philadelphia
1987–88	Grant Fuhr, Edmonton
1988–89	Patrick Roy, Montreal
1989–90	Patrick Roy, Montreal
1990–91	Ed Belfour, Chicago
1991–92	Patrick Roy, Montreal
1992–93	Ed Belfour, Chicago
1993–94	Dominik Hasek, Buffalo
1994–95	Dominik Hasek, Buffalo
1995–96	Jim Carey, Washington
1996–97	Dominik Hasek, Buffalo
1997–98	Dominik Hasek, Buffalo
1998–99	Dominik Hasek, Buffalo
1999–00	Olaf Kolzig, Washington
2000–01	Dominik Hasek, Buffalo
2001–02	Jose Theodore, Montreal
2002–03	Martin Brodeur, New Jersey
2003–04	Martin Brodeur, New Jersey
2004–05	No winner (lockout season)
2005–06	Miikka Kiprusoff, Calgary
2006–07	Martin Brodeur, New Jersey
2007–08	Martin Brodeur, New Jersey
2008–09	Tim Thomas, Boston
2009–10	Ryan Miller, Buffalo

was by a single goal, thanks to the brilliance of Hall.

Philadelphia's Reggie Leach won the Smythe in a losing cause in 1976 and 11 years would pass before another Cup loser got his hands on the Smythe. The Wayne Gretzky-led Edmonton Oilers dominated the NHL in the mid-1980s and looked to be on their way to a third Cup in 1987 when 23-year-old goalie Ron Hextall almost single-handedly stole the show. Edmonton won the first two games at home and split the next two in Philadelphia. Poised to win on home ice in Game 5, the Oilers were stymied when Hextall made 31 stops in a 4–3 Flyers win. Philadelphia won Game 6 at home 3–2, setting the stage for a possible epic comeback. The Oilers outshot Philadelphia 43–20 in Game 7 and won 3–1, but it was clear to everyone, Hextall was the best player of the playoffs.

Jennings Winners

1981–82	Rick Wamsley, Denis Herron, Montreal
1982–83	Roland Melanson, Billy Smith, NY Islanders
1983–84	Al Jensen, Pat Riggin, Washington
1984–85	Tom Barrasso, Bob Sauve, Buffalo
1985–86	Bob Froese, Darren Jensen, Philadelphia
1986–87	Patrick Roy, Brian Hayward, Montreal
1987–88	Patrick Roy, Brian Hayward, Montreal
1988–89	Patrick Roy, Brian Hayward, Montreal
1989–90	Andy Moog, Réjean Lemelin, Boston
1990–91	Ed Belfour, Chicago
1991–92	Patrick Roy, Montreal
1992–93	Ed Belfour, Chicago
1993–94	Dominik Hasek, Grant Fuhr, Buffalo
1994–95	Ed Belfour, Chicago
1995–96	Chris Osgood, Mike Vernon, Detroit
1996–97	Martin Brodeur, Mike Dunham, New Jersey
1997–98	Martin Brodeur, New Jersey
1998–99	Ed Belfour, Roman Turek, Dallas
1999–00	Roman Turek, St. Louis
2000–01	Dominik Hasek, Buffalo
2001–02	Patrick Roy, Colorado
2002–03	Martin Brodeur, New Jersey; Roman Cechmanek, Robert Esche, Philadelphia
2003–04	Martin Brodeur, New Jersey
2004–05	No winner (lockout season)
2005–06	Miikka Kiprusoff, Calgary
2006–07	Niklas Backstrom, Manny Fernandez, Minnesota
2007–08	Dominik Hasek, Chris Osgood, Detroit
2008–09	Tim Thomas, Manny Fernandez, Boston
2009–10	Martin Brodeur, New Jersey

"I said earlier Ron Hextall may be the best goaltender I've ever played against," Gretzky said in honor of the Conn Smythe Trophy winner that season.

The fifth and most recent Cup loser to win the Conn Smythe was Anaheim's Jean-Sébastien Giguère in 2003. The Cup final went the distance that year and New Jersey goalie Martin Brodeur earned three shutouts in the seven games, including 3–0 in Game 7, but Giguere was a force for all four playoff rounds. In 21 games, Giguere allowed just 38 goals, had a 1.62 goals-against average, .945 save percentage and five shutouts.

Other goalie winners of the Conn Smythe Trophy include: Montreal's Ken Dryden (1971), Philadelphia's Bernie Parent (1974 and 1975), New York Islanders' Billy Smith (1983), Patrick Roy with Montreal (1986 and 1993) and with Colorado (2001), Edmonton's Bill Ranford (1990), Detroit's Mike Vernon (1997) and Carolina's Cam Ward (2006). All were Stanley Cup champions as well.

The Hart Trophy rarely gets awarded to a goaltender, despite all the talk you hear about the goalie being the most important player in the game. Only two goalies since 1962 (and just seven in 86 seasons) have won the Hart as the league's MVP. Why is that?

"Goaltending is such a unique position that I think it almost should be separated from the Hart Trophy," Sinden said. "I've heard it said there isn't a player in the league who is as important as any of the goalies, so what do you do, give the Hart to a goalie every year? Isn't that what the Vezina is for?

"It's like the game of golf. You can be an excellent putter, but if you don't have a good swing with the other clubs or don't know how to swing a club, you [won't score well]. Playing hockey is a different game from stopping pucks. Goalies are excellent at what they do, but it's not the same as what the [skaters] do."

The list of goalies who have won the Hart is a select group. They include: New York Americans' Roy Worters (1928–29), New York Rangers' Chuck Rayner (1949–50), Chicago's Al Rollins (1953–54), Montreal's Jacques Plante (1961–62), Buffalo's Dominik Hasek (1996–97 and 1997–98) and Montreal's Jose Theodore (2001–02).

"Original Six" Stars

BY CHRIS MCDONELL

COMPETITION FOR goaltending positions was never so competitive as it was between 1942, when the NHL had six teams, and 1967, when it expanded to 12. Over those two-plus decades, with a few exceptions, the NHL netminding fraternity consisted of only six men at any one time.

A few newcomers got their shot when stalwarts such as Chuck Rayner, Frank Brimsek and Turk Broda served in the military during World War II, but even a seasoned All-Star such as Terry Sawchuk had constant worry about his job security, for there were always talented youngsters lurking impatiently in the wings. Playing with pain and disguising injuries was common, and the pressure to perform perfectly for fear of being replaced added to the heavy mental and physical strain.

The goaltender's paraphernalia had improved dramatically by the 1940s, with thick leather leg pads and a defined trapper and blocker being standard issue. Perhaps no goaltender has ever been as innovative with his equipment as the remarkably ambidextrous Bill Durnan, who had a unique pair of fingered gloves that could both catch the puck and hold his stick. But it took a stalwart netminder like Jacques Plante to literally change the face of goaltending when he donned a mask in late 1959. Of all the changes in over a century to the goalie's tools of the trade, this evolution is arguably the most profound. Thanks to Plante, a goalie today can put his head in harm's way in hopes of blocking a shot — a suicidal strategy in the Original Six era.

A goaltender's style of play also underwent a major metamorphosis during this period. Rayner and Plante got out of their crease to field pucks and feed passes to their teammates, Glenn Hall developed the butterfly stance, while Johnny Bower perfected the poke check. The Hall of Fame stars of the Original Six era proved puckstopping is an ever-evolving vocation.

Chicago's Glenn Hall charges out from the net to clear the puck from danger at the Montreal Forum.

INDUCTED 1976

JOHNNY BOWER

Wizened Yet Forever Young

JOHNNY "THE CHINA WALL" Bower seemed as ageless as the Asian landmark. Most remember him as a veteran goaltender, for he didn't begin his golden years as a Toronto Maple Leaf until he was almost 35 years old and past retirement age for most goaltenders. But Bower also had a distinguished career as a young man.

Dirt poor and the only boy in a family of nine children, somehow, at age 15, he managed to enlist in the Canadian army during World War II. In 1944, after four years of service, he was discharged due to illness. Still a teenager, he returned to his junior hockey team in Prince Albert, Saskatchewan, for the remainder of the 1944–45 campaign and made the jump to the American Hockey League (AHL) the following season.

"You had to bide your time," recalled Bower, who rode the buses with the Cleveland Barons for nine

seasons before getting his first chance in the NHL. He made the 1951 AHL Second All-Star Team and joined the First Team in the following two seasons, at which point the New York Rangers swung a deal for his services. Bower posted a strong 1953–54 campaign for the Rangers, playing all 70 games even though goalie Gump Worsley had been the NHL's Rookie of the Year with the Rangers the previous season. Later on, Bower faced a similar disappointment to Gump's, when, to his surprise, he found himself back in the minors the following season, and Worsley got his NHL job back. Although Bower won a multitude of AHL awards over the following four seasons, the perennial All-Star and three-time AHL MVP played only seven games as a call-up for the Rangers over that span.

Bower, like many professionals in the six-team era, was resigned to having a rewarding minor league career, but fate intervened in 1958. He had played a particularly

strong playoff series that spring against the Springfield Indians. Punch Imlach, who ran the Indians, was hired as coach and general manager of the Toronto Maple Leafs that year, and he drafted Bower. Although initially reluctant to join the Leafs, Bower was persuaded to report to training camp. "I was scared, literally shaking in my boots, for my first game in Maple Leaf Gardens," confessed Bower, but he quickly established himself as a No. 1 NHL goalie in the fall of 1958. Over the next 11 seasons, he won four Stanley Cup rings and two Vezina Trophies.

Bower was a standup goalie with surprisingly quick reflexes. He worked as hard in practice as he did in games, a habit that endeared him to Imlach, and although he was as affable a man as any who ever played in the NHL, he had an equally strong competitive streak. Bower is remembered for his famous poke check, a move he says

he learned from his New York Ranger mentor Chuck Rayner at a training camp early in his career. But Bower certainly made the dangerous but effective technique his own. Diving headfirst — and maskless of course — he'd spear the puck off the stick of an attacking forward's stick, and frequently take out the forward at the skates right after. Although facial injuries were common — from cuts and bruises to broken teeth — Bower never donned a mask until the very tail end of his career. His lined and scarred face led many to suspect he was even older than his reported age, and Bower was intentionally vague about dates, but his play was stellar, and Imlach never hesitated to use veteran players.

Bower helped the last-place Leafs into the playoffs his first season in Toronto, and then backstopped them to two consecutive Stanley Cup final, winning the 1960–61

Vezina Trophy along the way. Then, in 1962, he led the Leafs to the Promised Land. "It was such a thrill to win the Cup," said Bower. "I got so excited that at the end of the game, I threw my stick up in the air. I saw my teammates coming toward me to celebrate and realized I'd better get my stick. I looked up and — boom! — it came down on my forehead and cut me for seven stitches. I didn't feel a thing, bleeding all over the guys who were hugging me."

Toronto won the Cup in 1962, 1963 and 1964, with Bower averaging 2.01 goals-against in the playoffs. "Anytime you win in the Stanley Cup, the goaltender is the big reason," said Imlach. "We've got a lot of good hockey players on our team, but they're not worth a darn unless the old guy is making the big saves."

"I wasn't all that glad to see the two-goalie system come in," maintained Bower. "I wanted to play in all the games I possibly could." But Imlach was always alert to squeezing the last juice possible from NHL veterans and Bower shared the Vezina with Terry Sawchuk in 1964–65. While Sawchuk was ever the loner and not really willing to offer tips to Bower, both benefited by watching the other, and resting while the other flashed a hot hand. In what would prove to be the last hurrah for both, the two goalies combined efforts to help an underdog team of old-timers win the Cup again in 1966–67. That victory remains to date the last time the Stanley Cup belonged to the Toronto Maple Leafs.

Bower retired in 1970 as the oldest goalie ever to play in the NHL at the age of 45. He remained with the Leafs for many years as a scout and then goalie coach, putting the pads on and helping Leaf goalies in practice. He entered the Hockey Hall of Fame in 1976, but later, during the Maple Leafs' injury riddled 1979–80 season, the China Wall came within a whisker of dressing as Toronto's backup goalie — and had he been called to action, no one would have been surprised if the 56-year-old stoned the opposition.

Career Stats

REGULAR SEASON

Season	Age	Team	Lg	GP	W	L	T	SO	GA	GAA	G	A	PTS	PIM
1953-54	29	New York Rangers	NHL	70	29	31	10	5	182	2.60	0	0	0	0
1954-55	30	New York Rangers	NHL	5	2	2	1	0	13	2.60	0	0	0	0
1956-57	32	New York Rangers	NHL	2	0	2	0	0	6	3.00	0	0	0	0
1958-59	34	Toronto Maple Leafs	NHL	39	15	17	7	3	106	2.72	0	0	0	2
1959-60	35	Toronto Maple Leafs	NHL	66	34	24	8	5	177	2.68	0	0	0	4
1960-61	36	Toronto Maple Leafs	NHL	58	33	15	10	2	145	2.50	0	0	0	0
1961-62	37	Toronto Maple Leafs	NHL	59	31	18	10	2	151	2.56	0	1	1	4
1962-63	38	Toronto Maple Leafs	NHL	42	20	15	7	1	109	2.60	0	0	0	2
1963-64	39	Toronto Maple Leafs	NHL	51	24	16	11	5	106	2.11	0	0	0	4
1964-65	40	Toronto Maple Leafs	NHL	34	13	13	8	3	81	2.38	0	0	0	6
1965-66	41	Toronto Maple Leafs	NHL	35	18	10	5	3	75	2.25	0	1	1	0
1966-67	42	Toronto Maple Leafs	NHL	27	12	9	3	2	63	2.64	0	0	0	0
1967-68	43	Toronto Maple Leafs	NHL	43	14	18	7	4	84	2.25	0	1	1	14
1968-69	44	Toronto Maple Leafs	NHL	20	5	4	3	2	37	2.85	0	0	0	0
1969-70	45	Toronto Maple Leafs	NHL	1	0	1	0	0	5	5.00	0	0	0	0
NHL Career – 15 Seasons				552	250	195	90	37	1340	2.51	0	3	3	36

PLAYOFFS

Season	Age	Team	Lg	GP	W	L	T	SO	GA	GAA	G	A	PTS	PIM
1958-59	34	Toronto Maple Leafs	NHL	12	5	7		0	38	3.06	0	0	0	0
1959-60	35	Toronto Maple Leafs	NHL	10	4	6		0	31	2.88	0	0	0	0
1960-61	36	Toronto Maple Leafs	NHL	3	0	3		0	8	2.67	0	0	0	2
1961-62	37	Toronto Maple Leafs	NHL	10	6	3		0	20	2.07	0	0	0	0
1962-63	38	Toronto Maple Leafs	NHL	10	8	2		2	16	1.60	0	1	1	0
1963-64	39	Toronto Maple Leafs	NHL	14	8	6		2	30	2.12	0	0	0	0
1964-65	40	Toronto Maple Leafs	NHL	5	2	3		0	13	2.43	0	0	0	0
1965-66	41	Toronto Maple Leafs	NHL	2	0	2		0	8	4.00	0	0	0	0
1966-67	42	Toronto Maple Leafs	NHL	4	2	0		1	5	1.64	0	0	0	2
1968-69	44	Toronto Maple Leafs	NHL	4	0	2		0	11	4.29	0	0	0	0
NHL Career – 10 Seasons				74	35	34		5	180	2.47	0	1	1	4

Page 52: A fresh-faced Johnny Bower of the Cleveland Barons, where he spent nine AHL seasons.

Page 53: Bower knocks the puck away from the onrushing Camille Henry with a poke check, his specialty.

Page 54: Bower gets the paddle down on Henri Richard's wraparound attempt while the Toronto defense looks on.

INDUCTED 1966

FRANK BRIMSEK

Mr. Zero Made His Mark

FRANK BRIMSEK MADE AN auspicious NHL debut in the fall of 1938. Although initially unheralded as a replacement for the legendary Tiny Thompson, he made such a strong impression in two games as a substitute that the Boston Bruins traded the veteran Thompson to Detroit.

"The kid had the fastest hands I ever saw," said Boston coach and general manager (and former NHL star) Art Ross. "Like lightning." The Beantown fans were irate at the trade, however, and so were many of the Boston players, some of whom even threatened to quit in frustration.

"When I hit the ice, things were so quiet that I could hear the people breathing," recalled Brimsek, looking back at a game against the Montreal Canadiens on December 1, 1938. "They were just waiting for me to blow one." Under incredible pressure from both his uncertain teammates and the usually raucous fans, Brimsek and the Bruins

lost the game 2–0, and the crowd was on Brimsek's back throughout.

But Brimsek shut out his opponents in each of the next three games. When he finally surrendered a goal, after 231 minutes and 54 seconds of shutout hockey (breaking Thompson's team record), the Boston fans paused only a moment before breaking out into a prolonged ovation. Brimsek had won his doubters over. He posted a victory that game, too. In his first eight NHL games the rookie posted six shutouts.

Henceforth tagged with the moniker "Mr. Zero," Brimsek finished the 1938–39 season with a league-leading 10 shutouts. He was awarded the Calder Trophy as Rookie of the Year, the Vezina Trophy for the best goals-against average (1.56) and a First All-Star Team berth. More important, he took the Bruins to Stanley Cup victory, which they won four games to one over Toronto

and his heavy custom-made stick was used to sweep away pucks — or the skates of a foe taking liberties near his net. He played a smart mental game, too, always looking for an edge. "I tried to make the opposition player do what I wanted him to," he once explained. "I always felt that the glove side was the strongest side for a goaltender. And I would make the shooter believe this, too. In that way, I would make most shooters fire the puck to my stick side, which is what I wanted them to do in the first place."

Brimsek earned All-Star status in each of his first eight seasons, an unprecedented streak, winning a second Stanley Cup ring in 1941 and another Vezina Trophy in 1941–42. The latter season may have been his most spectacular, as the Boston lineup had lost the famed Kraut Line of Milt Schmidt, Bobby Bauer and Woody Dumart to the Canadian Armed Forces. Brimsek enlisted the following season. "You just get established in a business like hockey, and you have to give it all up," complained Brimsek. "A damned war comes along." World War II interrupted Brimsek's NHL hockey career for two seasons. He played for the U.S. Coast Guard Cutters for the 1943–44 season, on a team that was intended to bolster morale, but when American participation in the war intensified and casualties were increasing, Brimsek found himself on active duty in the South Pacific in 1944–45.

A year on a patrol boat left Brimsek "jumpy" when

in the league's first best-of-seven final series. Boston's biggest challenge that year came in the semifinal, when it took three overtime wins to vanquish the New York Rangers. Tiny Thompson was not forgotten, but Frank Brimsek had passed every test with flying colors.

One of the first NHL stars ever to hail from the United States, Brimsek was born in Eveleth, Minnesota, the home of the U.S. Hockey Hall of Fame (where he was enshrined as a charter member in 1973). A classic stand-up goalie, he showed great confidence, often leaning back calmly against his net when an opponent started in on a breakaway or a penalty shot. There was nothing passive about Brimsek's play, however. His glove hand, often described as "Brimmy's lightning," was a potent weapon, he returned to the NHL early in 1946. "I was a little shaky when I got back," he said later. "My legs and my nerves were shot." Although he later confessed that he came back too soon, primarily because he needed the money, Brimsek picked up much where he had left off. The Bruins made it to the 1946 Stanley Cup final but were vanquished by the Montreal Canadiens, who were led by a star who had emerged during Brimsek's military years: Maurice "Rocket" Richard.

Brimsek felt his skills were diminishing, and the Bruins overall were a shadow of their pre-war squad. Nevertheless, "Mr. Zero" continued to keep his team in many games. He finished second to the New York Rangers' Buddy O'Connor in the 1947–48 Hart Trophy voting for the NHL's Most Valuable Player, and made the NHL's Second All-Star Team in three consecutive seasons. Brimsek saw the end in sight, though. "When I got out of the war, I knew I wasn't going to play long. I didn't have

that same feeling for the game," he said. "I had a hard time even going back to training camp."

Thinking of future career opportunities, Brimsek had the first of his conversations with Art Ross about his post-Boston career in 1947, but he more or less demanded a trade to Chicago in 1949. "My brother was starting a business there," he explained, "and I thought I might help him open a few doors." Soon sold to the Black Hawks, reportedly for the largest cash outlay since Toronto's $35,000 purchase of King Clancy from Ottawa in 1930, Brimsek played every game of the 1949–50 season, adding five shutouts to his career record despite Chicago's last-place standing. Brimsek then retired, but left an indelible mark on the game. In 1966, his decade of NHL service was recognized when he became only the third American elected to the Hockey Hall of Fame. In Minnesota, the Frank Brimsek Award is presented annually to the state's top high-school goalie.

Career Stats

REGULAR SEASON

Season	Age	Team	Lg	GP	W	L	T	SO	GA	GAA	G	A	PTS	PIM
1938–39	23	Boston Bruins	NHL	43	33	9	1	10	68	1.56	0	0	0	0
1939–40	24	Boston Bruins	NHL	48	31	12	5	6	98	1.99	0	0	0	0
1940–41	25	Boston Bruins	NHL	48	27	8	13	6	102	2.01	0	0	0	0
1941–42	26	Boston Bruins	NHL	47	24	17	6	3	115	2.35	0	0	0	0
1942–43	27	Boston Bruins	NHL	50	24	17	9	1	176	3.52	0	0	0	0
1945–46	30	Boston Bruins	NHL	34	16	14	4	2	111	3.26	0	0	0	0
1946–47	31	Boston Bruins	NHL	60	26	23	11	3	175	2.92	0	0	0	2
1947–48	32	Boston Bruins	NHL	60	23	24	13	3	168	2.80	0	0	0	0
1948–49	33	Boston Bruins	NHL	54	26	20	8	1	147	2.72	0	0	0	2
1949–50	34	Chicago Black Hawks	NHL	70	22	38	10	5	244	3.49	0	0	0	2
NHL Career – 10 Seasons				514	252	182	80	40	1404	2.70	0	0	0	6

PLAYOFFS

Season	Age	Team	Lg	GP	W	L	T	SO	GA	GAA	G	A	PTS	PIM
1938–39	23	Boston Bruins	NHL	12	8	4		1	18	1.25	0	0	0	0
1939–40	24	Boston Bruins	NHL	6	2	4		0	15	2.50	0	0	0	0
1940–41	25	Boston Bruins	NHL	11	8	3		1	23	2.04	0	0	0	0
1941–42	26	Boston Bruins	NHL	5	2	3		0	16	3.13	0	0	0	0
1942–43	27	Boston Bruins	NHL	9	4	5		0	33	3.54	0	0	0	0
1945–46	30	Boston Bruins	NHL	10	5	5		0	29	2.67	0	0	0	0
1946–47	31	Boston Bruins	NHL	5	1	4		0	16	2.80	0	0	0	0
1947–48	32	Boston Bruins	NHL	5	1	4		0	20	3.79	0	0	0	0
1948–49	33	Boston Bruins	NHL	5	1	4		0	16	3.04	0	0	0	0
NHL Career – 9 Seasons				68	32	36		2	186	2.54	0	0	0	0

Page 56: Frank Brimsek in 1949–50, his last NHL season and his only season not in Boston.

Page 57: Brimsek angles the puck to the corner with his skate blade in a pre-game action shot.

Page 58: Game action from above the goal judge's booth in Maple Leaf Gardens. Brimsek makes a save with Leaf captain Syl Apps on the doorstep.

INDUCTED 1967

TURK
BRODA

The Brilliant Bulging Battler

THERE ARE A FEW TALES as to how Walter Broda earned his nickname, "Turk," and one of the more popular is that he got it for his freckles, which resembled the spots on a turkey egg. Turk was small as a child (he only grew to be 5-foot-9), and the other origin story for the famous moniker came from his school days in Brandon, Manitoba. There, Broda was a skinny, short-legged boy with a large upper body, which prompted his friends to dub him "Turkey Legs," and then, of course, "Turk."

The stout Broda was deemed too short to play any position other than goal, and he ended up playing his junior and minor league hockey with the Detroit Red Wings organization before Toronto Maple Leafs' owner Conn Smythe bought him for $7,500 to replace George Hainsworth for the 1936–37 season. Broda was a mainstay for the Leafs for the next 15 years, interrupted only by two years of military service.

Broda's outgoing style made him hugely popular with Leafs fans. They tossed cigars onto the ice in appreciation after a game, and Broda was quick to scurry around and gather them up. He was equally loved by his teammates, who knew firsthand his dedication to the team. Despite his chubby appearance, Broda worked harder than most in practice. "The Leafs pay me for my work in practices," he joked, "and I throw in the games for free." In truth, Broda established himself as a "money" goaltender, as his best games came when it mattered most. Although he backstopped the Leafs to the Stanley Cup final three times in his first four seasons, to his coach's dismay, Broda was notorious for getting distracted and letting in some long shots when the game wasn't on the line.

"Turk has been known to boot the odd soft one, miss a two-foot putt and trump a partner's ace," teased his coach Hap Day, who took over the Leafs' bench duties in the fall of 1940 and worked on his goaltenders reflexes and

awareness by having him play without a stick while team-mates fired shots from 20 and 30 feet out.

In 1940–41, Broda won his first of two Vezina Trophies, but the Leafs were eliminated in the first round of the playoffs. The team seemed destined, again, to also-ran status the following year, falling behind three games to none against Detroit in the 1942 Cup final. Broda, however, allowed only seven goals in the next four games, as Toronto executed an unprecedented comeback. Broda notched a shutout in the sixth game and let in only a single goal in the deciding seventh match, and Toronto had its first Stanley Cup victory in 10 years.

In 1943, Broda joined the army, as did many of his contemporaries. A public controversy erupted when the Royal Canadian Mounted Police stopped his train en route to Montreal and arrested Broda, who had been offered

a $2,400 bonus to enlist in Montreal and tend net for a Quebec military team. Returned to Toronto so that he would join the Toronto Army Daggers, Broda was sent off to England for two years, primarily to play hockey.

When Broda was discharged in 1945, he went straight to Maple Leaf Gardens and resumed practicing with the team. He was back in the nets, and there he stayed for four more Stanley Cup final, winning three in a row from 1947 to 1949. Broda played the entire season in goal in 8 of his 11 seasons, and part of two others, leading the league in shutouts twice. But for all his fame and glory, he's also remembered for his weight problems, which Conn Smythe used as a publicity stunt.

When the Leafs stumbled early in the 1949–50 season, Smythe ended Broda's run of more than 200 starts in a row by ordering five of his players onto diets, including his star netminder, who was reported to weigh 197 pounds. "The honeymoon is over," blustered Smythe. "I'm taking Broda out of the nets and he's not coming back until he shows some common sense. Two seasons ago, Broda weighed 185 pounds. Last season he went up to 190 — and now this. A goalie has to have fast reflexes and you can't move fast when you're overweight." Smythe added some gravitas to his decision by calling up the slim Gil Mayer, goaltender for the farm club team in Pittsburgh, and then sending four players and cash to the AHL's Cleveland Barons for up-and-coming lanky netminder Al Rollins.

For days afterward, however, newspaper articles showed Broda smiling, sometimes sitting on a scale. His wife, Betty, became famous for being the one person who could help him win "The Battle of the Bulge" and save the city's team. "I don't know what I can cut off Turk," lamented Mrs. Broda. "He hardly eats a darn thing now and has the smallest appetite in the house. Why, the girls

and I eat more than he does." After getting down to the prescribed weight of 190 pounds in a well-publicized weigh-in, Broda started his first game in a week.

"There may be better goalies around somewhere," laughed Smythe, "but there's no greater sportsman than the Turkey. If the Rangers score on him tonight, I should go out and buy him a malted milk just to show I'm not trying to starve him to death." Broda posted a shutout that night, and with the permission of his boss, announced he'd be enjoying a small steak that evening. He went on to notch a career-best nine shutouts that season.

Although reduced to backup status in the following campaign, Broda sparkled in the 1951 playoffs, playing 8 of the 11 games it took the Leafs to win the Stanley Cup. All five games of the final against Montreal went into overtime. "I couldn't beat him. Toe Blake couldn't. None of the Canadiens could," Maurice Richard said after that series. It was Broda's swan song, however, and he retired after playing only half a game the next season.

Career Stats

REGULAR SEASON

Season	Age	Team	Lg	GP	W	L	T	SO	GA	GAA	G	A	PTS	PIM
1936–37	22	Toronto Maple Leafs	NHL	45	22	19	4	3	106	2.30	0	0	0	0
1937–38	23	Toronto Maple Leafs	NHL	48	24	15	9	6	127	2.56	0	0	0	0
1938–39	24	Toronto Maple Leafs	NHL	48	19	20	9	8	107	2.15	0	0	0	0
1939–40	25	Toronto Maple Leafs	NHL	47	25	17	5	4	108	2.23	0	0	0	0
1940–41	26	Toronto Maple Leafs	NHL	48	28	14	6	5	99	2.00	0	0	0	0
1941–42	27	Toronto Maple Leafs	NHL	48	27	18	3	6	136	2.76	0	0	0	0
1942–43	28	Toronto Maple Leafs	NHL	50	22	19	9	1	159	3.18	0	0	0	0
1945–46	31	Toronto Maple Leafs	NHL	15	6	6	3	0	53	3.53	0	0	0	0
1946–47	32	Toronto Maple Leafs	NHL	60	31	19	10	4	172	2.87	0	0	0	0
1947–48	33	Toronto Maple Leafs	NHL	60	32	15	13	5	143	2.38	0	0	0	2
1948–49	34	Toronto Maple Leafs	NHL	60	22	25	13	5	161	2.68	0	0	0	0
1949–50	35	Toronto Maple Leafs	NHL	68	30	25	12	9	167	2.48	0	0	0	2
1950–51	36	Toronto Maple Leafs	NHL	31	14	11	5	6	68	2.23	0	0	0	4
1951–52	37	Toronto Maple Leafs	NHL	1	0	1	0	0	3	6.00	0	0	0	0
NHL Career – 14 Seasons				629	302	224	101	62	1609	2.53	0	0	0	8

PLAYOFFS

Season	Age	Team	Lg	GP	W	L	T	SO	GA	GAA	G	A	PTS	PIM
1936–37	22	Toronto Maple Leafs	NHL	2	0	2		0	5	2.26	0	0	0	0
1937–38	23	Toronto Maple Leafs	NHL	7	4	3		1	13	1.73	0	0	0	0
1938–39	24	Toronto Maple Leafs	NHL	10	5	5		2	20	1.94	0	0	0	0
1939–40	25	Toronto Maple Leafs	NHL	10	6	4		1	19	1.74	0	0	0	0
1940–41	26	Toronto Maple Leafs	NHL	7	3	4		0	15	2.05	0	0	0	0
1941–42	27	Toronto Maple Leafs	NHL	13	8	5		1	31	2.38	0	0	0	0
1942–43	28	Toronto Maple Leafs	NHL	6	2	4		0	20	2.73	0	0	0	0
1946–47	32	Toronto Maple Leafs	NHL	11	8	3		1	27	2.38	0	0	0	0
1947–48	33	Toronto Maple Leafs	NHL	9	8	1		1	20	2.15	0	0	0	10
1948–49	34	Toronto Maple Leafs	NHL	9	8	1		1	15	1.57	0	0	0	2
1949–50	35	Toronto Maple Leafs	NHL	7	3	4		3	10	1.33	0	0	0	0
1950–51	36	Toronto Maple Leafs	NHL	8	5	1		2	9	1.10	0	0	0	0
1951–52	37	Toronto Maple Leafs	NHL	2	0	2		0	7	3.50	0	0	0	0
NHL Career – 13 Seasons				101	60	39		13	211	1.98	0	0	0	12

Page 60: Turk Broda, well out to cut the angle, looks on as a shot sails wide of the net.

Page 61: Broda seen in net enjoying a large stack of pancakes. Broda's weight was the subject of much ridicule during his career with the Leafs, but the star netminder took it all with good humor.

Page 62: Broda in a staged action shot making a blocker save.

BILL
DURNAN

The Quick Change Artist

WHEN THE MONTREAL Canadiens came calling, Bill Durnan was not eager to enter professional hockey, despite earning at most $15 per week between playing hockey, softball and doing a variety of odd jobs. Initially signed by the Toronto Maple Leafs, Durnan was invited to attend his first pro camp in 1936 at age 20. Just before camp, he injured his knee in a playful tussle on the beach with a friend.

When the Leafs heard he had torn all the ligaments in his knee and displaced some cartilage, they dropped Durnan like a hot potato. Durnan felt he'd been treated shabbily and lost his enthusiasm for the pro game, even drifting completely away from hockey for a spell. He then spent four seasons in the northern Ontario mining town of Kirkland Lake, where he helped the Blue Devils win the 1940 Allan Cup, senior hockey's top prize.

Friends in Montreal then convinced Durnan to take a job with the Royals in their city, and after three years in the Quebec senior league, he had the full attention of the Montreal Canadiens' general manager Tommy Gorman. Durnan's play at the Habs' training camp in 1943 had Gorman convinced he had a new starting goalie, but Durnan drove a hard bargain. He was content to make less money as an amateur in return for less stress, but he did have his price. Gorman made a final counteroffer ten minutes before the Canadiens' first game of the season. The ink on his $4,200 contract was barely dry when Durnan stepped between the pipes of the Montreal net for what would prove to be a brief but brilliant NHL career.

Durnan was skilled at cutting off angles and a superb athlete, but unusual ambidexterity was one of the keys to his goaltending mastery. Hockey hasn't seen this skill, before or since, but Durnan wore specially fingered trappers

that allowed him to hold his stick or catch the puck with either hand, and he could make the switch with lightning speed. No matter which way a shooter came in at him, Durnan would ensure he had his catching hand at the optimum side. He credited Steve Faulkner, his boyhood coach in a Toronto church league, for the development of his unique skill. "He worked me by the hour," recalled Durnan, "until I had the technique down pat, and we won five city championships in six years. At first, it felt as though I was transferring a telephone pole from one hand to the other, but after a while, I'd hardly realize I was doing it."

Over seven seasons at the NHL level, from 1943–44 to 1949–50, Durnan confounded shooters enough to win the Vezina Trophy six times, including his first year when he finished runner-up as Rookie of the Year and earned his first of six First All-Star Team berths. In the playoffs that year, he posted a 1.53 goals-against average and won his first Stanley Cup ring.

"Durnan was toughest for me," recalled Boston's Milt Schmidt, when asked about goaltenders during his lengthy playing career. "I could never do much with the guy. At the outset, he troubled me, and it got to be a complex, I guess. It got to the point where I'd break through on him and have the feeling he had me beaten anyway. Durnan had an uncanny way of cutting off all the angles, and waiting patiently for you to commit yourself."

Durnan backstopped the Habs to Stanley Cup victory again in 1945–46, and to the final the following season. Although genial in temperament off the ice, Durnan was serious during games and constantly vocal in directing his teammates on the ice. His leadership was acknowledged when Toe Blake suffered a broken leg in January 1948 and Durnan was handed the captain's "C." Durnan's frequent forays to discuss game matters with the referee had the opposition fuming and arguing he was just seeking an opportunity to catch his breath. The league instituted a new rule for the following season, disallowing a goaltender from executing the captain's duties on the ice.

Montreal failed to make the playoffs in 1947–48 and Durnan received sustained booing for the first time. "I don't know whether you've ever heard 13,000 people all calling you the same bad name at the same time," he later recalled, "but it sure makes a loud noise." He was an easygoing man by nature, but with his heavy workload and extra responsibilities as captain, compounded with the team faltering, Durnan felt the pressure starting to get to him. "It got so bad," he said, "that I couldn't sleep the night before a game or the night afterwards, either. Nothing is worth that kind of agony." He contemplated quitting but the Canadiens talked him out of it — temporarily.

"I'll admit, if they were paying the kind of money goaltenders get today, they'd have to shoot me to get me out of the game," conceded Durnan in 1972. "But at the end of any given season, I never had more than $2,000 in the bank, I wasn't educated and had two little girls to raise. All this worried me a great deal, and I was also hurting."

Durnan posted career highs in 1948–49, with 10 shutouts and a 2.10 goals-against average, but looked back at the 1949–50 season as "the beginning of the end." Although he tallied eight shutouts and led the league with a 2.20 goals-against average, most of the fun of the game had gone for him. A bad gash in his head from an errant skate, late in the season, had him pondering retirement, but more significant, he felt his play was faltering and he was letting down his teammates.

When Montreal fell behind three games to none in the playoff semifinal in 1950, Durnan abruptly quit. Montreal had signed a promising young goalie named Gerry McNeil, and Durnan felt McNeil might as well get started. This time, despite McNeil's and his coach and teammates' protestations, there was no convincing Durnan to change his mind again. McNeil won one match before the Canadiens were eliminated that season, and Durnan never played another game.

Career Stats

REGULAR SEASON

Season	Age	Team	Lg	GP	W	L	T	SO	GA	GAA	G	A	PTS	PIM
1943–44	28	Montreal Canadiens	NHL	50	38	5	7	2	109	2.18	0	0	0	0
1944–45	29	Montreal Canadiens	NHL	50	38	8	4	1	121	2.42	0	0	0	0
1945–46	30	Montreal Canadiens	NHL	40	24	11	5	4	104	2.60	0	0	0	0
1946–47	31	Montreal Canadiens	NHL	60	34	16	10	4	138	2.30	0	0	0	0
1947–48	32	Montreal Canadiens	NHL	59	20	28	10	5	162	2.77	0	0	0	5
1948–49	33	Montreal Canadiens	NHL	60	28	23	9	10	126	2.10	0	0	0	0
1949–50	34	Montreal Canadiens	NHL	64	26	21	17	8	141	2.20	0	1	1	2
NHL Career – 7 Seasons				383	208	112	62	34	901	2.36	0	1	1	7

PLAYOFFS

Season	Age	Team	Lg	GP	W	L	T	SO	GA	GAA	G	A	PTS	PIM
1943–44	28	Montreal Canadiens	NHL	9	8	1		1	14	1.53	0	0	0	0
1944–45	29	Montreal Canadiens	NHL	6	2	4		0	15	2.41	0	0	0	0
1945–46	30	Montreal Canadiens	NHL	9	8	1		0	20	2.07	0	0	0	0
1946–47	31	Montreal Canadiens	NHL	11	6	5		1	23	1.92	0	0	0	0
1948–49	33	Montreal Canadiens	NHL	7	3	4		0	17	2.18	0	0	0	0
1949–50	34	Montreal Canadiens	NHL	3	0	3		0	10	3.33	0	0	0	0
NHL Career – 6 Seasons				45	27	18		2	99	2.07	0	0	0	0

Page 64: Canadiens captain Bill Durnan shares a laugh in the Habs dressing room with coach Dick Irvin (top) Maurice Richard (left) and Butch Buchard (right).

Page 65: Durnan strikes a game ready pose. Notice his ambidextrous catching gloves.

Page 66: Durnan sets himself to clear the puck from harm's way.

GLENN
HALL

INDUCTED 1975

Ironman and the Butterfly

GLENN "MR. GOALIE" HALL earned his nickname for his consistently sterling play over more than 1,000 games, including an "ironman" record that will likely stand the test of time. Beginning with the first game of 1955–56, through part of the 1962–63 season, Hall played every minute of every game before a back injury forced him out of action. His streak ended at 502 games (552 including playoffs) and what is even more significant is that Hall played those games without a mask. There was nothing cautious about his play, either.

Hall pioneered the "butterfly" style of goaltending when he discovered that crouching and keeping his legs spread below the knees allowed him to go down rapidly but keep his body erect to cover more of the net, and then spring back up again quickly. Hall's innovative method was ridiculed by many, who saw it as "flopping" and contrary to the accepted stand-up style. "I didn't realize at the time how much criticism was being directed at me through the media, because I didn't read the hockey section of the newspaper until I retired," he recalled. "I'm thankful for that. I knew the style was good for me. The critics didn't

understand what I was doing. The butterfly keeps the body erect. When the body is erect, you can recover easily. It's actually the opposite of flopping."

Of course, Hall's butterfly method also put his unprotected face directly into harm's way. "The styles have changed so much since the mask came in," Hall said. "We tried to get our feet over in front of the puck and the head out of the way. Making the save was thought number two; it was survival, number one. Sometimes you sacrificed that to stop the puck, but survival was always on our mind."

Hall grew up in Saskatchewan, but played his junior hockey with the Windsor Spitfires in the Ontario Hockey Association and was signed by the Detroit Red Wings in 1951. He entered Detroit's farm system, where he continued to perfect his style. "I liked the deep crouch that I saw Terry Sawchuk use," recalled Hall. "Most goalies would try to look over the players screening them, but Terry would often look underneath the screen. That worked well for me too,

but in those days, goalies never talked about goaltending. I was called up a few times to fill in for Terry when he was injured, but he never told me a thing. No goalie ever did."

Hall was called up for six games with the Wings in 1952–53, and just two more in 1954–55, posting a 6–1–1 record over those eight games. And even with the small sample size, Detroit thought highly enough of his potential that the great Sawchuk was deemed expendable. Hall began his ironman streak in the Detroit net in 1955 and won the Calder Trophy as Rookie of the Year with a league-leading 12 shutouts. He made the First All-Star Team the following season, yet it was his last in Detroit.

Annoyed at Hall's outspokenness when his teammate Ted Lindsay was forging the first NHL Players' Association, Red Wings' general manager Jack Adams traded both players to the lowly Chicago Black Hawks, a move at the time comparable in NHL terms to exile in Siberia.

"Being around Ted Lindsay did a lot for my approach to the game," recalled Hall. "I think I was reasonably talented, but he taught me that if you forced yourself to play harder, you'd get better results." Hall's mental

preparation before a game involved getting so keyed up that he would be sick to his stomach, but it wasn't nervousness. For him, this was a sign that he was ready to compete to the best of his ability. "I always felt I played better if I was physically sick before the game," he said, and Hall's vomit bucket became part of goaltending lore. "I had no trouble getting 'up' for a game," he added. "I was always completely ready. Five minutes before a game or between periods, I didn't hear what a coach was saying because I was in total preparation. All I would be thinking about was what I had to do. During a game, when someone got ready to shoot, I'd already looked at the shot in my mind. I tried to prepare myself for every option."

Hall didn't miss a beat — or a game — with the move to the Windy City and the Hawks were immeasurably improved by the addition of other "rebels" from various teams and the arrival of junior sensations such as Bobby Hull and Stan Mikita. Hall made the First All-Star Team in 1958 and 1960, and the Second Team in 1961, when he also backstopped the Hawks to the team's first Stanley Cup victory since 1938. Before the decade was out, Hall made both the First and Second All-Star Teams three more times, and thrice got his name on the Vezina Trophy.

The St. Louis Blues wisely chose Hall as their first pick in the expansion draft of 1967. At age 36, "Mr. Goalie" showed he still had plenty of game left. He backstopped the Blues to the Stanley Cup final three seasons in a row, earning the 1968 Conn Smythe Trophy as the playoffs' Most Valuable Player even though his heroics couldn't prevent his club being swept 4–0 in the best-of-seven series. "The Original Six teams gave nothing to the expansion clubs but old guys they thought couldn't play anymore or young kids they didn't think would ever amount to much," recalled Hall. "We had a team of 20- and 40-year-olds, but I feel good about how well the Blues represented the expansion teams. I don't think the NHL would be

enjoying the success it is today if we hadn't done so well."

Fellow veteran Jacques Plante came out of retirement and joined the Blues for the 1968–69 season, and the veteran tandem shared the Vezina with Hall snagging a First All-Star selection. Perhaps it was Plante's influence, but Hall finally donned a face mask that season and continued to wear it until his retirement in 1971. "I had no confidence in the masks we wore," he said, "but the game was changing. Instead of beating the defenseman wide, the forwards often put the puck back to the point and went for the screen and the deflection. As a result, there were more injuries to the goalies." At the time of Hall's retirement, his 84 career shutouts was second best in NHL history, behind only Terry Sawchuk's remarkable 103; he is currently fourth on the all-time list.

Career Stats

REGULAR SEASON

Season	Age	Team	Lg	GP	W	L	T	SO	GA	GAA	G	A	PTS	PIM
1952–53	21	Detroit Red Wings	NHL	6	4	1	1	1	10	1.67	0	0	0	0
1954–55	23	Detroit Red Wings	NHL	2	2	0	0	0	2	1.00	0	0	0	0
1955–56	24	Detroit Red Wings	NHL	70	30	24	16	12	147	2.10	0	0	0	14
1956–57	25	Detroit Red Wings	NHL	70	38	20	12	4	155	2.21	0	0	0	2
1957–58	26	Chicago Black Hawks	NHL	70	24	39	7	7	200	2.86	0	0	0	10
1958–59	27	Chicago Black Hawks	NHL	70	28	29	13	1	208	2.97	0	0	0	0
1959–60	28	Chicago Black Hawks	NHL	70	28	29	13	6	179	2.56	0	1	1	2
1960–61	29	Chicago Black Hawks	NHL	70	29	24	17	6	176	2.51	0	1	1	0
1961–62	30	Chicago Black Hawks	NHL	70	31	26	13	9	184	2.63	0	0	0	12
1962–63	31	Chicago Black Hawks	NHL	66	30	20	15	5	161	2.47	0	0	0	0
1963–64	32	Chicago Black Hawks	NHL	65	34	19	11	7	148	2.30	0	2	2	2
1964–65	33	Chicago Black Hawks	NHL	41	18	17	5	4	99	2.43	0	0	0	2
1965–66	34	Chicago Black Hawks	NHL	64	34	21	7	4	164	2.63	0	2	2	14
1966–67	35	Chicago Black Hawks	NHL	32	19	5	2	5	66	2.38	0	0	0	10
1967–68	36	St. Louis Blues	NHL	49	19	21	9	5	118	2.48	0	0	0	0
1968–69	37	St. Louis Blues	NHL	41	19	12	8	8	85	2.17	0	2	2	20
1969–70	38	St. Louis Blues	NHL	18	7	8	3	1	49	2.91	0	0	0	0
1970–71	39	St. Louis Blues	NHL	32	13	11	8	2	71	2.42	0	1	1	0
NHL Career – 18 Seasons				906	407	326	163	84	2222	2.49	0	9	9	88

PLAYOFFS

Season	Age	Team	Lg	GP	W	L	T	SO	GA	GAA	G	A	PTS	PIM
1955–56	24	Detroit Red Wings	NHL	10	5	5		0	28	2.78	0	0	0	0
1956–57	25	Detroit Red Wings	NHL	5	1	4		0	15	3.00	0	0	0	10
1958–59	27	Chicago Black Hawks	NHL	6	2	4		0	21	3.50	0	0	0	0
1959–60	28	Chicago Black Hawks	NHL	4	0	4		0	14	3.37	0	0	0	0
1960–61	29	Chicago Black Hawks	NHL	12	8	4		2	26	2.02	0	0	0	0
1961–62	30	Chicago Black Hawks	NHL	12	6	6		2	31	2.58	0	0	0	0
1962–63	31	Chicago Black Hawks	NHL	6	2	4		0	25	4.17	0	0	0	0
1963–64	32	Chicago Black Hawks	NHL	7	3	4		0	22	3.24	0	0	0	0
1964–65	33	Chicago Black Hawks	NHL	13	7	6		1	28	2.21	0	0	0	0
1965–66	34	Chicago Black Hawks	NHL	6	2	4		0	22	3.80	0	0	0	0
1966–67	35	Chicago Black Hawks	NHL	3	1	2		0	8	2.73	0	0	0	0
1967–68	36	St. Louis Blues	NHL	18	8	10		1	45	2.43	0	0	0	0
1968–69	37	St. Louis Blues	NHL	3	0	2		0	5	2.29	0	0	0	0
1969–70	38	St. Louis Blues	NHL	7	4	3		0	21	2.99	0	0	0	0
1970–71	39	St. Louis Blues	NHL	3	0	3		0	9	3.00	0	0	0	0
NHL Career – 15 Seasons				115	49	65		6	320	2.78	0	0	0	10

Page 68: Glenn Hall collects himself after making a save against the Leafs' Gerry James.

Page 69: Hall gets set in his revolutionary butterfly position to stop the Montreal attack.

Page 70: Hall uses his butterfly to thwart a backhand shot by Toronto's Frank Mahovlich.

INDUCTED 1980

HARRY LUMLEY

The Nomadic Netminder

H ARRY LUMLEY DIDN'T LOOK as though he was NHL material at first, but he fashioned a Hall of Fame career for himself before he was done. Known as "Apple Cheeks" for his ruddy complexion when he blushed, Lumley holds the record as the youngest goalie to play an NHL game. He signed his first professional contract at age 16 and was a 17-year-old rookie when he was called up for two games in 1943–44 with the Detroit Red Wings.

After giving up 13 goals and losing both games, Lumley had been officially sent back to the minors but was still in town when Detroit hosted the New York Rangers. Watching from the stands, he saw Detroit take the lead before the Rangers' goalie went down with an injury near the end of the second period. As teams only carried one goalie in those days, it was expected that the home team would provide a substitute, should one be necessary.

Detroit called upon Lumley, who donned a Ranger sweater for the third period as a "loaner." He blanked the Wings, causing coach Jack Adams to rage to his team that, "the best Red Wing player tonight wasn't even wearing a Red Wings uniform!"

Lumley was sent back to the Indianapolis Capitols of the AHL for half of the next season before earning a starting job with the Wings. He was especially effective in the playoffs, backstopping Detroit to within a game of the 1945 Stanley Cup. The Toronto Maple Leafs rookie goalie, Frank McCool, won the first three games of the series by shutouts to set an NHL record. Lumley, the first teenager to ever play goal in the Stanley Cup final, rebounded and posted a shutout of his own in Game 5. Toronto's owner and manager Conn Smythe thought he could rattle the young netminder in the following game and seal the Leafs win.

"Smythe lurked behind Lumley's net in the late

stages of the game and gave Harry the full benefit of his inimitable verbal blasts," wrote Jim Coleman of *The Globe and Mail.* "Every time Lumley turned aside another Maple Leaf thrust, he would turn and smile sweetly upon Smythe." Lumley posted his second consecutive shutout, making a lasting impression upon Smythe, and forcing a seventh and deciding game, a 2–1 thriller won by Toronto.

Over the next five years, Lumley and the Red Wings established themselves among the league's best in a very competitive era. Considered large in his day, at six feet tall and 200 pounds, Lumley was not noted for quickness or a flashy style, but he was consistently effective. Twice with Detroit he led the league in wins and games played and he had the most shutouts (seven) in 1947–48. Near the end

of the 1949–50 regular season, Lumley was injured and young Terry Sawchuk was called up to guard the Detroit net for seven games. He showed great promise, but it was Lumley back in net for the 1950 Stanley Cup playoffs, as Detroit overcame the loss of Gordie Howe to a serious injury in the semifinal series against Toronto, and then beat New York in the final. Lumley won his first and only Stanley Cup ring, with three playoff shutouts and a minuscule 1.85 goals-against average.

Only a week after hoisting the Cup, Lumley was traded to the lowly Chicago Black Hawks in a nine-player deal. He spent two seasons in the league basement, facing a nightly barrage of rubber behind the NHL's weakest offense and defense. Lumley fashioned only 29 victories over 134 games with the Hawks before being traded to another struggling franchise in 1952. Conn Smythe sent four players — Al Rollins, Gus Mortson, Cal Gardner and Ray Hannigan — in return for Lumley, who had foiled Toronto so many times while with Detroit. Lumley rewarded Smythe's judgment by posting his best individual seasons with the Maple Leafs.

In 1953–54, Lumley won his only Vezina with a 1.86 average and led the league while posting a modern-day record of 13 shutouts, a feat not bettered until Tony Esposito notched 15 in 1969–70. Lumley also was selected to the league's First All-Star Team, a distinction he'd earn again the following season. Unfortunately, he lost the 1954–55 Vezina to Detroit's Sawchuk by a single goal (unlike today where the NHL GMs vote for the best goalie, the trophy then went to the netminder(s) that allowed the fewest goals), despite the fact that he led the league with a 1.94 goals-against average over 69 games versus Sawchuk's

1.96 average over 67 games and one period. To further illustrate Lumley's dominance in 1954–55, the rouge-cheeked netminder posted his league-low goals against while back-stopping the weakest offense in the NHL, as Toronto only scored 147 times compared to Detroit's 204 goals (Montreal notched 228). Lumley kept his team in every game, posting 23 wins, 24 losses, and a still-standing record of 22 ties.

As perhaps the most under-rated goalie of his era, Lumley found himself cast off once again in the summer of 1956. He was sold (along with Eric Nesterenko) back to Chicago. Lumley wanted no part of the struggling Black Hawks again, however, and refused to report. He played instead with the AHL's Buffalo Bisons for most of the next two seasons. Lumley returned to the NHL in 1957 when Boston needed help, his fifth club of the Original Six, and he split duties with Don Simmons for the Bruins until he retired in 1960. Lumley's 71 career shutouts leave him currently in the number-12 spot in NHL history.

Career Stats

REGULAR SEASON

Season	Age	Team	Lg	GP	W	L	T	SO	GA	GAA	G	A	PTS	PIM
1943–44	17	Detroit Red Wings	NHL	2	0	2	0	0	13	6.50	0	0	0	0
1943–44	17	New York Rangers	NHL	1	0	0	0	0	0	0.00	0	0	0	0
1944–45	18	Detroit Red Wings	NHL	37	24	10	3	1	119	3.22	0	0	0	0
1945–46	19	Detroit Red Wings	NHL	50	20	20	10	2	159	3.18	0	0	0	6
1946–47	20	Detroit Red Wings	NHL	52	22	20	10	3	159	3.06	0	0	0	4
1947–48	21	Detroit Red Wings	NHL	60	30	18	12	7	147	2.46	0	0	0	8
1948–49	22	Detroit Red Wings	NHL	60	34	19	7	6	145	2.42	0	0	0	12
1949–50	23	Detroit Red Wings	NHL	63	33	16	14	7	148	2.35	0	0	0	10
1950–51	24	Chicago Black Hawks	NHL	64	12	41	10	3	246	3.90	0	0	0	4
1951–52	25	Chicago Black Hawks	NHL	70	17	44	9	2	241	3.46	0	0	0	2
1952–53	26	Toronto Maple Leafs	NHL	70	27	30	13	10	167	2.39	0	0	0	18
1953–54	27	Toronto Maple Leafs	NHL	69	32	24	13	13	128	1.86	0	0	0	6
1954–55	28	Toronto Maple Leafs	NHL	69	23	24	22	8	134	1.94	0	0	0	9
1955–56	29	Toronto Maple Leafs	NHL	59	21	28	10	3	157	2.67	0	0	0	2
1957–58	31	Boston Bruins	NHL	24	11	10	3	3	70	2.92	0	0	0	2
1958–59	32	Boston Bruins	NHL	11	8	2	1	1	27	2.45	0	0	0	0
1959–60	33	Boston Bruins	NHL	42	16	21	5	2	146	3.48	0	0	0	12
NHL Career – 16 Seasons				803	330	329	142	71	2206	2.75	0	0	0	95

PLAYOFFS

Season	Age	Team	Lg	GP	W	L	T	SO	GA	GAA	G	A	PTS	PIM
1944–45	18	Detroit Red Wings	NHL	14	7	7		2	31	2.14	0	0	0	0
1945–46	19	Detroit Red Wings	NHL	5	1	4		1	16	3.10	0	0	0	0
1947–48	21	Detroit Red Wings	NHL	10	4	6		0	30	3.00	0	0	0	10
1948–49	22	Detroit Red Wings	NHL	11	4	7		0	26	2.15	0	0	0	2
1949–50	23	Detroit Red Wings	NHL	14	8	6		3	28	1.85	0	0	0	0
1953–54	27	Toronto Maple Leafs	NHL	5	1	4		0	15	2.80	0	0	0	0
1954–55	28	Toronto Maple Leafs	NHL	4	0	4		0	14	3.50	0	0	0	0
1955–56	29	Toronto Maple Leafs	NHL	5	1	4		1	13	2.57	0	0	0	2
1957–58	31	Boston Bruins	NHL	1	0	1		0	5	5.00	0	0	0	0
1958–59	32	Boston Bruins	NHL	7	3	4		0	20	2.75	0	0	0	4
NHL Career – 10 Seasons				76	29	47		7	198	2.49	0	0	0	18

Page 72: Harry Lumley makes a save for the lowly Chicago Black Hawks. Despite Lumley's solid puckstopping, Chicago could only muster a 29-85-19 mark with him in net.

Page 73: A young Lumley suits up for the Detroit Red Wings. 17 when he played his first NHL match, Lumley stayed in Detroit for seven seasons.

Page 74: Lumley spent his prime years in Toronto. Here he blocks a scoring attempt from his former team.

INDUCTED 1978

JACQUES
PLANTE

Jake the Snake

JACQUES PLANTE MARCHED to the tune of his own drum, all the way to the Hockey Hall of Fame. As well as being one of the best goalies of all time, Plante was among the most innovative. He is best known today as the first NHL goalie to regularly wear a mask.

His approach to the mask was that it could prevent injury, not just protect an injury, which had previously been its use when Clint Benedict debuted his leather contraption in 1930. "They figured a goalie had to be scared to play well," Plante later recalled. "When shots are coming at you at 100 miles per hour, you're scared whether you have a mask or not." But it took an ultimatum to overcome the notion that a mask was a sign of cowardice.

On November 1, 1959, New York Rangers' sniper Andy Bathgate ripped open Plante's nose with a backhand shot. Plante had worn a mask in practice since 1956, never in a game, but, while getting stitched up in the dressing room, he told his Montreal Canadiens coach Toe Blake that he wouldn't go back into the net without his mask on. In the single-goalie era, Blake had little choice but to capitulate, with the stipulation that the mask came off when Plante's nose was healed. The Habs then went on an 11-game win streak, yet Blake held Plante to their deal, and the mask came off. When Montreal lost the following game, Blake allowed Plante to decide whether the mask was a help or a hindrance. The mask soon became standard equipment, not just for Plante, but for goalies everywhere.

Of course, it took a premier netminder to change the face of the game. Plante, known as "Jake the Snake" for his quick reflexes, made his first appearances with the Canadiens in November 1952, playing three games and going undefeated. He spotted starter Gerry McNeil for four games in the 1953 playoffs, notching a shutout against

the Chicago Black Hawks in his post-season debut, and earned his first of six Stanley Cup rings. Plante started the 1953–54 campaign with the AHL's Buffalo Bisons, but before season's end, he was with the Habs to stay. He backstopped his team to within one win of the Stanley Cup that spring — falling to Detroit in seven games — and then an unequalled string of five consecutive Stanley Cup victories (1954–55 to 1958–59). "For five years, he was the greatest goalie the league has ever seen," observed Montreal coach Toe Blake.

Plante also changed the game with the way he interacted with the puck and opposing shooters. While other goalies before him periodically came out of their crease to play the puck, Plante made it a regular practice. He was the first to skate in behind the net to stop the puck from ringing the boards on a shoot-in, and was the first goalie to raise his arm to signal an icing call for his defensemen. Plante perfected a stand-up style of goaltending that emphasized positional play, cutting down the angles and staying square to the shooter. "So often, your skilled

players are not dedicated," noted fellow netminder Glenn Hall. "But Plante was."

His eccentricities were legendary, some harmless, such as knitting his own hats and undershirts (although his first Canadiens coach, Dick Irvin, forbade him from wearing his tuque on the ice, as Plante desired). Some other "quirks" were deemed harmful to team camaraderie, such as staying in a different hotel than his teammates because he felt the air was better for his asthma (a questionable practice at the time). It was actually Plante's asthma that had led him to become a goaltender in the first place, as the ailment prevented him from skating for long periods. He gravitated to the net, where he quickly found his niche.

Although he picked up his sixth Vezina Trophy and won the Hart Trophy as the league's MVP in 1961–62, Plante eventually wore out his welcome in Montreal. Traded to New York in June 1963, Plante bragged that he would win another Vezina Trophy in Manhattan. Instead, tired of losing with the sad-sack Rangers, he retired in 1965 and took care of his ailing wife.

Three years later, Plante was lured out of retirement by the St. Louis Blues to share goaltending duties with the great Glenn Hall. Plante shared the 1968–69 Vezina Trophy with Hall at the age of 40, his seventh, and a new NHL record. "I don't think I ever played better than I did with St. Louis," claimed Plante, "even in my best years with the Canadiens." The veteran tandem took the Blues to the 1969 and 1970 Stanley Cup final. In the latter series, against the Boston Bruins, Phil Esposito tipped a blazing Fred Stanfield slap shot, splitting Plante's mask in two. When he regained consciousness in hospital, the doctors and Plante concurred that the mask had saved his life. That proved to be Plante's final game in a St. Louis uniform.

Sold to Toronto in May 1970, Plante made the NHL's Second All-Star Team the following season. At the age of 42, he led the league with a 1.88 goals-against average. He also tutored fellow Maple Leaf up-and-coming goaltender Bernie Parent, who soon afterward emerged as the NHL's premier netminder. Plante finished his NHL career with the Boston Bruins at the tail end of the 1972–73 campaign, then came out of retirement one last time to play a season for the Edmonton Oilers in the World Hockey Association in 1974–75. Plante was inducted into the Hockey Hall of Fame in 1978. He died of stomach cancer in 1986 and the Montreal Canadiens recognized his outstanding contribution by officially retiring his No. 1 in 1995.

Career Stats

REGULAR SEASON

Season	Age	Team	Lg	GP	W	L	T	SO	GA	GAA	G	A	PTS	PIM
1952–53	24	Montreal Canadiens	NHL	3	2	0	1	0	4	1.33	0	0	0	0
1953–54	25	Montreal Canadiens	NHL	17	7	5	5	5	27	1.59	0	0	0	0
1954–55	26	Montreal Canadiens	NHL	52	33	12	7	5	110	2.14	0	0	0	2
1955–56	27	Montreal Canadiens	NHL	64	42	12	10	7	119	1.86	0	0	0	10
1956–57	28	Montreal Canadiens	NHL	61	31	18	12	9	122	2.00	0	0	0	16
1957–58	29	Montreal Canadiens	NHL	57	34	14	8	9	119	2.11	0	0	0	13
1958–59	30	Montreal Canadiens	NHL	67	38	16	13	9	144	2.16	0	1	1	11
1959–60	31	Montreal Canadiens	NHL	69	40	17	12	3	175	2.54	0	0	0	2
1960–61	32	Montreal Canadiens	NHL	40	23	11	6	2	112	2.80	0	0	0	2
1961–62	33	Montreal Canadiens	NHL	70	42	14	14	4	166	2.37	0	0	0	14
1962–63	34	Montreal Canadiens	NHL	56	22	14	19	5	138	2.49	0	1	1	2
1963–64	35	New York Rangers	NHL	65	22	36	7	3	220	3.38	0	1	1	6
1964–65	36	New York Rangers	NHL	33	10	17	5	2	109	3.37	0	1	1	6
1968–69	40	St. Louis Blues	NHL	37	18	12	6	5	70	1.96	0	0	0	2
1969–70	41	St. Louis Blues	NHL	32	18	9	5	5	67	2.19	0	2	2	0
1970–71	42	Toronto Maple Leafs	NHL	40	24	11	4	4	73	1.88	0	0	0	2
1971–72	43	Toronto Maple Leafs	NHL	34	16	13	5	2	86	2.63	0	0	0	2
1972–73	44	Toronto Maple Leafs	NHL	32	8	14	6	1	87	3.04	0	0	0	0
1972–73	44	Boston Bruins	NHL	8	7	1	0	2	16	2.00	0	2	2	2
1974–75	46	Edmonton Oilers	WHA	31	15	14	1	1	88	3.32	0	1	1	2
Career – 19 Seasons				868	452	260	146	83	2052	2.36	0	9	9	94

PLAYOFFS

Season	Age	Team	Lg	GP	W	L	T	SO	GA	GAA	G	A	PTS	PIM
1952–53	24	Montreal Canadiens	NHL	4	3	1		1	7	1.75	0	0	0	0
1953–54	25	Montreal Canadiens	NHL	8	5	3		2	15	1.88	0	0	0	0
1954–55	26	Montreal Canadiens	NHL	12	6	3		0	30	2.82	0	0	0	0
1955–56	27	Montreal Canadiens	NHL	10	8	2		2	18	1.80	0	0	0	2
1956–57	28	Montreal Canadiens	NHL	10	8	2		1	17	1.66	0	0	0	4
1957–58	29	Montreal Canadiens	NHL	10	8	2		1	20	1.94	0	0	0	2
1958–59	30	Montreal Canadiens	NHL	11	8	3		0	26	2.33	0	0	0	0
1959–60	31	Montreal Canadiens	NHL	8	8	0		3	11	1.35	0	0	0	0
1960–61	32	Montreal Canadiens	NHL	6	2	4		0	16	2.33	0	0	0	2
1961–62	33	Montreal Canadiens	NHL	6	2	4		0	19	3.17	0	0	0	0
1962–63	34	Montreal Canadiens	NHL	5	1	4		0	14	2.80	0	0	0	0
1968–69	40	St. Louis Blues	NHL	10	8	2		3	14	1.43	0	1	1	0
1969–70	41	St. Louis Blues	NHL	6	4	1		1	8	1.48	0	0	0	2
1970–71	42	Toronto Maple Leafs	NHL	3	0	2		0	7	3.13	0	0	0	0
1971–72	43	Toronto Maple Leafs	NHL	1	0	1		0	5	5.00	0	0	0	0
1972–73	44	Boston Bruins	NHL	2	0	2		0	10	5.00	0	0	0	0
Career – 16 Seasons				112	71	36		14	237	2.14	0	1	1	12

Page 76: A white plaster mold of Jacques Plante's face and a thin fiberglass prototype mask made by Bill Burchmore, the maker of the original Plante mask. The prototype mask was never used as it was deemed by Plante to be too light.

Page 77: Plante makes a pre-mask kick save (and a beauty).

Page 78: Plante demonstrates his roaming ability, beating a Leaf forward to the puck to nullify a scoring chance.

CHUCK
RAYNER

Bonnie Prince Charlie

CHUCK RAYNER HAD a Hall of Fame career despite playing exclusively for a variety of weak teams. He got his professional start with the Springfield Indians of the American Hockey League in 1940–41, where he earned a Second Team All-Star selection. More important, he received instruction from legendary defenseman Eddie Shore, who had taken over the club after finishing his own stellar playing career the previous season.

Shore's "creative" but notorious coaching methods and parsimonious ways generally made enemies of his students, but Rayner acknowledged him as "the greatest goaltending coach I ever had. Before that, there wasn't such a thing as a goaltending coach. Nobody told you anything. You went out and did your best, got hell for the goals you didn't stop, and no praise for the ones you did."

"Tap-dancing improves balance and balance is the foundation of an athlete's ability," said Shore, explaining one of his more extreme coaching methods. "From balance you get power and maneuverability. I want a player who can move forward, backward, one side or the other without actually taking a step; just shifting his balance." Shore once tethered a goalie to the crossbar with a rope around his neck to train him not to fall to the ice, but as a four-time NHL MVP, Shore also had genuine skills, insights and a fierce work ethic. Through Shore's insistence, Rayner participated in every skating drill with his teammates, and fired pucks until he couldn't move from fatigue. This training helped Rayner develop outstanding skating and shooting abilities, which became hallmarks of his own innovative style. In turn, fellow Hall of Famers Gump Worsley and Johnny Bower both credit Rayner with teaching them invaluable lessons in what we now know

are essential NHL goaltending skills, like the poke check.

Rayner was called up from Springfield to the New York Americans for a 12-game tryout in 1940–41, and became a full-time NHLer in 1941–42. That season Rayner appeared in 36 games and posted a 3.47 goals-against average for the newly-christened Brooklyn Americans, who didn't enjoy any more success financially or on the ice with the franchise name change. Rayner notched one shutout for the lackluster squad, but the team remained in the league basement with a 16–29–3 record over the 48-game season.

The Americans folded after that 1941–42 campaign, marking the actual beginning of the "Original Six" era, but Rayner was changing his address regardless. He enlisted in the Canadian Navy and missed three NHL seasons. He played some hockey for Navy teams in Halifax and Victoria, but eventually shipped out on a frigate that traversed the North Atlantic. When the war ended, he signed with

the New York Rangers, where he split goaltending duties with "Sugar" Jim Henry for three seasons. The pioneering move toward the "two-goalie" system was instituted by Ranger coach Frank Boucher, who, like Eddie Shore, was a former star player and creative thinker. The system worked well as the two goalies became close friends, but the Rangers eventually decided they couldn't afford the luxury of two NHL netminders on the payroll and traded Henry.

Although the Rangers had fallen into the league cellar during the war years, Rayner often brought the crowd to its feet with his unprecedented roaming from the crease. Boucher called him "brilliantly aggressive," and Rayner's poke check became a signature move. He surprised many attacking forwards when he dove headfirst, his goal stick outstretched in front of him, to knock the puck away. "Bonnie Prince Charlie" led the league with five shutouts in 1946–47, although he also had an offensive flair. He went behind his net for pucks, fielded them in the corner, and fired passes to his teammates, and he even made rink-long rushes, attempting to become the first NHL netminder to score a goal. Boucher didn't need to pull his goalie when there was a delayed-penalty call, as Rayner functioned effectively as a sixth attacker.

Rayner lost much of the 1947–48 season recovering from a broken cheekbone, and was one of the first goaltenders to use a face mask, although he wore it only in practice. He made the NHL's Second All-Star Team in 1949, 1950 and 1951, playing almost every single game for the Rangers. He guided New York to a surprisingly successful trip to the 1950 playoffs, helping to vanquish the Montreal Canadiens in surprisingly short order (leading to the resignation of his friend Bill Durnan in the Canadiens' net). After falling behind two games to Detroit in the Stanley Cup final, a team that had finished 21 points ahead of them in the 70-game regular season, Rayner backstopped the Rangers to three straight wins, including two overtime victories. Sadly, New York lost the Cup to the Red Wings in the second overtime period of the seventh game. Their near win was all the more remarkable when one realizes the Rangers had to play all the games of the final on the road because the circus had taken over Madison Square Garden. Rayner received the 1950 Hart Trophy as the league's Most Valuable Player, the second goalie after Roy "Shrimp" Worters to win the prestigious award, and one of only five to receive the trophy to date.

The Rangers didn't qualify for the playoffs again during Rayner's tenure, and in the 1952–53 season he played only 20 games, replaced by Gump Worsley, who won Rookie of the Year honors. Rayner went back to his home province of Saskatchewan the following season, signed as a free agent by the Saskatoon Quakers of the Western Hockey League. He played a handful of games spread over the following two campaigns with the WHL's Nelson Maple Leafs before hanging up his skates.

Career Stats

REGULAR SEASON

Season	Age	Team	Lg	GP	W	L	T	SO	GA	GAA	G	A	PTS	PIM
1940–41	20	New York Americans	NHL	12	2	7	3	0	44	3.42	0	0	0	0
1941–42	21	Brooklyn Americans	NHL	36	13	21	2	1	129	3.47	0	0	0	0
1945–46	25	New York Rangers	NHL	40	12	21	7	1	149	3.76	0	0	0	6
1946–47	26	New York Rangers	NHL	58	22	30	6	5	177	3.05	0	0	0	0
1947–48	27	New York Rangers	NHL	12	4	7	0	0	42	3.65	0	0	0	0
1948–49	28	New York Rangers	NHL	58	16	31	11	7	168	2.90	0	0	0	2
1949–50	29	New York Rangers	NHL	69	28	30	11	6	181	2.62	0	0	0	6
1950–51	30	New York Rangers	NHL	66	19	28	19	2	187	2.85	0	0	0	6
1951–52	31	New York Rangers	NHL	53	18	25	10	2	159	3.00	0	0	0	4
1952–53	32	New York Rangers	NHL	20	4	8	8	1	58	2.90	0	0	0	2
NHL Career – 10 Seasons				424	138	208	77	25	1294	3.05	0	0	0	26

PLAYOFFS

Season	Age	Team	Lg	GP	W	L	T	SO	GA	GAA	G	A	PTS	PIM
1947–48	27	New York Rangers	NHL	6	2	4		0	17	2.83	0	0	0	0
1949–50	29	New York Rangers	NHL	12	7	5		1	29	2.25	0	0	0	0
NHL Career – 2 Seasons				18	9	9		1	46	2.43	0	0	0	0

Page 80: Chuck Rayner and Neil Colville give chase for a loose puck in the New York zone.

Page 81: Rayner posing for a portrait photograph.

Page 82: Ever creative with his stick, Rayner hooks a Leaf forward during action at Maple Leaf Gardens.

INDUCTED 1971

TERRY SAWCHUK

The Agony and the Glory

TERRY SAWCHUK'S NAME WAS evoked numerous times in 2009, as Martin Brodeur encroached upon, and then surpassed, Sawchuk's almost 40-year-old career record of 103 regular-season shutouts. The mark, long considered unassailable, was the last of the major goaltending records Sawchuk had established as, arguably, the greatest goalie of the Original Six era, and perhaps the best ever. Sadly, however, Sawchuk's career was as noteworthy for tragedy as glory.

Terry Sawchuk's brother died of a heart attack at age 17, and 10-year-old Terry inherited his goalie equipment. Within five years, the superbly talented athlete was playing junior hockey, and he signed his first pro contract with a Detroit Red Wings farm club while still a teenager. Sawchuk got his first NHL action when Detroit's Harry Lumley sprained an ankle near the end of the 1949–50 season. Sawchuk sparkled in seven games, notching his first shutout, and despite the fact that Detroit was an NHL powerhouse, winning the Stanley Cup that season with Lumley back between the pipes, Sawchuk was handed the full-time job for 1950–51.

The pressure of joining the defending Cup champs and replacing a future Hall of Famer didn't faze the 20-year-old Sawchuk an iota. He not only won the Calder Trophy as top rookie, he led the league with 44 wins and

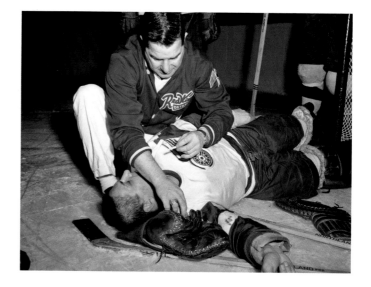

11 shutouts and made the First All-Star Team. Over the next four seasons, Sawchuk won the Vezina Trophy three times while backstopping the Red Wings to three Stanley Cup victories. He had brilliant reflexes, but he also pioneered a new goaltending stance.

"I found that I could move more quickly from the crouch position," explained Sawchuk. "It gave me better balance to go both ways, especially with my legs. Scrambles and shots from the point were becoming the style in hockey when I broke into the NHL. From the crouch, I could keep the puck in my vision much better when it was coming through a maze of players."

Of course, this new stance put Sawchuk's unmasked face in danger, and he bore the scars to prove it. In truth, none of his successes came easily. Battling through a long list of physical injuries, his life was fraught with pain. Additionally, although generally weighing about 195 pounds, he

had to work hard to maintain that weight, ballooning to 230 in the fall of 1951 before dropping to a gaunt 175 pounds. But his internal demons were also a constant pressure.

"The first time I met Terry Sawchuk," recalled Joe Falls of the *Detroit Free Press*, "he was raging with anger and shouting obscenities and throwing his skates at a reporter. This was in 1953. In all the years to follow, he never really changed."

Despite his tremendous success with Detroit, Adams tried to maximize his assets and sent Sawchuk to Boston, as part of a then-record, nine-player trade, two months after his star netminder helped hoist the 1955 Stanley Cup. Sawchuk, as usual, had played hurt many nights for Detroit, but, partly because of frayed nerves, there were occasions when he just couldn't play. Glenn Hall filled in for him twice in his last season in Detroit, and Adams liked what he saw in the younger netminder.

Sawchuk's confidence was severely shaken when

he joined the Bruins, a far weaker team than Detroit. Although he still tallied nine shutouts in his first season in Boston (1955–56), he suffered a nervous breakdown and then temporarily quit midway through the 1956–57 campaign. Sawchuk's wife and children had remained in Detroit after the trade, and he felt that their support would help him cope better. At Sawchuk's request, Boston traded him back to Detroit for John Bucyk the following summer. The Red Wings sent Hall to Chicago, where he became a star, and Sawchuk spent seven more seasons as a Red Wing. While his skills were still remarkably sharp, the team was heading into some lean years, and Sawchuk was plagued with injuries. "When it came time to waken him," his wife later recalled, "I often had to help him out of bed and, later, into the car for the trip to the rink. Then he'd take a painkiller pill, timing it so he would unstiffen by the time the buzzer sounded to skate out onto the ice." Needless to say, with such a regimen, Sawchuk earned no accolades as a practice goalie, but he made the Second All-Star Team in 1959 and 1963, as he established the career records for wins and shutouts.

With the emergence of the two-goalie system, Toronto claimed Sawchuk in the 1964 intra-league draft, and he shared the net with Johnny Bower for three seasons. "Terry was a real loner," recalled Bower, who is quick to acknowledge he learned lots just from watching his teammate. "He was certainly a great competitor whose record speaks for itself, but I just couldn't talk to him. I asked him for help a couple of times, but he only reassured me without really offering any insight or assistance." The two shared the 1965 Vezina Trophy, and Sawchuk relieved Bower in the 1967

playoffs to help the underdog Leafs unexpectedly defeat the Montreal Canadiens for the Stanley Cup. That victory would prove to be the last highlight of his career.

Sawchuk was picked in the NHL's expansion draft by Los Angeles, where he played the 1967–68 campaign, but at 38, his age was beginning to show. He bounced back to Detroit for 13 games the following season and concluded his career with the New York Rangers in 1969–70, appearing in only eight games. Sadly, shortly after the end of the season, he died of heart failure following two operations that were the result of a wrestling match with teammate Ron Stewart. The usual waiting period was waived and Sawchuk entered the Hall of Fame, posthumously, in 1971.

Career Stats

REGULAR SEASON

Season	Age	Team	Lg	GP	W	L	T	SO	GA	GAA	G	A	PTS	PIM
1949-50	20	Detroit Red Wings	NHL	7	4	3	0	1	16	2.29	0	0	0	0
1950-51	21	Detroit Red Wings	NHL	70	44	13	13	11	139	1.99	0	0	0	2
1951-52	22	Detroit Red Wings	NHL	70	44	14	12	12	133	1.90	0	0	0	2
1952-53	23	Detroit Red Wings	NHL	63	32	15	16	9	120	1.90	0	0	0	5
1953-54	24	Detroit Red Wings	NHL	67	35	19	13	12	129	1.93	0	1	1	31
1954-55	25	Detroit Red Wings	NHL	68	40	17	11	12	132	1.96	0	1	1	10
1955-56	26	Boston Bruins	NHL	68	22	33	13	9	177	2.60	0	0	0	20
1956-57	27	Boston Bruins	NHL	34	18	10	6	2	81	2.38	0	0	0	14
1957-58	28	Detroit Red Wings	NHL	70	29	29	12	3	206	2.94	0	0	0	39
1958-59	29	Detroit Red Wings	NHL	67	23	36	8	5	207	3.09	0	0	0	12
1959-60	30	Detroit Red Wings	NHL	58	24	20	14	5	155	2.67	0	0	0	22
1960-61	31	Detroit Red Wings	NHL	37	12	16	8	2	112	3.13	0	1	1	8
1961-62	32	Detroit Red Wings	NHL	43	14	21	8	5	141	3.28	0	0	0	12
1962-63	33	Detroit Red Wings	NHL	48	22	16	7	3	118	2.55	0	0	0	14
1963-64	34	Detroit Red Wings	NHL	53	25	20	7	5	138	2.64	0	0	0	0
1964-65	35	Toronto Maple Leafs	NHL	36	17	13	6	1	92	2.56	0	2	2	24
1965-66	36	Toronto Maple Leafs	NHL	27	10	11	3	1	80	3.16	0	1	1	12
1966-67	37	Toronto Maple Leafs	NHL	28	15	5	4	2	66	2.81	0	0	0	2
1967-68	38	Los Angeles Kings	NHL	36	11	14	6	2	99	3.07	0	0	0	0
1968-69	39	Detroit Red Wings	NHL	13	3	4	3	0	28	2.62	0	0	0	0
1969-70	40	New York Rangers	NHL	8	3	1	2	1	20	2.91	0	1	1	0
NHL Career – 21 Seasons				971	447	330	172	103	2389	2.51	0	7	7	229

PLAYOFFS

Season	Age	Team	Lg	GP	W	L	T	SO	GA	GAA	G	A	PTS	PIM
1950-51	21	Detroit Red Wings	NHL	6	2	4		1	13	1.68	0	0	0	0
1951-52	22	Detroit Red Wings	NHL	8	8	0		4	5	0.62	0	0	0	0
1952-53	23	Detroit Red Wings	NHL	6	2	4		1	21	3.39	0	0	0	10
1953-54	24	Detroit Red Wings	NHL	12	8	4		2	20	1.60	0	0	0	2
1954-55	25	Detroit Red Wings	NHL	11	8	3		1	26	2.36	0	0	0	12
1957-58	28	Detroit Red Wings	NHL	4	0	4		0	19	4.52	0	0	0	0
1959-60	30	Detroit Red Wings	NHL	6	2	4		0	20	2.96	0	0	0	0
1960-61	31	Detroit Red Wings	NHL	8	5	3		1	18	2.32	0	0	0	0
1962-63	33	Detroit Red Wings	NHL	11	5	6		0	35	3.18	0	0	0	0
1963-64	34	Detroit Red Wings	NHL	13	6	5		1	31	2.75	0	0	0	2
1964-65	35	Toronto Maple Leafs	NHL	1	0	1		0	3	3.00	0	0	0	0
1965-66	36	Toronto Maple Leafs	NHL	2	0	2		0	6	3.00	0	0	0	0
1966-67	37	Toronto Maple Leafs	NHL	10	6	4		0	25	2.65	0	0	0	0
1967-68	38	Los Angeles Kings	NHL	5	2	3		1	18	3.86	0	0	0	0
1969-70	40	New York Rangers	NHL	3	0	1		0	6	4.50	0	0	0	0
NHL Career – 15 Seasons				106	54	48		12	266	2.54	0	0	0	26

Page 84: Detroit trainer Lefty Wilson gives smelling salts to Terry Sawchuk during Game 1 between Toronto and Detroit in the first round of the 1959–60 playoffs. Detroit won the game, but Toronto took the series 4–2.

Page 85: Sawchuk, masked late in his career, clears the puck to the corner as Allan Stanley keeps the forechecker at bay.

Page 86: Sawchuck leaps head first to make a dangerous and dazzling save in 1960.

INDUCTED 1980

GUMP
WORSLEY

Goaltending Gump-tion

L ORNE "GUMP" WORSLEY may have been the funniest man to play in the NHL. He picked up his nickname as a child for his resemblance to Andy Gump of the funny papers, and his round face, short stature and pudgy physique made him appear to be more of a wit than an athlete.

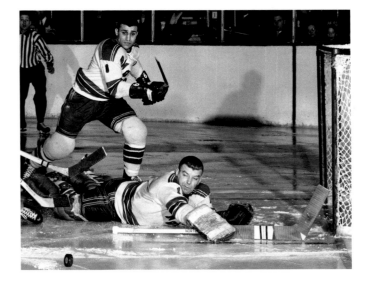

Yet his accomplishments were exemplary and his longevity was rare. Worsley played 21 years in the NHL, but his career didn't begin until he was 23 years old. Born in Montreal in 1929, Worsley played his first amateur hockey in Verdun (a borough of Montreal), but was signed into the New York Rangers' organization when he was 19 and played the rest of his amateur hockey with the New York Rovers. Prior to his 1952–53 NHL rookie season in the Big Apple, Worsley played in five different semi-pro leagues, winning honors and trophies at virtually every stop along the way.

Worsley attended the Ranger's training camp for three straight seasons before he was given a real crack at the NHL. The month-long camps gave the up-and-coming netminder some time to develop his game alongside pro players. "Charlie Rayner tutored me on how to play goal," said Worsley, recalling the Rangers' star netminder. "I had

some of the basics, but he taught me most of what I know. Charlie was very good to me, staying after practice and getting a couple of guys to shoot on us. He showed me how to cut the angles and play the position. He was coming to the end of his career, and I eventually took his spot on the Rangers when he retired." Although New York was mired deep in the league basement, Worsley won the Calder Trophy in 1953 as NHL Rookie of the Year. Thinking he'd earned a raise, Worsley asked for more money but was instead sent back to the minors (Vancouver Canucks of the WHL) for a season, where he led the Western Hockey League with 39 wins and a 2.40 goals-against average.

In 1954–55, he resumed his NHL career in the New York net and spent most of the next decade there. "Facing a lot of shots was an occupational hazard in New York," recalled Worsley, who often saw the opposition put 50 to 60 shots on net, but his sense of humor remained

intact. Asked by a reporter which team gave him the most trouble, Worsley quipped, "The Rangers."

At first it looked as if "The Gumper" had won the lottery when the stalwart Montreal Canadiens sent Jacques Plante to New York in 1963 in a multi-player swap that sent Worsley to the Habs. "I've yet to be informed by the Rangers," claimed Worsley in 1996, saying the Rangers never informed him and he only ever got the news from Montreal's Frank Selke Sr., who welcomed him to his new club. Worsley got off to a strong start as a Hab, but only eight games into the 1963–64 season, he suffered a knee injury. Sent to the AHL's Quebec Aces to get into shape after his injury healed, Worsley had a difficult time breaking back into the Montreal lineup. "I was 34 years old and thought it was the end of my career," he said. "I didn't get the callback for a year." When he did, midway through the 1964–65 season, Worsley performed heroically, backstopping Montreal all the way to Stanley Cup victory. "The last five minutes of the seventh game seemed to last five

years. I kept looking at the clock, and the hands never seemed to move. We were leading 4–0, and I was sure I'd never let five goals in, but I was incredibly nervous. I was 13 years in the league by then. I can't really put the feeling in words, but I could have walked home without my feet touching the ground. Every Cup win was the same."

In 1965–66, Worsley shared the Vezina Trophy with Charlie Hodge and made the Second All-Star Team, before playing every playoff game and again sipping from the Stanley Cup. "Worsley wasn't even tested," griped Detroit's great defenseman Bill Gadsby. "His underwear can't even be wet." Told of the comment, Worsley joked, "What most people don't know is that my underwear is wet even before the game begins."

Worsley shared the 1968 Vezina with the up-and-coming Rogie Vachon, and made the First All-Star Team with a league-best and career-low 1.98 goals-against average. He went on to win another Cup ring that season and the next. But the pressure of playing for the Canadiens is often relentless. "Montreal can be a difficult place to be if you're not winning," said Worsley, whose wife at times would have strangers shouting at her in the grocery store, and even his son once faced pressure to get playoff tickets for his school teachers or see his marks suffer. "I had to go raise hell at the school," he said.

Worsley suffered an emotional collapse midway through the 1968–69 season but came back to contribute important playoff wins for the Canadiens. However, Vachon started getting most of the work. When Montreal attempted to send Worsley to the minors in November 1969, he retired instead.

The Minnesota North Stars convinced Worsley to join them late that season, and he went on to play four more

seasons with them. "I loved it there," said Worsley. "Cesare Maniago and I became a 'Mutt and Jeff' goaltending tandem." Maniago, a lanky 6-foot-3 veteran, but 10 years younger, was indeed a comical counterpart to 5-foot-7 Worsley — much like the famed comic-strip odd couple. "Cesare eventually convinced me to have a mask made, and I tried it in practice but couldn't get used to it," said Worsley. "I found it very warm and couldn't see the puck between my feet." But just before he hung up his pads for good, and almost 45 years old, Worsley donned a mask for the final six games of the 1973–74 season. "I knew I was retiring, and Minnesota was mathematically eliminated from the playoffs. [General manager] Wren Blair said, 'Save your eyes, Gump. Put it on.' But I didn't like it."

Career Stats

REGULAR SEASON

Season	Age	Team	Lg	GP	W	L	T	SO	GA	GAA	G	A	PTS	PIM
1952-53	23	New York Rangers	NHL	50	13	29	8	2	153	3.06	0	0	0	2
1954-55	25	New York Rangers	NHL	65	15	33	17	4	197	3.03	0	0	0	2
1955-56	26	New York Rangers	NHL	70	32	28	10	4	198	2.83	0	0	0	2
1956-57	27	New York Rangers	NHL	68	26	28	14	3	216	3.18	0	0	0	19
1957-58	28	New York Rangers	NHL	37	21	10	6	4	86	2.32	0	0	0	10
1958-59	29	New York Rangers	NHL	67	26	30	11	2	198	2.97	0	0	0	10
1959-60	30	New York Rangers	NHL	39	7	23	8	0	135	3.52	0	0	0	12
1960-61	31	New York Rangers	NHL	59	20	29	8	1	190	3.28	0	0	0	10
1961-62	32	New York Rangers	NHL	60	22	27	9	2	172	2.92	0	0	0	12
1962-63	33	New York Rangers	NHL	67	22	34	10	2	217	3.27	0	0	0	14
1963-64	34	Montreal Canadiens	NHL	8	3	2	2	1	22	2.97	0	0	0	0
1964-65	35	Montreal Canadiens	NHL	19	10	7	1	1	50	2.94	0	0	0	0
1965-66	36	Montreal Canadiens	NHL	51	29	14	6	2	114	2.36	0	1	1	4
1966-67	37	Montreal Canadiens	NHL	18	9	6	2	1	47	3.18	0	0	0	4
1967-68	38	Montreal Canadiens	NHL	40	19	9	8	6	73	1.98	0	0	0	10
1968-69	39	Montreal Canadiens	NHL	30	19	5	4	5	64	2.25	0	0	0	0
1969-70	40	Montreal Canadiens	NHL	6	3	1	2	0	14	2.33	0	0	0	0
1969-70	40	Minnesota North Stars	NHL	8	5	1	1	1	20	2.65	0	0	0	0
1970-71	41	Minnesota North Stars	NHL	24	4	10	8	0	57	2.50	0	0	0	10
1971-72	42	Minnesota North Stars	NHL	34	16	10	7	2	68	2.12	0	1	1	2
1972-73	43	Minnesota North Stars	NHL	12	6	2	3	0	30	2.88	0	1	1	22
1973-74	44	Minnesota North Stars	NHL	29	8	14	5	0	86	3.22	0	0	0	0
NHL Career – 21 Seasons				861	335	352	150	43	2407	2.88	0	3	3	145

PLAYOFFS

Season	Age	Team	Lg	GP	W	L	T	SO	GA	GAA	G	A	PTS	PIM
1955-56	26	New York Rangers	NHL	3	0	3		0	14	4.67	0	0	0	2
1956-57	27	New York Rangers	NHL	5	1	4		0	21	3.99	0	0	0	0
1957-58	28	New York Rangers	NHL	6	2	4		0	28	4.60	0	0	0	0
1961-62	32	New York Rangers	NHL	6	2	4		0	21	3.28	0	0	0	0
1964-65	35	Montreal Canadiens	NHL	8	5	3		2	14	1.68	0	0	0	0
1965-66	36	Montreal Canadiens	NHL	10	8	2		1	20	1.99	0	0	0	0
1966-67	37	Montreal Canadiens	NHL	2	0	1		0	2	1.50	0	0	0	0
1967-68	38	Montreal Canadiens	NHL	12	11	0		1	21	1.88	0	0	0	10
1968-69	39	Montreal Canadiens	NHL	7	5	1		0	14	2.27	0	0	0	5
1969-70	40	Minnesota North Stars	NHL	3	1	2		0	14	4.67	0	0	0	0
1970-71	41	Minnesota North Stars	NHL	4	3	1		0	13	3.25	0	0	0	0
1971-72	42	Minnesota North Stars	NHL	4	2	1		1	7	2.16	0	0	0	0
NHL Career – 12 Seasons				70	40	26		5	189	2.78	0	0	0	17

Page 88: A young Gump Worsley in his early years with the New York Rangers. Worsley played his first 10 seasons on Broadway.

Page 89: Worsley in his final NHL years with the Minnesota North Stars. Lured out of retirement to play for the expansion club, Worsley posted a very respectable 39–37–24 record for the North Stars.

Page 90: Worsely swats a puck out of the air in an exhibition match against the Soviets.

GEARING UP

BY BOB DUFF

WHEN THE GAME OF hockey was in its infancy, the only thing that separated the goaltender from the rest of those on his team was the courage of his convictions — or the craziness within his cranium, depending upon your perspective.

To the naked eye, early netminders didn't appear to be any different than the other players on the ice. Study a team photo of the 1892–93 Montreal Amateur Athletic Association (MAAA), first winners of the Stanley Cup, and you wouldn't be able to pick goalie Tom Paton out of the crowd without the identifying names at the bottom of the portrait. Paton is holding the same stick, wearing the same skates, hockey pants and MAAA sweater adorned with its winged wheel logo as all the other players.

Marc-André Fleury's yellow RBK trapper that he used throughout the 2006–07 NHL season holds the brown Cooper-Weeks leather trapper of journeyman goaltender Ed Chadwick from his time with the AHL's Buffalo Bisons. Chadwick played in Buffalo at the end of his pro career from 1964–68.

The 1892–93 Stanley Cup champion Montreal AAA.
Goaltender Tom Paton is seated third from the left.

The 1896 Winnipeg Victorias. Whitey Merritt is seated
in the middle wearing cricket leg protectors.

In reality, there was little need for much in the way of protective gear during that era, as the hockey of the day was all about passing and the puck rarely left the ice surface. But as the quality of sticks improved, players soon discovered that by backhanding the puck they could get some loft and put some velocity into their shots. For the first time in hockey history, the goalie was becoming a moving target and slowly but steadily, his appearance between the pipes began to change.

GOALIE PADS

It's interesting to note that throughout hockey's history, innovations in goaltending equipment started from the ground up. The first protective gear donned by netminders in order to give them a leg up on the competition was an item you might still find around the house: catalogues. Goalkeepers would stuff the latest thick-paper edition from Simpson's, Eaton's or the Hudson Bay Company inside their hockey socks prior to taking the ice, in order to absorb the pain of a six-ounce piece of vulcanized rubber ricocheting off their previously unprotected legs. A goalie in Dartmouth, Nova Scotia, was reported to have worn some sort of shin guard in an 1889 game and there is documented evidence of goalies in Winnipeg donning leg guards as early as 1891. By the time the Manitoba and North-West Amateur Hockey Association officially

formed on November 11, 1892, it was commonplace for the goaltenders in that loop, borrowing from the popular English sport of cricket, to don the leg pads worn by wicket keepers to help their shins and ankles survive the onslaught of rubber biscuits. It was around the same time period that Winnipeg skaters began to develop the early intricacies of the wrist shot, so the donning of the pads was as much about self-preservation as it was about innovation.

When an All-Star Team from the three clubs in the Winnipeg senior league — the Winnipegs, the Victorias and Fort Osborne — toured the eastern Canadian provinces in February 1893, the locals were astonished to see Winnipeg netminder A.M. Stowe wearing these leg guards. After the All-Stars played the Montreal AAA on Febuary 15, 1893, the *Montreal Gazette* reported, "The goalkeeper wore a pair of cricket greaves and every man on the team wore shin pads."

These early pads were a hard shell, covering the shin from the ankles to just below the knees, and by the next season, some Ontario Hockey Association goaltenders began wearing this type of leg coverage.

Winnipeg Victorias goaltender George "Whitey" Merritt wore a similar pair of leg protectors onto the ice February 14, 1896, when they challenged the champion Montreal Victorias for the Stanley Cup. The Montreal club originally protested their use, feeling it gave the Winnipeg goaler an unfair advantage, but the game went on as scheduled, and backstopped by their padded net protector, Winnipeg won the showdown by a 2–0 count, taking Lord Stanley's mug to Western Canada for the first time. In the process, Merritt posted the first shutout in Stanley Cup history. "Many shots were rained in on Merritt, but none got behind the posts," the *Winnipeg Free Press* noted.

Added *The Montreal Herald*, "Merritt carries a great many memories of his stubborn and successful battle between his posts. Winnipeg ought to put a statue to his memory. Never was there such a goalkeeper. The Winnipegs owe their victory to the really marvelous work of their goalkeeper during the second half of the match."

While Merritt is often mistakenly referred to as the first goalie to wear pads in a match, the reality is that he was the first to wear them in a Stanley Cup game, which, with its vast audience of interested spectators and followers was certainly the catalyst that made goal pads standard gear for the netminder.

Soon, goal pads evolved to where they were constructed of a canvas material and strapped around the leg, covering from the base of the hockey pants (mid-thigh) to the ankle. The 1913 Spalding Equipment Catalog featured goalkeepers leg guards for $5 per pair, describing them as follows: "Made of finest quality buckskin, extra heavy can strips, covering well up over the knee. This guard is used by leading goalkeepers and is undoubtedly the finest guard made." A similar pair constructed from a lesser stock of canvas retailed for $3.50.

The cricket-style pad stayed as the goaltenders' leg protector of choice into the 1920s, when the man who would become the maven of goalie pads revolutionized the method in which this piece of equipment was designed.

Emil "Pop" Kenesky was two years old when his family emigrated from a town near the German-Polish border. Settling in Hamilton, Ontario, he eventually opened a harness-making and bicycle repair business on Barton Street in 1916. In 1920, Hamilton gained an NHL team when a Quebec franchise relocated there. The Tigers, as they were known, didn't enjoy much success on the ice, and during the 1923–24 season, Kenesky approached

Hamilton manager Percy LeSueur and goaltender Vernor "Jake" Forbes with an idea.

Kenesky suggested they flatten out and thicken the cricket pads, noting there was nothing in the rules to govern this area, and created a set of pads for Forbes that were wider and flatter, jutting out to the sides. The outside of the pads were leather in front and felt in the back, and the thickness was provided by stuffing of kapok and deer hair.

Too thick, as it turned out. Wearing his new gear, Forbes struggled desperately to start the season. The Tigers opened 0–4 and critics lampooned the goaltender for his poor play. Prior to Hamilton's December 29th game at Ottawa, LeSueur and Kenesky performed major surgery of the open-pad variety. Forbes allowed two goals in a 3–2 victory over the Senators in which Ottawa players professed that the Hamilton goaltender had turned in a display of netminding as impressive as they'd ever seen. The January 2, 1924, edition of the *Hamilton Spectator* delved into Forbes' padded stats: "Was Vernor Forbes carrying too much weight?" the paper asked. "The fact of the matter is that his pads were too big and too heavy. He could not get his feet together and some of the goals that were scored against him [previously] were due to that. The day before the game at Ottawa, a gang of workmen started in to rebuild the pads and they evidently made a good job of it, for the little fellow showed better form … due to the fact that he wasn't handicapped by having a couple of mattresses in front of him."

Kenesky and LeSueur removed 17 pounds of stuffing from Forbes' pads, reducing their combined weight to seven pounds.

Forbes was the ideal netminder to hand this revolutionary piece of gear to, largely because he was a born rebel. In 1920, after a strong rookie season with the Toronto St. Patricks, Forbes balked at his contract offer and indignantly refused to sign it, opting to sit out the season. In 1925, when Hamilton players felt they'd been shortchanged in their paychecks by owner Percy Thompson, Forbes was among the ringleaders who took the team out on strike prior to the playoffs, eventually forfeiting the NHL title to the Montreal Canadiens.

When other netminders got an eyeful of Forbes' new look, Kenesky became a popular fellow. Over the years, netminders suggested modifications to Kenesky's design, and he proved an apt listener. In the 1930s, Montreal Canadiens goalie Wilf Cude convinced him to lengthen the pads to provide better coverage of the leg above the knee. New York Americans goalie Earl Robertson offered his own quirk: he demanded his pads include a rabbit's foot sewn inside each leg for good luck.

Kenesky's business began to grow and so did the size of goal pads — until 1925 when the NHL finally put a stop to the enlarged leg protection, when it passed a rule that prohibited pads from exceeding a 12-inch width. Two years later, the league reduced the width to 10 inches. The 10-inch rule was seldom challenged, but it became a cause célèbre during the opening round of the 1973 Stanley Cup playoffs between the Buffalo Sabres and Montreal Canadiens.

With five minutes remaining in regulation time in a 2–2 tie in Game 5 of the series, Sabres coach Joe Crozier sent back-up goalie Dave Dryden to the dressing room to retrieve a copy of the NHL rule book. At a stoppage in play with 29 seconds to go until overtime, Crozier got the attention of referee Bruce Hood and pointed out Section Three, Rule 22B under equipment, which noted, "The leg guards worn by a goalkeeper shall not exceed 10 inches in extreme width when on the leg of the player."

Crozier requested a measurement of the pads of Montreal goalie Ken Dryden, Dave's younger brother.

At the conclusion of regulation time, the pads were measured and the left leg pad was found to be three-quarters of an inch too wide. Montreal was assessed a two-minute penalty and Dryden's pads were thinned out and taped up for the overtime period. Though the Sabres didn't score on the ensuing power play, they did win in overtime.

The measurement was a bit of tit-for-tat between the clubs. During a regular-season game, Montreal coach Scotty Bowman had called for a measurement of Dave Dryden's stick.

"What I used to say to the people making my equipment was, 'Look, just make it to the specifications of the rule book,'" Dave Dryden recalled. "One night in Montreal,

we were playing the Canadiens and Scotty Bowman called for a stick measurement on me. I was really ticked. I told Louisville to make them to the right size and I trusted Louisville. They were a great company. Referee Ron Wicks measured the stick and said it was all right.

"After the game, I said to Ken, 'That really rips me that Scotty didn't trust me. I wonder if we had called a measurement on you, Ken, if your stuff would be legal?' Well, Ken went and measured his pads and discovered that they were about half an inch too wide. He decided that he was going to get them made smaller, which he did. I went back to Buffalo, took out the tape measure and realized that my sticks were an inch too big. Scotty had actually been right and Ron Wicks had measured them wrong. I had to take all my sticks and cut them down to the right size."

Crozier was determined to get even, and waited for the right moment. "In the playoffs, Joe Crozier said to us, 'Do you think Ken's pads are too big?' The consensus around the room was, 'Yeah, I think they probably are.' Joe called a measurement on Ken and when the measurement happened, Ken was sort of chuckling and saying, 'I got you this time.' But I'll be damned if when they measured, his pads were still too wide, because he leaned on his pads and they popped out."

After the game, it was Ken's turn to vent at Dave. "He was so pissed off at me," Dave remembered, though the passage of time has softened Ken's anger. Currently a Canadian Member of Parliament, Ken holds no grudge over the call. "That didn't bother me," Ken said. "The rule exists, if you want to use it."

The Kenesky family would rule the legs of NHL goalies for nearly five decades. The Kenesky model became the pad of choice for NHL netminders and it became a status symbol among amateur goalies to own a pair of Pop's handcrafted pads. A goalie seeking a set might have to order them a year in advance, the demand for the product was so high.

The design of the pad changed little over that time, other than to mold them better to the feet to offer increased protection and coverage for along-the-ice shots. Kenesky pads were all the rage well into the mid-1980s, when synthetic products began to take over. Calgary

Flames goalie Réjean Lemelin was among the first of the pros to utilize pads made from nylon material and filled with foam. The edge synthetic pads offered was their lightweight construction. Modern Kenesky pads weighed 11 pounds each and could absorb as much as six pounds of water during a game. That's why goalies would pound their pads with their sticks, seeking to lighten their load by smacking some of the moisture out. The addition of Sofrina, a Japanese-made fiber that repelled water, also made the new synthetic pads attractive. A current pair of synthetic, machine-made pads weigh less than half of one of Kenesky's hand-stitched models.

The leather pad has gone the way of the maskless goaltender and the six-team NHL — merely a memory of days long ago.

GOALIE STICKS

Incorrectly looked upon as the father of the goalie pad, Winnipeg Victorias goalie Whitey Merritt may in fact be the standard-bearer of the goalie stick.

Photographic evidence documents Merritt in a team photo with the 1894–95 Victorias holding a stick with a wider base than that of his teammates. Merritt had taken a second piece of wood and fastened it to one side of the lower half of his stick. This design eventually progressed to a point where the bottom half of the shaft of the stick widened creating a larger lower shaft and blade at the base. This was the first piece of hockey equipment designed solely for use by the goalkeeper, but as much as it made sense, other goaltenders were still slow to follow Merritt's lead. As late as 1905, during the infamous Dawson City Klondikers–Ottawa Silver Seven Stanley Cup series, Dawson City goaltender Albert Forrest utilized a wide-based goal stick, while Bouse Hutton, his opposite number, protected his cage with a regular player's stick. The extra size didn't work to Forrest's advantage, however. In the two-game series, he was beaten for 32 goals.

Eventually, all goalkeepers went to the wider-based style of stick, and that led hockey's regulators to govern its growth. In 1921, NHL rules prohibited goal sticks from being wider than 3.5 inches.

There were few changes to sticks over the next several decades, other than the laminating of sticks, which began in the 1940s and fiberglass coating, which was first added during the 1960s. The curved stick was all the rage at this time and it wasn't long before goaltenders began experimenting with curved blades. Doug Sauter, goaltender for the Western Hockey League's Calgary Centennials in 1972–73, claims he was the first to utilize a curved blade, a fact that puzzled his coach, Albert "Scotty" Munro, himself a former netminder. "Scotty asked me one day why I needed a curved stick," Sauter recalled. "And I told him it made it easier to scoop the puck out of the back of the net."

Former NHLer Don McLeod is believed to be the first netminder to employ a curved blade in the professional ranks, with the Vancouver Blazers of the World Hockey Association during the 1974–75 season. McLeod found he was able to handle the puck much more efficiently and he was able to get more loft on his clearing attempts. During the following season, he recorded 13 assists, a major-pro hockey record until Grant Fuhr of the Edmonton Oilers collected 14 helpers in 1983–84. "The curved blade comes in handy," McLeod told Milt Dunnell of *The Toronto Star* in a 1975 interview, "especially when we're shorthanded."

By the end of that decade, curved goalie sticks were standard, allowing superb puckhandling goalies such as Ron Hextall, Martin Brodeur, Marty Turco and Rick DiPietro to operate as a third defenseman in their own end, clearing the puck from harm's way before enemy attackers could gain the zone.

As with players' sticks, goal sticks today are available in composite designs, though wood sticks haven't faded from the goaltending scene as rapidly as they departed from the hands of the other skaters on the ice.

GOALIE PANTS

When goalies began to drop to the ice to stop the puck, padding was added along the hip and tailbone of regular hockey pants. The pants were made from reinforced canvas and the padding was sponge rubber covered with felt.

Today, goalie pants are larger and heavily-lined with

padding to aid the netminder in puckstopping, complete with solid pieces of padding lining the inside of each leg to help prevent pucks from sneaking through the five-hole.

GOALIE SKATES

Early skates were merely metal blades strapped to a walking boot, which caused a myriad of problems for the netminder. "In one game, the goalie was using his skates to block the ice-hugging shots," wrote Captain James T. Sutherland, one of organized hockey's pioneers, in his memoirs about early hockey played in Kingston, Ontario, during the mid-1880s. "The impact would release the trigger-type fastener and the skate would fly off the goalie's boot, or go sailing across the rink. The referee would have to stop play, the skate would be put back on the goalkeeper's boot, and the game would proceed."

The invention of the tube skate at the turn of the 20th century resulted in the first skate blade that was held to a boot with rivets. Both players and netminders wore these skates, though netminders began to increase their ability to stop the puck by adding a piece of canvas or sheet metal to prevent pucks from slipping through between the boot and blade.

The 1931 book, *Ice Hockey: How To Play And Understand The Game*, written by coach Alexander Sayles of Williams College in Massachusetts and St. Nicholas, New York, Hockey Club captain Gerard Hallock III, described goal skates in the following manner: "The skates should have no radius and between the blade and the shoe there should be a leather or metal strap about a half to three-quarters of an inch wide running the length of the skate. This is to prevent the puck from passing between the skate and the shoe. The shoe should have a heavy box toe, and it is also advisable to have the sides of the shoe covered with heavy leather, high enough to meet the bottom of the goal pad."

During the 1938 Stanley Cup final, after breaking a toe, Chicago Black Hawks goalie Mike Karakas returned to action with the toe of his skate reinforced with steel. By the 1940s, goalie skates featured the protective plastic cowling around the boot that is still used today.

Emile Francis is seen with a coach and teammates wearing his modified first baseman's mitt with gauntlet cuff.

GOALIE GLOVES

At the outset, goalies wore the same style gloves as all hockey players. There really wasn't a need for added protection since most shots were aimed below the waist and the rules of the day prohibited handling of the puck by any player on the ice. By the early 1900s, gloves that extended further up the forearm became available, and by 1910, the innovative Percy LeSueur was tending goal in Ottawa with the gauntlet-style gloves he designed. Offering extra padding in the hand, LeSueur's gloves also featured a lengthy piece of solid, padded protection that extended from the wrist up each arm until just below the elbow.

By the 1920s, stick-side goalie gloves grew wider on the front and featured felt padding to help absorb the blows of wicked shots, while catching gloves still resembled players' gloves, but with longer padding up the arm and extra padding in the hand area. In 1927 the rules changed to permit netminders to handle and catch the puck. Boston's Cecil "Tiny" Thompson, who arrived on the NHL scene in 1928, was also an excellent baseball player and proved to be the first goalie to make snaring drives with his glove hand a regular occurrence.

In 1935, Mike Karakas debuted with the Chicago Black Hawks, winning the Calder Trophy as the NHL's top rookie. Three years later, he changed the way the puck was stopped when he introduced a rounded glove with a webbed pocket between the thumb and index finger. It was a baseball-mitt-like innovation that allowed him to catch the puck — an innovation that was also seen on the left hand of Bruins' rookie stopper Frank Brimsek in the 1938–39 season. Both Karakas and Brimsek hailed from Eveleth, Minnesota, where they were battery mates on the same baseball team and were both known for their lightning-quick catching hand. By the 1939–40 season, this style of catching glove was worn by all NHL netminders.

A decade after Karakas and Brimsek's innovation, another Chicago goalie came along to further advance the catching-hand glove. Emile Francis, a prominent baseball player in Saskatchewan, adapted a first baseman's mitt into a goalie trapper, which he first used while playing senior hockey in Regina. "It was a George McQuinn model made by Rawlings," Francis recalled to author Kevin Shea. "He played for the New York Yankees. At training camp, I asked the trainer to take the glove to a shoemaker and have him take the cuff off an old hockey glove and sew it onto the baseball glove. I used that glove."

Signed late in the 1946–47 season by the Black Hawks, Francis took the warm-up for a game against Detroit wearing his modified catching glove, but before game time, Detroit coach Jack Adams protested to referee King Clancy that the glove was a piece of illegal equipment. Clancy skated to the net Francis was tending, and demanded to see the glove.

"King came over to me and said, 'Let me see that glove you've got there,'" Francis remembered. "I showed him the glove. He said, 'You can't use that.' I said, 'What do you mean, I can't use it?' He said, 'It's too big.' I said, 'If I can't use this glove, you've got no game tonight. I don't have any other glove and I have no intention of using any other glove. I'm not using a forward's glove to play goal.'"

The game went on, and the next day, Francis and Clancy met with NHL president Clarence Campbell in Montreal. Campbell studied Francis's glove and ruled that it was legal.

As Francis tells it, "the story got out and within a month, all the sporting goods companies were making

those goal gloves. I should have copyrighted the idea. All I wanted was to be a better goalkeeper. From then on, every goalkeeper started using the catching glove."

The blocker took a little longer to develop into the hardened plastic pad that became standard for all modern-era blockers. Brimsek is credited with being the first to add an extra layer of padding to the outside of his blocker, and Al Rollins, who won the Hart Trophy in goal for the Black Hawks in 1953–54, took this development one step further. He added a fiber backing covered with a piece of leather, which aided him in controlling and deflecting rebounds to safety. Prior to that, most blocker pads were constructed of felt or sponge rubber, making the control of rebounds virtually impossible. Further into the Original Six era, the blocking surface became more rigid and continued to be covered with leather to help create the forerunners of the blockers we see today. By the mid-1950s, the flat hardened surfaces made first of wood, and later of plastic, began to appear on the front of blockers.

Perhaps the most unique goalie glove innovation in NHL history was brought about by Montreal Canadiens goalie Bill Durnan. A six-time winner of the Vezina Trophy between 1943–44 and 1949–50, Durnan was ambidextrous and had specially-designed gloves that could operate as both blocker and trapper (see page 65), allowing him to switch hands and always play his strong side to a shooter's weakness. It was a trait taught to him by Steve Faulkner, one of Durnan's youth hockey coaches growing up in Toronto.

"It wasn't easy at first, because I was so young, and the stick seemed so heavy," Durnan once explained in an interview with the Canadian Press. "But Steve kept after me and gradually, the stick became lighter and I could switch it automatically. It was a tremendous asset."

Necessity was also the mother of invention for Dan Blackburn, a first-round draft pick of the New York Rangers in 2001, whose career was derailed by a 2003 shoulder injury that caused nerve damage, prohibiting him from making the motions necessary to make glove-hand saves.

When Blackburn returned to the ice with the East Coast League's Victoria Salmon Kings during the 2004–05 season, he did so wearing blockers on both hands at the suggestion of Rangers GM Glen Sather. The glove-side blocker was modified to include webbing and a pocket on the inside.

With these modifications, Blackburn was able to deflect high shots without having to lift and turn his arm, while maintaining the ability to catch low shots. Sadly, the innovation couldn't salvage Blackburn's once-promising career. He played just 12 games with Victoria, then announced his retirement in September 2005 at the age of 24.

HEAD GEAR

One of the last innovations in goalie equipment was among the first to enter the development stage.

By the turn of the 20th century, there already were rumblings within hockey circles that goaltenders might want to consider donning some sort of facial protection. When Eddie Geroux, goalkeeper for the Toronto Marlboros, was cut in the face by a shot from the stick of Tommy Phillips during a December 9, 1903, Ontario Hockey Association senior practice, two stitches were required to close the wound, and Geroux experimented with returning to the ice wearing additional protection. "Goalkeeper Geroux will be unable to play for a few days on account of the cut which he received the other day," reported the December 12, 1903, edition of the *Toronto Globe*. "He is talking of wearing a baseball mask as a protection in future." A few days later, Geroux underwent a change of heart. "Goalkeeper Geroux has discarded his baseball mask," said the *Toronto Globe* on December 17, 1903. "He wore it at a couple of practices, but found it unsatisfactory owing to the difficulty in locating shots from the side."

Further mask use came about in 1912, as Kingston Frontenacs forward George Richardson donned facial protection to ensure his eyeglasses weren't damaged during play, and in 1919, another goalie experimented with the mask. Morris Jones donned a baseball catcher's mask during an Upper Ottawa Valley League game.

The mask was becoming an issue that hockey moguls found worthy of discussion. In fact, at its 1920 annual meeting, the OHA passed a resolution regarding the subject: "Goalkeepers may wear a mask for protection."

One of the "forefathers" of the goalie mask was, in fact, a woman. Elizabeth Graham tended goal for the Queen's University women's team in Kingston, Ontario, and she turned more than a few heads by covering hers up for a February 7, 1927, game.

Graham wore a fencing mask to protect her from pucks at the insistence of her father George, who didn't want to see any of her dental work dislodged by an errant puck. "She gave the fans a surprise," *The Kingston Whig-Standard* reported. "It was safety first with her, and even at that she can't be blamed for her precautionary methods." Around the same era, Charles Fasel, playing for the Swiss club HC Davos, wore a face mask. Soon, an NHL netminder would get in on the cover up.

The Montreal Maroons were taking on the rival Montreal Canadiens on January 7, 1930, when a shot from the stick of Canadiens star Howie Morenz shattered the nose of Maroons' goalie Clint Benedict — whose nose had already taken a wallop in a game three days earlier against the Boston Bruins from a puck shot by Dit Clapper. "Someday," reported the January 8, 1930, edition of the *Montreal Gazette*, "the league will authorize masks for netminders as baseball does for its catchers."

Someday soon, as it turned out.

Benedict sat out the next 14 games recuperating, and when he returned to the ice February 20 for a game against the New York Americans at Madison Square Garden — which ended in a 3–3 tie — he did so with protection for his wounded proboscis (see page 14, 193).

"Benedict, the Maroons goalie, played his first game since his injuries over a month ago, wearing a huge mask to protect his injured nose," said *The New York Times* the next morning.

Benedict explained himself during a 1976 interview with the *Montreal Gazette*, "I asked a firm in Boston to create a mask. It was leather and wire with a big nose piece."

He wore the mask for five games, and on March 4, 1930, he was injured during a goalmouth scramble in a 6–2 loss to the Ottawa Senators when his mask was driven hard into his nose. "The nosepiece proved the problem, because it obscured my vision," Benedict said.

Benny played the next season in the minor leagues with the Windsor Bulldogs, the Maroons' farm club, and was released at season's end, but in 1932, indicated he was plotting a comeback, armed with a new face mask. "Benedict … may become the first 'Man in the Mask' of the ice sport," said the *Winnipeg Free Press* in 1932, "He is practicing daily and believes he can come back with all his old ability. He is wearing glasses and has had a mask specially constructed to protect the glasses. The mask is of his own design."

Benedict's dream never came true. No team was willing to give him and his mask a chance and he never played again.

Nearly three decades would pass before the mask would return to pro hockey, but it wasn't gone from the hockey world. Franklin Farrell wore a wire mask for the United States during the 1932 Winter Olympics in Lake Placid and four years later at the 1936 Winter Olympiad in Garmisch-Partenkirchen, Germany, Japan's Teiji Honma donned a baseball-style mask to protect his eyeglasses while tending goal. Roy Musgrove of the British National League club, the Wembley Lions, also wore a wire base-ball-style mask in the mid-to-late 1930s.

Clarkson College goaltender Ed MacDonald, an all-tournament team selection at the 1957 NCAA final four, did so while wearing a face mask during practice that season. One-piece Plexiglas shields for practice work were commonplace for NHL netminders in this era, though they fogged up easily and weren't feasible for game action.

During the 1958–59 season, Gene Long, trainer for New York's Hamilton College hockey team, developed a fiberglass mask for netminder Don Spencer, who'd suffered facial fractures when hit by a puck. Spencer utilized the mask in practice, but never in game action. The mask featured rectangular openings for the eyes and mouth, two small openings at the end of the nose, and several smaller holes throughout the mask for ventilation. Long's idea grew from work he'd done to develop fiberglass heel protectors for long jumpers with the school's track and field team.

Plante protects the goal while wearing his infamous mask in 1959–60.

At the same time, Jacques Plante of the Montreal Canadiens was experimenting with a face mask designed by the Montreal-based Fiberglass Canada. He'd donned the mask in training camp for the 1959–60 season and had been using it ever since in practice, much to the chagrin of Canadiens coach Toe Blake, who was dead set against the idea of a masked man guarding his team's net.

Plante's moment came on November 1, 1959, at Madison Square Garden — the same building where Clint Benedict had debuted his mask 29 years earlier. Smacked in the nose by a rising shot from the stick of Rangers star Andy Bathgate, Plante had to be taken off the ice for emergency repairs. As he was being patched up, Plante informed Blake that without the aid of his mask, he wasn't going back between the posts. Without a capable back-up man, Blake had no choice but to relent, especially after Plante returned to perform splendidly in a 3–1 victory over the Rangers.

The original Plante mask was hardly a thing of beauty — drab gray in color, with two eyeholes and one more below the nose. "I designed it for protection, not good looks," noted Bill Burchmore of Fiberglass Canada.

Plante immediately launched a 10–0–1 run as a masked man, helping stave off the criticism heaped his way. The attitude of hockey people in Plante's era made it so that it actually took more courage for Plante to stand in the way of pucks wearing his mask than it would have for him to stare down the rubber directed his way barefaced. "It's completely ridiculous for anyone to think that a goalie who wants to wear a mask is chicken, because anyone who would stand up to a 100-mile-an-hour projectile is no coward," NHL president Clarence Campbell said in defense of the character of goaltenders who chose to wear facial protection.

With Plante leading the way, the 1959–60 season became the campaign in which the mask went mainstream. New York Rovers' goalie Don Rich briefly wore the Plexiglas bubble visor in Eastern League action. Hamilton College goalie Herbie Heintz donned a Gene Long-model mask in an NCAA game, as did Toronto Varsity Blues' goaltender Bob Giroux in OUAA play. Belleville McFarlands goaltender Gordie Bell returned to OHA Senior A action wearing a mask after suffering a lacerated eyeball, and Peterborough TPTs goalie George Holmes was the first netminder to don facial protection in an OHA Junior A game.

Just over a month after Plante debuted his mask in New York, Boston goalie Don Simmons became the second NHL goalie to regularly wear a mask, donning one for the Bruins' 4–3 loss to the Rangers on December 13, 1959. That game curiously enough, was also played at Madison Square Garden. The same week, Emile Francis of Spokane became the first Western League goalie to wear a mask. By the end of December, Cleveland Barons goalie Gil Mayer brought the mask into action in the American League.

In January, Plante switched to a fiberglass, pretzel-style bar mask. Eastern League goalie Norm DeFelice of Clinton became a masked man, and Montreal Royals netminder Gerry McNeil brought the mask to the Eastern Pro League.

Even Blake would become a fan. "I don't care what kind of mask he wears in the future," the Canadiens coach said after Plante won his fifth consecutive Vezina Trophy while backstopping the Habs to their fifth straight Stanley Cup.

Through the 1960s, goaltenders became known for the style of mask they wore: Was it a pretzel mask? A full fiberglass face covering? Did it have square eyeholes? Round eyeholes?

But as the decade was concluding, a new form of brand was identifying these masked men — artwork.

The first attempts were crude, but effective, and definitely noticeable. During the 1968–69 season, Boston Bruins goalie Gerry Cheevers was looking for a way out of practice, something that was commonplace for him. A shot glanced off his mask and he made a beeline for the dressing room, closely followed by Bruins trainer John "Frosty" Forristall.

Within seconds, Bruins coach Harry Sinden joined them, demanding that Cheevers get back on the ice. While Cheevers was sheepishly suiting up for his return to duty, Forristall grabbed his mask and with a black magic marker, quickly sketched 10 stitch marks where the puck had deflected off of it.

With one stroke of a Sharpie, an icon was born — hockey's most memorable mask.

With each shot to the face, Forristall added more faux stitches. "When [wearing a] mask finally became big [in the late 1960s], everyone was wearing a white one," Cheevers said. "I was someone who never cared for the color white."

Others soon followed his lead. Philadelphia Flyers goalie Doug Favell painted his mask orange for Halloween in 1970. "Two days before Halloween, at the morning skate, [Flyers trainer] Frank Lewis and I were sitting around and I said, 'Frankie, why not paint this mask orange for Halloween?'" Favell explained to *The Hockey News*. The next season, Favell switched to an orange-and-white starburst design while teammate Bobby Taylor added a black starburst pattern to his mask a year later.

Then in 1974, Jim Rutherford took things to the next level. Traded by Pittsburgh to the Detroit Red Wings in January, Rutherford, whose mask was painted blue to match the Penguins' colors of the time, dropped it off to designer Greg Harrison with instructions to paint it white.

Harrison did so — but added two wings, one coming off each eye.

"I wore it and everyone loved it," Rutherford said. "After that, all goalies started having things painted on their masks."

Swedish netminder Goran Hogosta wears a helmet-and-cage style mask while stopping pucks for the Quebec Nordiques in 1979–80.

Today's goaltenders are identified by the artwork on their mask, whether it be the savage bear of Boston's Tim Thomas, or the flame-red skull of Calgary's Miikka Kiprusoff.

Chris Osgood stands alone among NHL goalies and he isn't willing to change. As stubbornly as Jacques Plante was married to the idea of initially using the mask, Osgood is attached to the old-school birdcage mask.

"I'm getting too old to change," said Osgood, who entered the NHL wearing his Bauer helmet-and-cage mask in 1993. "I've tried [the modern fiberglass-and-kevlar mask with wire cage] a couple of times, but I didn't like it."

The so-called birdcage mask was first seen on a regular basis in North America during the 1972 Summit Series, when Soviet goalie Vladislav Tretiak starred while wearing one. As European goalies slowly began to migrate across the Atlantic Ocean, they brought the helmet-and-cage style with them. "We had a Swedish goalie [Goran Hogosta] come to camp with us [in 1977]," recalled former New York Islanders goalie Glenn "Chico" Resch. Both Resch and counterpart Billy Smith noticed that when the

puck hit Hogosta's helmet-and-cage, he didn't receive the sting from the blow of the puck the way they did in their all-fiberglass, form-fitting masks.

Both made the switch to the birdcage, and more goalies followed after a 1979 incident in which the stick of New York Rangers forward Don Maloney got into the right eyehole of the fiberglass mask of Philadelphia's Bernie Parent, causing a career-ending eye injury.

By the 1980s, the birdcage mask was all the rage, but its decline was in full swing by the early 1990s with the rise of the modern mask. Arturs Irbe, one of the last birdcage loyalists, got so desperate for parts for his out-of-stock Jofa helmet-and-mask that he took out an ad in a goaltending periodical, seeking to buy models that he could cannibalize for parts.

Irbe eventually retired and so did prominent helmet-and-cage user Dominik Hasek, and Dan Cloutier, another bird cage user, faded from the scene, leaving Osgood to stand alone.

"I'll never change," he said.

When it came to his gear, Dave Dryden could best be described as a tinkerer. "It was one aspect of goaltending that I really enjoyed, experimenting with the equipment," he said.

During the summer of 1978, while tending goal for the Edmonton Oilers of the World Hockey Association, Dave Dryden teamed up with mask designer Greg Harrison to unveil the latest and, as it would turn out, the greatest, advance in goalie-mask technology.

Just ask his brother.

"Dave completely revolutionized how a goaltender plays," Hall of Fame netminder Ken Dryden, today a Canadian Member of Parliament, told the *Hamilton Spectator*. "That is something that should not be underestimated at all.

"People think of goaltending being transformed by Jacques Plante with the mask and Glenn Hall with the butterfly, but the third transformational figure in goaltending is my brother."

Dave Dryden wasn't merely the first big-league goaltender to don the modern fiberglass mask with cage opening, the mask of choice today for all but one current

NHL goalie, he was the creator of this quintessential piece of goalie gear.

"I had been hit on the face a couple of times in the previous year," he explained. "I was getting toward the end of my career and I thought, 'This is silly, especially since I could maybe get an eye injury.'

"I'd always liked the idea of a cage, and a lot of the European goalies in the WHA were wearing the cage mask, but when I put it on and it was attached to the helmet, it just didn't make sense to me, because it was padded on the top of my head. The ring of padding went around my head like a halo, and I figured the ring of padding should be around the face, because that's where we were getting hit. I just started experimenting in Edmonton and got some solder, jigged myself up a model and really kind of thought it would work. I had always made my masks in the past, but I didn't know how I would make the cage part, so I came to Toronto that summer and worked with Greg Harrison."

Harrison took Dryden's rough design and made it workable for NHL goalies, devising a method to make the cage of strong enough metal to resist the hardest of shots.

Goalies no longer had to fear a shot to the face, because utilizing Dryden's and Harrison's design, the cage sat out away from the face, protecting the eyes, and the fiberglass head coverage, which was designed to deflect (as opposed to block) shots straight to the face, safely deflected away pucks without the netminder absorbing the shock of the blow.

"I wore it to training camp in September of 1978 and it was great," Dave Dryden said. "I just never had any problems with it. The Oilers went over to Finland for a series of pre-season games and the very first game, a guy got a rolling puck in the slot and slapped it — just drilled it — and it hit me right in the face. I went down, and then I thought, 'It didn't even hurt.'"

Slowly, the butterfly became an accepted way to play goal, because it was no longer folly for a goalie to play with his head within the shooting area. "The difference today is that the whole body stops the puck, whereas in our day, really, it was our pads and our hands that did the stopping," Dave Dryden said. "We didn't play everything off our chest."

BODY ARMOR

As early as the late 1800s, about 20 years before the chest protector would become a standard piece of the goalie's armor, baseball catchers were wearing the chest protector to help absorb blows from foul balls. Jack Clements of the Philadelphia Phillies is credited with being the first major-league backstop to don this piece of protective gear in 1885.

For netminders, there really was no need for such upper-body protection until well into the 1900s, since goaltenders were prohibited from leaving their feet to stop the puck and thus, seldom were hit with a shot above the waist.

Once goalies were permitted to drop to the ice to make a save — 1913 in the Pacific Coast Hockey Association and 1918 in the National Hockey League — it became necessary to add another element to their protective gear. By the early 1920s, bulging belly pads constructed of leather, canvas and felt were commonplace under the sweaters of netminders. Some goaltenders had their belly pads long enough so that when kneeling on the ice, the chest protector hung down between the goaltender's legs to help cover any openings.

Arm protection came along shortly after, first in the form of elbow pads, then in the long, mostly felt, arm pads that extended from the shoulder down to the wrist and fit across the chest like the shoulder pads of a forward or defenseman. These early pads covered the whole arm, but offered little in the way of protection. Former NHL goalie John Davidson remembered doctors thinking the bruises all over his arms were symptoms of leukemia.

Radical change in goalie chest and arm gear came forth in the 1990s with the introduction of upper-body armor, in which the shoulder and chest protector were combined into one piece of equipment that was thicker, reinforced with Kevlar for added protection and designed to better cover key areas such as the elbow, collarbone and shoulder. The advances in upper-body protection helped to make the butterfly technique the goaltending style of choice. "To me, there were two components — the face, and then the arm and shoulder protection," explained Dave Dryden, when talking of the evolution of goaltending styles.

"The upper-body armor. That, combined with the mask, and guys just don't get hurt anymore, except on the rare occasion. If we [goaltenders wearing old, two-piece upper body gear] anticipated a shot coming toward our shoulders, we tried to get our hands in the way. The same with our face. Now, the guys don't have to worry about that. They just take it off the shoulder and when it bounces down in front of them, they cover it."

The days of goaltenders covered with upper-body welts and abrasions have quickly faded into the sunset. "It is totally different," Dave Dryden said.

THE KIM CROUCH COLLAR

The Markham Waxers were playing the Royal York Royals in a Metro Toronto Jr. A League game on January 5, 1975. Markham's Kip Churchill and Bob Todd of Royal York were tussling for the puck near the Markham net when Waxers netminder Kim Crouch dove into the fray in an attempt to freeze the biscuit. One of the players' skates caught Crouch in the throat, slicing into his jugular vein.

Quick work by Markham trainer Joe Piccininni Jr., who applied pressure to the wound with gauze, kept Crouch from bleeding to death while medical help arrived. Police roadblocks cleared a route to the hospital for Crouch's ambulance, and his life was saved with two hours of surgery.

"I was no doubt saved on the ice by the trainer," said Crouch, a retired firefighter now living in Whitby, Ontario. "After 30 years in the fire service, I've really developed an appreciation for the severity of that type of injury, and the likelihood that you're going to survive is not very good. [The trainer] did what he had to do. I'm still here and I'm still playing."

That near tragedy was the impetus for one of the more recent innovations in goaltender safety equipment — the Kim Crouch Collar, designed to prevent skate cuts to the neck and throat area. Kim's father, Ed Crouch, the Whitby fire chief at the time of his son's accident, was the original creator of the product. "He was the inventor of the neck guard," Kim says proudly. "After I was injured, he had the first prototype put together in about two weeks. That's where it all originated."

Designed to get his son back on the ice, it quickly evolved into a piece of equipment many considered vital if they were to play the position. Ed Crouch, himself a former netminder who played for the Oshawa Generals in 1949–50, constructed the guards from ballistic nylon and similar materials and slowly made a business out of the protective gear.

"I think his initial plan was to just get me fixed up and able to play, but there was so much publicity from the actual injury and then the follow-up stories, that it sort of created interest in the product," Kim said. "I still think we were well ahead of our time. It didn't become mandatory [in minor hockey] until 1992. For 17 years, we were struggling along, just getting by. Nobody was going at this full-time by any means in the early days. We certainly weren't getting numbers like we do now."

The unique aspect of the Crouch collar is that it evolved from a piece of goalie equipment into protective wear that makes sense for everyone on the ice. "I make them for everybody right across the board," Kim said.

Sadly, it took two other near tragedies to spark further interest in the product. When Buffalo Sabres goalie Clint Malarchuk — who wasn't wearing neck protection at the time — suffered a severed jugular vein in a 1989 game against the St. Louis Blues, it led to a surge in demand for Crouch's product. After Florida Panthers forward Richard Zednik suffered a skate cut to the throat in 2008 (curiously, also in Buffalo) the Ontario Hockey League moved quickly to make neck guards mandatory for all players. In 2009, when linesman Kevin Brown suffered a slashed throat from a skate, the Ontario Hockey Association deemed neck guards mandatory for all its officials.

"We do see a spike in sales whenever there is a serious injury," Crouch said. "It puts the safety issue back at the front of people's minds. Once it became mandatory, that really was the turning point."

Crouch retired from the fire department in 2008 to run the company full time. "I retired early because I had this business to keep me busy," he said. "It's become a year-round business for me."

Garth Snow illustrates the extreme of mid-to-late 1990s equipment modification with his gigantic, angular shoulder pads.

HALTING A GROWING TREND

As equipment grew lighter in the late 1980s, it also grew bigger. In the early 1990s, goal-scoring in the NHL dried up dramatically. Some of it was due to stifling defensive systems employed by teams, and some of it was caused by a proliferation of on-ice obstruction; but some of it was caused by goaltenders who had ballooned into Michelin Men on skates, virtually obscuring the view of the net from the shooter.

"We always wanted to be as light as possible," recalled Phil Myre, an NHL goaltender for 14 seasons from 1969–83, and former NHL goalie coach. "Today, they want to be as big as possible."

The limit on leg pad width was increased from 10 to 12 inches in 1989, but it wasn't strictly enforced. "I remember taking my pads out that I wore my last season in the league [1988–89]," recalled former Chicago Blackhawks goalie and current NHL broadcaster Darren Pang. "I measured them. They were 14 inches wide."

Blocker pads and catching gloves grew to oversized proportions. "Glove hands were used more for knocking the puck down, as opposed to catching the puck," recalled former NHL goalie John Davidson, today president of the

St. Louis Blues. Goaltenders ordered sweaters in as large a size as was available, and body armor also swelled up.

Something had to be done to halt the inflating goaltenders, and it was. The NHL began random spot checks of goaltending equipment in 1996. "That was exactly my issue when I got in there — exactly how much is for protection, and how much is for puck-stopping and covering areas," recalled Dave Dryden, who was serving on the NHL's safety council at the time. "It is a fine line. The one that is really difficult from my perspective is the shoulder protection. It does have to be somewhat bulky … The only way you can protect [those areas] is by overlap, so it gets bulkier than you want."

The shoulder pads worn by Philadelphia Flyers goalie Garth Snow in the mid-1990s rose up several inches from his shoulders to become level with his ears.

"The guys for a while were really abusing it," Dave Dryden said. "They were puffing that stuff up, putting wood in there, doing everything. I really felt that once we got into policing it, that sort of disappeared, but the question I always had was, 'Why don't the referees have the final say in this?' I could go in and measure a guy's equipment, but who's to say that as he steps out on the ice, he doesn't take a sock and stuff it in his shoulders?"

The fear of goaltenders cheating after policing was dampened with the implementation in 1998 of a two-minute penalty for any goalie found to be wearing illegal equipment during a game. Enforcement was taken a step further for the 2003–04 season, as NHL goalie pads were limited to 38 inches in length. If a goaltender's pads were found to exceed the limit, his team was fined $25,000.

Further changes in equipment specifications came prior to the 2005–06 campaign, when pads, blockers, catching gloves and sweaters were all cut down in size once more. Pad width was limited to 11 inches. Blockers were downsized one inch in length to eight inches, catching gloves by three inches to a maximum of eight inches in width and all body armor and sweaters were required to be contoured to the individual goaltender's size.

Myre was one who believed that this growing trend among netminders required continued adjustment, especially with catching gloves and upper-body gear.

"Surely there's some science today to make the padding a little bit smaller without taking any protection away," Myre said. "I think it should all be rounded out. They're allowed eight inches, but nobody's got an eight-inch wide arm. To me, they can have anything they want up front, but you want to avoid anything that makes them wider."

Apparently, the NHL was listening. Going even further, the league instituted sweeping equipment regulation changes again prior to the 2008–09 season. All inner-knee pads were restricted to be a maximum of 2.5 inches thick. Leg pads could only be 10.5 inches deep, a measurement taken from the front face of the pad to the last edge of the calf/inner-knee protection. Calf-wing protectors could no longer be attached to the five-hole or five-hole seam, and were limited to one inch in thickness.

A number of changes were also instituted regarding chest and arm protectors. One action was to round off all straight edges. The clavicle protector/shoulder floater must have a flexible seam without becoming an extension beyond the normal shape of the shoulder, contoured to the shape of the torso and away from the armpit. Rib protection is allowed as long as it wraps the body and is not used to provide additional blocking area. Chest and arm pads should be flat in the front and should wrap around the shoulder tightly.

The changes have had the desired effect. "Getting around has become more important," former NHL goalie and current Detroit Red Wings goalie coach Jim Bedard said. "Guys have to be good athletes and be able to move laterally much quicker because of the (smaller) size of the equipment. Quickness, athleticism and agility have become more important."

Former NHL coach and current NHL television analyst Harry Neale noticed an immediate difference in the game. "They looked a lot more like the old goalies," Neale said. "They were forced to move to make saves, rather than just get into position." In a sense, Dave Dryden believes some of the measures have served only to make goaltenders better and therefore, more difficult to beat. "Every time the league talks about making the pads smaller, they think it's going to solve [the lack of goal scoring], but all it does is that it allows the goalies to move even quicker," he explained. "There is a real balance and I think most of the goalies understand now that they can bulk their pads up a little bit height-wise, but you can build them up to a point where you can't move as well."

The 2008–09 season goalie-equipment regulation changes were just a start. "There will be more changes [in 2009–10], with more proportional fittings for protection only." NHL goaltending supervisor Kay Whitmore, who played goal in 155 NHL games for the Hartford Whalers, Vancouver Canucks, Boston Bruins and Calgary Flames, told the *Montreal Gazette*. Whitmore, with the aid of a committee of active goaltenders, shooters and general managers, created a list of immediate and long-term adjustments to goalie equipment that will be implemented incrementally, beginning with the 2009–10 NHL season.

An immediate change for the goalie's blocker is the contour of the thumb protector of the blocker will be held to a stricter standard. The blocker must not be more than seven inches deep. The measurement will be taken from the face of the blocker to the end of the thumb protector.

The NHL planned to work with manufacturers to develop a uniform set of pant sizes, and pants were to be more tapered from the waist. The catching glove will also be reduced in overall size without compromising safety, with emphasis on the cheater pad above the trapper.

Turning into an impromptu tailor, Whitmore charted the arm length, chest, waist and hip circumference, and skate-boot size for every NHL goaltender. He also measured every goalie from the floor beneath his feet to the center of his kneecap — with the knee slightly bent — then up from the knee to pelvic bone. This data was designed to create a record of maximum allowable length for an individual goalie's leg pads, with the aim being to corral the top of the pads at the goalie's mid-thigh, instead of covering the entire area up to the waist.

"We have to get back to the beginning of what equipment was for in the first place," Whitmore said.

That would be to protect the goalie, not to fill the net in order to prevent goals.

UP CLOSE & PERSONAL

PHOTOS BY MATTHEW MANOR

A look at the evolution of goalie gear taken from the archives of the Hockey Hall of Fame. Photo captions are on pages 148–151.

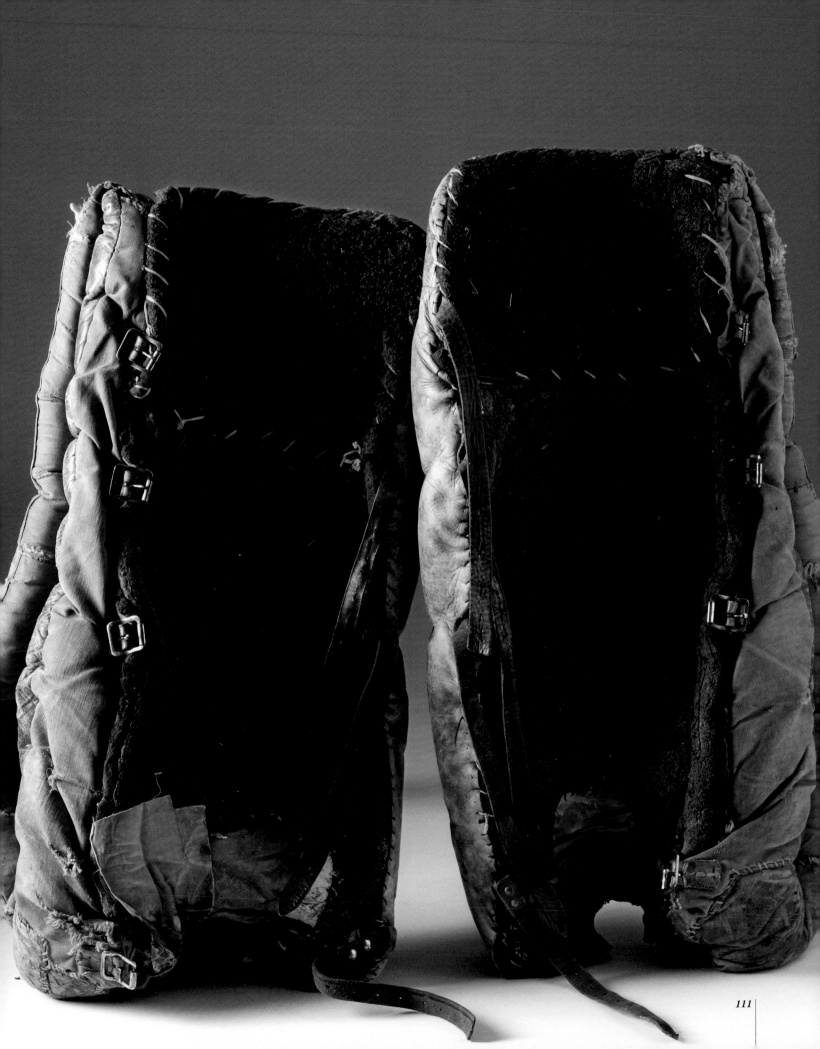

115

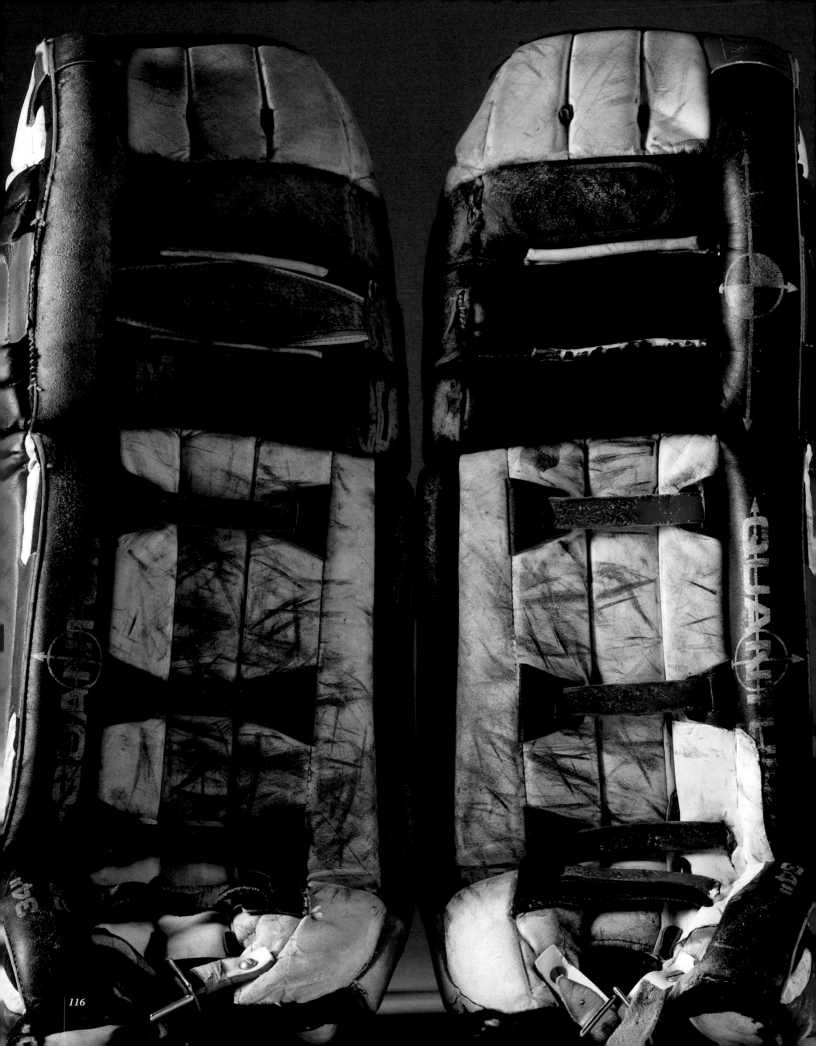

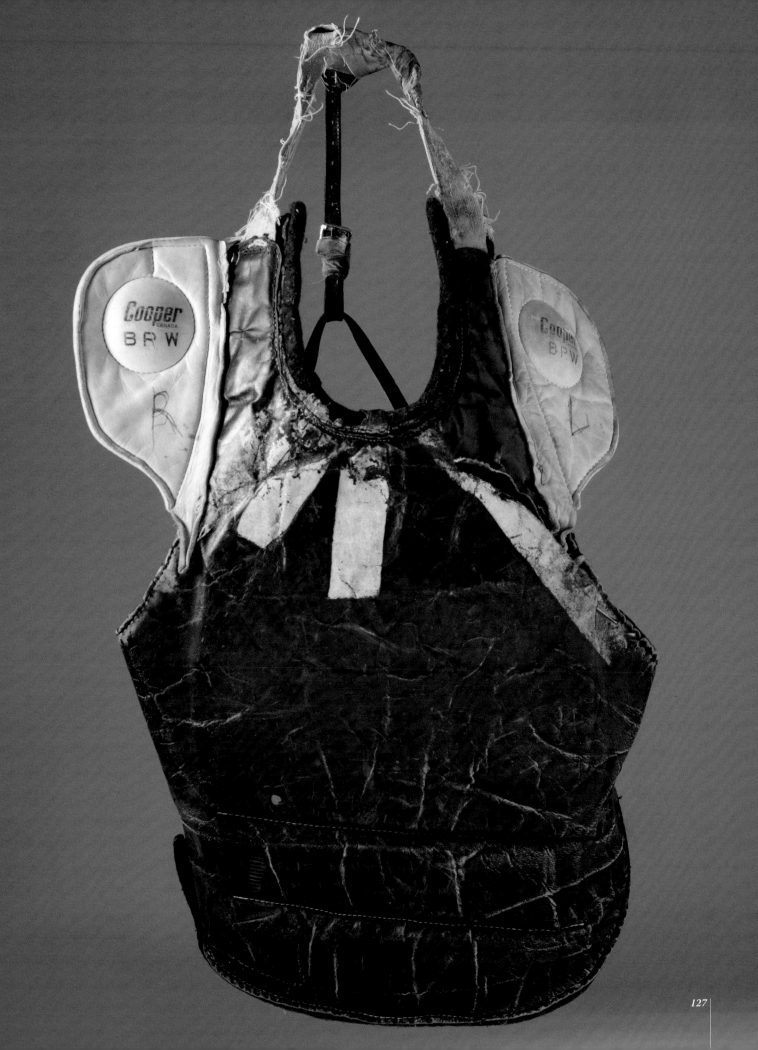

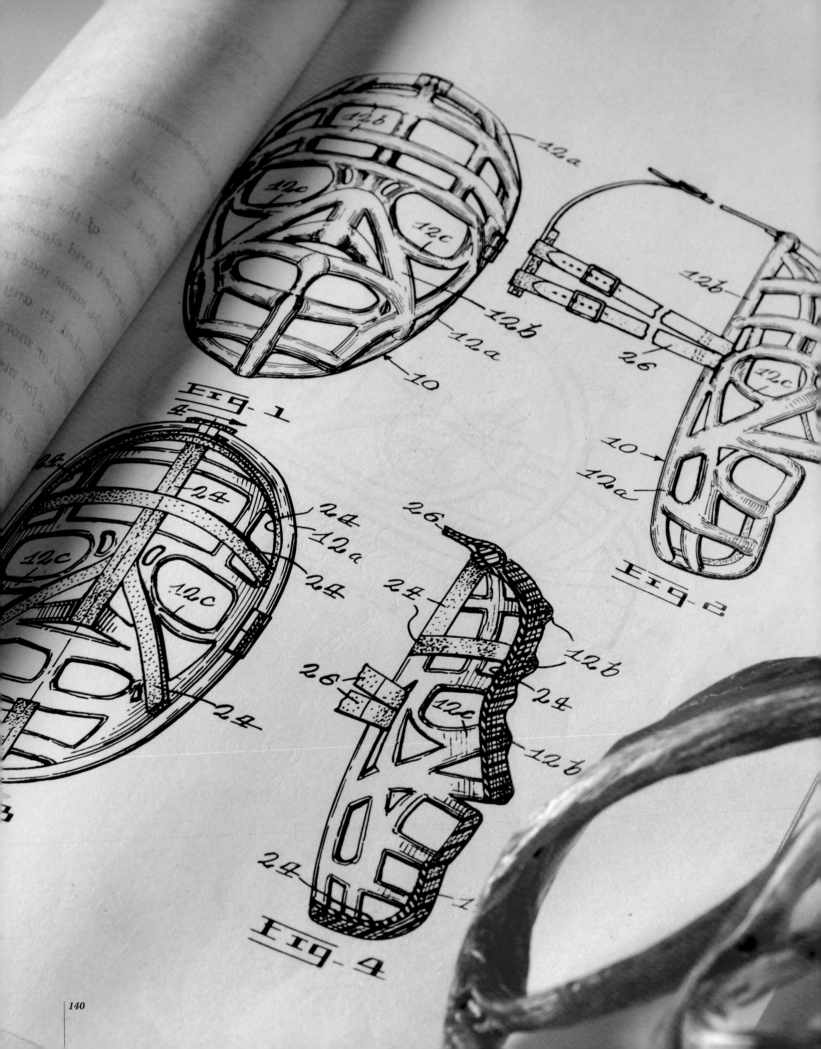

Fig-1

Fig-2

Fig-4

Gloves and pads worn by the Phoenix Coyotes' Brian Boucher during the 2003–04 season where he posted five consecutive shutouts. His streak of shutout hockey ended at 332:01 minutes, surpassing the mark of 309:21 set by Bill Durnan in 1949.

Captions

108–109

A close up of the knees of Bill Durnan's brown leather pads from his time manning the pipes in Montreal in the 1940s. The pads have no brand identification but are made in the style of the early Kenesky pads.

110

111

Durnan would have more than likely worn these pads for multiple seasons. Notice the patch jobs to keep the well-worn pads together.

The back of Durnan's pads, lined with felt, for comfort.

A close up of a 1960s Kenesky leg pad worn by Terry Sawchuk late in his career. By this time, Kenesky had become the most trusted brand of leg pads.

A mismatched set of Kenesky's: Sawchuck's pad is on the left and Brian Hayward's 1989–90 pad is on the right. Despite the age difference, the pads have an almost identical design.

Heaton Pro 90z worn by Canadian Corey Hirsch during the 1994 Lillehammer Olympics. Hirsch led Canada to silver after a 3–2 shootout loss to Sweden in the gold medal game.

Marc-André Fleury's 2006–07 pads. Fleury switched to white pads in 2008 after he was advised his yellow pads might be more noticeable to shooters.

A set of Gerry Cheevers' Kenesky pads from the 1975–76 AHL season. The pads owe their dark complexion to leather oil, used to keep the pads supple.

The first synthetic lightweight pads worn in the NHL, introduced by Réjean Lemelin in the 1986–87 season. Lemelin wore the Lowson pads for seven seasons.

A set of lightweight synthetic Aeroflex pads worn by Daren Puppa in his 24 games with the Buffalo Sabres in 1992–93.

Billy Smith became the first NHL goalie to be credited with a goal when he was the last Islander to touch this puck before it entered an empty Colorado net on November 28, 1979.

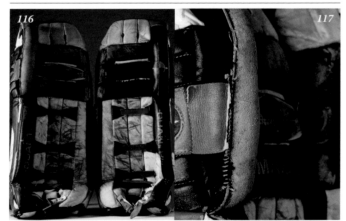

Martin Brodeur's battered 1993–94 rookie pads. With these pads Brodeur won 27 games and claimed the Calder trophy.

A close up of Brodeur's rookie pads shows the extreme wear of the horizontal and vertical blocker-side knee bars.

Marc-André Fleury's blocker from 2006–07 stands beside the blocker of Ed Chadwick from his time with the AHL's Buffalo Bisons (1964–68).

Trapper worn by Kelly Dyer of the Sunshine Hockey League's West Palm Beach Blaze in 1994–95 and 1995–96.

124 *125*

Dominik Hasek items: dressing room stool from his 2001–02 season in Detroit, trapper from his 2005–06 season in Ottawa and blocker from his 2006–07 season in Detroit.

Blue pants worn by Grant Fuhr in 1994–95 and red pants worn by Ed Giacomin in 1977–78. Giacomin's playing size was one inch taller and only 20 pounds lighter than Fuhr's.

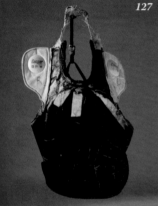

126 *127*

Bill Durnan's felt belly pad from the 1940s when he played in Montreal.

Johnny Bower's belly pad which he wore from 1958–59 to 1969–70. This was Bower's first ever belly pad despite having already played 13 seasons of pro hockey.

128 *129*

Marc-André Fleury's 2006–07 upper-body gear lies underneath the custom upper-body gear of Dave Dryden from 1970–71.

The New York American's barber-pole jersey of Roy Worters from the 1932–33 season.

130 *131*

Vladislav Tretiak's Team USSR jersey from the inaugural Canada Cup tournament in 1976. After a 3–1 round-robin loss to Canada, Tretiak traded this jersey with Canada's Denis Potvin.

Tony Esposito's 1980 Campbell Conference All-Star jersey. Esposito allowed two goals in the game.

132–133

Sticks (L to R): the original Victoriaville Curtis Curve; Kelly Dyer's 1990 Women's World Championship stick; Grant Fuhr's 1985 Stanley Cup final CCM; composite stick used by Megan Van Beusekom-Sweerin in the 2010 Clarkson Cup championship; Vladislav Tretiak's unused backup stick from the 1979 Izvestia Tournament; Terry Sawchuk's 1954 Stanley Cup stick.

134–135

Sticks (L to R): Patrick Roy's 1986 Stanley Cup stick; Bill Ranford's 1994 World Championship gold-medal stick; Jeff Reese's February 10, 1993, record stick with which he made three assists; John Ross Roach's 1922 Stanley Cup stick complete with commemorative ribbons; stick used by Tony Esposito to record his 76th shutout; Ron Hextall's December 8, 1987, goal-scoring stick.

Generations of goalie skates (left to right): Alfie Moore's leather skate with hard toe from his time with the New York Americans in 1936–37; Jaime Janiga's all-plastic Lange skate with liner from his junior career between 1977–81; Jean-Sébastien Giguère's RBK 9K Stanley Cup skate from 2007.

Jacques Plante's famous mask from the 1959–60 season, the first to be regularly worn in the NHL.

Ken Dryden's pretzel style mask that he wore during his time at Cornell University and as a rookie with the Montreal Canadiens.

The netting defended by Colorado's Patrick Roy during the first and third periods of a 4–3 victory over Washington. The win was Roy's 448th, surpassing Terry Sawchuk's record.

Gilles Meloche's mask from his time with the Cleveland Barons, 1976–78.

A late model form-fitting mask used by Grant Fuhr before he switched to a mask with a cage.

A late model form-fitting mask with elongated neck protection used by Billy Smith before he switched to helmet-and-cage style protection.

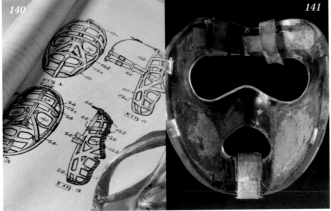

Schematics outlining a "Protective Face Mask" sent to the U.S. Patent office on March 22, 1960, by creator Bill Burchmore, and a prototype mask designed for Jacques Plante.

A view from inside Jacques Plante's early practice mask

Dave Dryden's take on head protection combined the cage elements of helmet-and-cage style protection and the form-fitting face elements of earlier masks.

A modern mask worn by Team Canada goalie Paul Rosen during the 2006 Paralympic Games sledge hockey tournament in Turin, Italy.

Expansion and Modern Era Greats

BY CHRIS MCDONELL

AVAILABLE POSITIONS between the pipes more than doubled in 1967 as the NHL expanded from six to 12 teams and many clubs began to adopt the two-goalie system. While this prolonged the careers of some Original Six stars, it also provided opportunities to a new generation. Gerry Cheevers, Ed Giacomin and Billy Smith fashioned Hall of Fame careers sharing duties with a partner who carried a considerable part of the goaltending load, while Tony Esposito, Ken Dryden and Grant Fuhr played the vast majority of their teams' games in a dominant fashion.

Fuhr and Patrick Roy bridge a gap between the Expansion and Modern eras of NHL hockey. Fuhr, spectacularly agile and arguably a throwback to a more acrobatic generation, reinvented himself more than once, while Roy single-handedly inspired an entire generation of goalies, particularly in his home province of Quebec, to emulate his butterfly style. "Whatever works" has always been a goalie's refrain.

Roy and Fuhr each benefitted from the coaching and equipment that NHL netminders enjoy in the 21st century. The improvement in the quality and design of equipment: the lighter, stronger, water-repellant and substantially larger pads, gloves, upper body armor, pants and sweaters — not to mention one-piece Kevlar-reinforced helmets — have done more to change the position of goaltending than almost any other trend or evolution before it. But hockey as a game has changed too. Players are stronger, faster, better on their skates and more dangerous with their tactics. And they too benefit from the use of lightweight, high-tech gear.

The Hall of Fame goaltenders of the Expansion and Modern eras have established a legacy of innovation, persistence and individual style. The performances of these players are especially memorable because they each navigated the challenges of stopping pucks in a style that made sense for the manner in which the game was played. The goaltending position has certainly changed since 1967, but keeping the puck out of the net has remained as hard a task as ever.

Ken Dryden stands in his now-famous pose as a rookie. Dryden led the Canadiens to a Stanley Cup in 1971 and was named playoff MVP, and took home the Calder Trophy in 1972.

INDUCTED 1985

GERRY
CHEEVERS

A Stitch in Time

ALTHOUGH HIS CAREER record shows little in the way of honors for personal accomplishment, Gerry Cheevers made an indelible mark on the game. Team victories were what he valued most, and so long as his club scored more goals than he let in, he was satisfied. "Circumstances dictated what I did," explained Cheevers, who was well known for his sense of humor. "When a goal meant nothing to the outcome, I wouldn't always play the puck.

My teammates laughed for a long time about one bouncing puck that I intentionally ignored. I heard it hit the post — closer to the net than I predicted — but I felt relieved that I had played it properly. Unfortunately, it was the middle post that it hit." But only a star can get away with playing the clown at times, and in truth, Cheevers was a clutch performer.

"I don't know how I got a reputation for being a 'money' goaltender, because I probably lost almost as many big games as I won," he maintained, humble enough to question his legacy. "Perhaps I'm remembered for playing well in some games that meant a lot to the team. If you aren't ready to perform well in a game that means elimination, then you shouldn't play professional hockey. I enjoyed

those games, but you never win them all — no one does."

While his Boston teammates Bobby Orr and Phil Esposito got more of the limelight, Cheevers was a critical component of the club that won the Stanley Cup in 1970 and 1972. In the latter campaign, he notched a remarkable 33-game undefeated streak, a record that still stands. It was an improbable peak to a career that began inauspiciously during the Original Six years.

Born in 1940 in St. Catharines, Ontario, Cheevers was raised in Toronto and grew up in the Maple Leafs organization. The Leafs sent him to the St. Michael's Majors in the Ontario Hockey Association to develop. The Majors' coach, trying to cure Cheevers of roaming so far from his crease (a skill that became part of his professional repertoire), and for his disinterest in practice, made him, as punishment, play a dozen games at left wing. Nevertheless, Cheevers acquired strong goaltending skills over his

five years at the famous hockey finishing school. But when he graduated in 1961, Johnny Bower was entrenched in the Toronto goal. Sent to the farm team in Pittsburgh, Cheevers played two games with Toronto in 1961–62, but without making much of an impression.

"I trusted that my day would come," recalled Cheevers, noting that with Bower, then Don Simmons and Terry Sawchuk, the Toronto goalies were getting old. But the Leafs left Cheevers exposed two years in a row in the intra-league draft (protecting Bower and Sawchuk), and he was claimed in 1965, much to his disappointment. "Not only would I not get my chance with the Leafs," he explained, "but the Bruins were a team going nowhere." Cheevers, however, found both a friend and a mentor in Boston teammate Eddie Johnston. "We competed in a friendly manner," said Cheevers, "but more than anyone, he helped me to become a big-league goaltender. He had an uncanny knowledge of the game that he was willing to share."

Cheevers played seven games for the Bruins in the 1965–66 season, and 22 the next before establishing himself as the number one man in Boston. "It wasn't until 'Number 4' showed up that I started to enjoy myself," said Cheevers. "I knew immediately that we were going to win a championship." Boston got the incomparable Orr in 1966–67 and, soon afterward, Esposito and a plethora of other great scoring stars, and while the team worked hard at putting the puck in the net, "Cheesy" was frequently left to his own devices to prevent goals. Acrobatic and aggressive, he swung his stick freely to clear his crease of opponents and accumulated a large number of penalties as one of the "Big Bad Bruins."

During practice in the 1968–69 season, Cheevers began creating his trademark mask. "I was trying to get out of practice one day," he explained, "when this shot that couldn't have broken an egg hit me in the mask. I faked a serious injury and went into the dressing room. I was sitting there having a Coke when [coach] Harry Sinden came in and told me to get back out onto the ice. All the guys were laughing, so I knew I had to do something. I told the trainer to paint a 30-stitch gash on the mask. Then I went out and told Harry, "See how bad it is?" In ensuing years, Cheevers periodically added more stitch marks and his mask became less a joke and more an iconic symbol of the first generation of mask-wearing goalies.

In the summer of 1972, fresh from a Stanley Cup victory, Cheevers was one of a number of superstars to leave the NHL and join the upstart World Hockey Association (WHA). He signed a massive, seven-year, $1.4 million contract with the Cleveland Crusaders and earned his only professional hockey All-Star nominations: First Team in 1973, and Second Team in 1974 and 1975. But when the team's finances got rocky, Cheevers asked for a buyout. He returned to the Bruins and the NHL in January 1976.

Although he wasn't in game shape, Boston immediately dressed him as backup against Toronto. "I never felt so badly for someone as I did for [Boston goalie] Dave Reese, but with every goal that went in, I went farther down the aisle," confessed Cheevers, recalling his first game back. Maple Leafs' captain Darryl Sittler had a game for the ages, tallying a record 10 points. "I didn't want our coach Don Cherry to see me. Don knew I wasn't ready, but if the Leafs had scored any more goals, I would have been hiding up in the stands with all my equipment on."

Cheevers helped the Bruins back to the Stanley Cup final in the spring of 1977 and 1978, but they lost both times. He retired after the 1979–80 campaign, then immediately stepped behind the Boston bench as coach for an impressive four-and-a-half seasons.

Career Stats

REGULAR SEASON

Season	Age	Team	Lg	GP	W	L	T	SO	GA	GAA	G	A	PTS	PIM
1961–62	21	Toronto Maple Leafs	NHL	2	1	1	0	0	6	3.00	0	0	0	0
1965–66	25	Boston Bruins	NHL	7	0	4	1	0	34	6.00	0	0	0	0
1966–67	26	Boston Bruins	NHL	22	5	10	6	1	72	3.33	0	0	0	12
1967–68	27	Boston Bruins	NHL	47	23	17	5	3	125	2.83	0	2	2	8
1968–69	28	Boston Bruins	NHL	52	28	12	12	3	145	2.80	0	0	0	14
1969–70	29	Boston Bruins	NHL	41	24	8	8	4	108	2.72	0	0	0	4
1970–71	30	Boston Bruins	NHL	40	27	8	5	3	109	2.72	0	0	0	4
1971–72	31	Boston Bruins	NHL	41	27	5	8	2	101	2.50	0	2	2	25
1972–73	32	Cleveland Crusaders	WHA	52	32	20	0	5	149	2.84	0	1	1	30
1973–74	33	Cleveland Crusaders	WHA	59	30	20	6	4	180	3.03	0	0	0	30
1974–75	34	Cleveland Crusaders	WHA	52	26	24	2	4	167	3.26	0	1	1	59
1975–76	35	Cleveland Crusaders	WHA	28	11	14	1	1	95	3.63	0	0	0	15
1975–76	35	Boston Bruins	NHL	15	8	2	5	1	41	2.73	0	0	0	2
1976–77	36	Boston Bruins	NHL	45	30	10	5	3	137	3.04	0	4	4	46
1977–78	37	Boston Bruins	NHL	21	10	5	2	1	48	2.65	0	1	1	14
1978–79	38	Boston Bruins	NHL	43	23	9	10	1	132	3.16	0	2	2	23
1979–80	39	Boston Bruins	NHL	42	24	11	7	4	116	2.81	0	0	0	62
Career – 17 Seasons				609	329	180	83	40	1765	2.90	0	13	13	348

PLAYOFFS

Season	Age	Team	Lg	GP	W	L	T	SO	GA	GAA	G	A	PTS	PIM
1967–68	27	Boston Bruins	NHL	4	0	4		0	15	3.75	0	0	0	4
1968–69	28	Boston Bruins	NHL	9	6	3		3	16	1.68	0	0	0	17
1969–70	29	Boston Bruins	NHL	13	12	1		0	29	2.23	0	1	1	2
1970–71	30	Boston Bruins	NHL	6	3	3		0	21	3.50	0	0	0	4
1971–72	31	Boston Bruins	NHL	8	6	2		2	21	2.61	0	0	0	0
1972–73	32	Cleveland Crusaders	WHA	9	5	4		0	22	2.41	0	0	0	4
1973–74	33	Cleveland Crusaders	WHA	5	1	4		0	18	3.56	0	0	0	6
1974–75	34	Cleveland Crusaders	WHA	5	1	4		0	23	4.60	0	0	0	0
1975–76	35	Boston Bruins	NHL	6	2	4		1	14	2.14	0	0	0	0
1976–77	36	Boston Bruins	NHL	14	8	5		1	44	3.08	0	0	0	4
1977–78	37	Boston Bruins	NHL	12	8	4		1	35	2.87	0	0	0	6
1978–79	38	Boston Bruins	NHL	6	4	2		0	15	2.50	0	0	0	0
1979–80	39	Boston Bruins	NHL	10	4	6		0	32	3.10	0	0	0	0
Career – 13 Seasons				107	60	46		8	305	2.85	0	1	1	47

Page 154: Gerry Cheevers wears his famous "stitch" mask in the Boston net.

Page 155: Cheevers as a Cleveland Crusader. His jump to the WHA came on the heels of Boston's 1972 Stanley Cup, and outraged many in Beantown.

Page 156: A young, mask-less Cheevers maintains good position as he reacts to a cross-crease pass.

KEN
DRYDEN

The Thinker

IN HIS DAY, KEN DRYDEN was considered by some to be too big to be an NHL goalie. At 6-foot-4 and over 200 pounds, he was certainly above average in size, and conventional wisdom would have seen him turned into a defenseman. Yet, Dryden's cerebral approach and remarkable athleticism combined to make him a netminder truly larger than life. His brief but spectacular NHL career was richly studded with both individual and team accomplishments, and his early retirement was almost as surprising as his NHL debut.

Boston drafted Dryden in 1964, but the Montreal Canadiens quickly acquired the 17-year-old's rights in a four-player trade. Perhaps it was Dryden's pedigree that caught their attention, as the other players in the swap were never heard of again. Dryden's brother Dave, six years older and also a goaltender, had already made one appearance in an NHL game for the New York Rangers and had posted

the lowest goals-against average the previous season in the Ontario Hockey Association's senior league. Regardless, the deal would prove to be one of Montreal's most astute.

Ken Dryden made an unusual move in the 1960s and, rather than join a quasi-professional junior team, he attended Cornell University. He had to sit out his freshman year, but over the next three All-American seasons, he went 76–4–1 while getting a history degree as a step to becoming a lawyer. His brother Dave, meanwhile, had secured a backup goaltending position with the Chicago Black Hawks, but Ken always followed his own path, playing for Canada's national team in order to continue his studies over the 1969–70 season. When the team was disbanded, he finally stepped into Montreal's farm system, where he proved that his apprenticeship had served him well.

Dryden made a strong impression with the AHL's Montreal Voyageurs in 1970–71, and was rewarded with

a six-game callup to the parent club late in the season. History was made when he faced his brother Dave, then with the Buffalo Sabres in their inaugural season, on March 20, 1971, the first time brothers had ever played goal against each other in the NHL. The two shook hands at center ice after the game, a ritual they repeated over the handful of times they met over the remainder of their careers. Ken won that first game, as well as the other five games he played for Montreal that campaign, allowing only nine goals in total, yet it was still a shocking decision when the Habs decided to start their rookie against the powerhouse Boston Bruins in the 1971 playoffs.

With Bobby Orr in his prime, Boston was the defending Stanley Cup champion and had scored a record 399 goals that season to establish themselves as one of the most powerful offensive clubs of all time. Dryden, however, seemed totally unfazed. After most whistles, he stood with his arms crossed and gloves stacked on the butt end of his stick, with the blade tip spearing the ice, looking completely calm and collected. In truth, the ritual served to stretch out his spine, a relief from his constant crouch in game action, but his unique pose served as further proof that here was someone very different, and Dryden managed to get into the heads of the opposition.

"That was the greatest save that's ever been made off me in my life," said sniper Phil Esposito after Game 4, who'd set a new record that season with 76 goals and 76 assists. "My God, he's got arms like a giraffe." Dryden got all the credit when his team defeated the Bruins in seven games, an enormous upset. He then backed Montreal to a six-game victory over the Minnesota North Stars, to face the heavily favored Chicago Black Hawks in the Stanley Cup final. Montreal once again prevailed in a seven-game series, and Dryden was presented with the Conn Smythe Trophy as the league's most valuable playoff performer

Dryden dispelled any notion of a sophomore jinx

when he won the 1972 Calder Trophy as top rookie and made the Second All-Star Team, leading the league with 64 appearances and 39 wins. He played in the famous 1972 Summit Series for Canada against the Soviets the following September, and then earned his first Vezina Trophy (with a 2.26 goals-against average) and a First All-Star Team berth while backstopping Montreal to another Cup victory over Chicago. Understanding his role on the team, Dryden grew disenchanted with his contract. When the Canadiens refused to renegotiate it, Dryden joined a law firm as an articling student and sat out the 1973–74 season, during which the Habs faltered. Dryden got the new contract he wanted, with his salary quadrupled in accordance with the going rate for the league's top talent.

From the 1975–76 season, up until the end of his career in 1979, Dryden performed impeccably. He never posted worse than a goals-against mark of 2.30 per game and his team won the Stanley Cup four times in a row, giving him six rings in eight seasons. Dryden was awarded

the Vezina Trophy and was on the First All-Star Team four more times. He blanked the opposition 46 times over his career, peaking with 10 shutouts in 1976–77, compiling a stellar 2.14 goals-against average during the regular season, and lowering it to 1.56 in the playoffs. His powerhouse club had no real weakness, but Dryden was inarguably a key to Montreal's success.

Dryden always had back problems, but they flared up more dramatically in 1979. So, too, did the awareness that he had little new to accomplish in the game. Although physically sound enough to continue to play, Dryden quit the game to pursue other interests. He launched what proved to be a successful writing and broadcasting career, penning *The Game* (one of hockey's most insightful books), and several other bestsellers on various topics. In 1997, he was lured back into NHL hockey as an executive with the Toronto Maple Leafs, and in 2004 he entered the political arena, where he has served as a Toronto Member of Parliament and a Liberal cabinet minister.

Career Stats

REGULAR SEASON

Season	Age	Team	Lg	GP	W	L	T	SO	GA	GAA	G	A	PTS	PIM
1970–71	23	Montreal Canadiens	NHL	6	6	0	0	0	9	1.65	0	0	0	0
1971–72	24	Montreal Canadiens	NHL	64	39	8	15	8	142	2.24	0	3	3	4
1972–73	25	Montreal Canadiens	NHL	54	33	7	13	6	119	2.26	0	4	4	2
1974–75	27	Montreal Canadiens	NHL	56	30	9	16	4	149	2.69	0	3	3	2
1975–76	28	Montreal Canadiens	NHL	62	42	10	8	8	121	2.03	0	2	2	0
1976–77	29	Montreal Canadiens	NHL	56	41	6	8	10	117	2.14	0	2	2	0
1977–78	30	Montreal Canadiens	NHL	52	37	7	7	5	105	2.05	0	2	2	0
1978–79	31	Montreal Canadiens	NHL	47	30	10	7	5	108	2.30	0	3	3	4
NHL Career – 8 Seasons				397	258	57	74	46	870	2.24	0	19	19	12

PLAYOFFS

Season	Age	Team	Lg	GP	W	L	T	SO	GA	GAA	G	A	PTS	PIM
1970–71	23	Montreal Canadiens	NHL	20	12	8		0	61	3.00	0	1	1	0
1971–72	24	Montreal Canadiens	NHL	6	2	4		0	17	2.83	0	0	0	0
1972–73	25	Montreal Canadiens	NHL	17	12	5		1	50	2.89	0	0	0	2
1974–75	27	Montreal Canadiens	NHL	11	6	5		2	29	2.53	0	0	0	0
1975–76	28	Montreal Canadiens	NHL	13	12	1		1	25	1.92	0	0	0	0
1976–77	29	Montreal Canadiens	NHL	14	12	2		4	22	1.55	0	0	0	0
1977–78	30	Montreal Canadiens	NHL	15	12	3		2	29	1.89	0	0	0	0
1978–79	31	Montreal Canadiens	NHL	16	12	4		0	41	2.48	0	3	3	2
NHL Career – 8 Seasons				112	80	32		10	274	2.40	0	4	4	4

Page 158: Ken Dryden's unique resting pose added to his mystique during his rookie season.

Page 159: The lanky Dryden watches the puck while he makes an awkward save as Henri Richard looks on.

Page 160: Dryden helps out his All-Star defense by charging out and knocking the puck away from the Blues' Garry Unger.

INDUCTED 1988

TONY
ESPOSITO

Shutouts, Chicago-Style

AS ONE HALF OF PERHAPS the most colorful brother act in NHL history, Tony Esposito was as sensational in keeping pucks out of the net as his older brother Phil was in scoring goals. When Phil joined the Chicago Black Hawks in 1963–64, Tony took the academic route to NHL hockey by attending Michigan Tech. He graduated four years later, with three All-American seasons and an NCAA championship under his belt. But he had also been keeping close tabs on Phil's teammate Glenn Hall.

"I'd go down and visit," he said. "I'd spend hours with Glenn Hall. We would go out and have a sociable beer, and he would talk goaltending and stuff with me." The tips from the well-seasoned Hall were not wasted on the college boy. "I tried to copy his style," admitted Esposito, who refined Hall's butterfly with an even wider stance and helped make it a critical component of his game. "I went down a lot," he said. "For me, if I'm screened or I can't see the shot, my instinct is to cover the lower half of the net. I stopped a lot of pucks without seeing them."

Although stocky in build — he was a successful halfback in high school football — he had quick reflexes and a lightning-fast glove hand, made all the more effective by the glove being on his right hand, an unusual look that confounded more than a few shooters. Esposito also

had a strong competitive streak, barking instructions to his teammates and in his later years unafraid to complain to management when he was dissatisfied with the team in front of him.

The Montreal Canadiens first signed Esposito in 1967 and, after some minor-pro seasoning, he made his NHL debut on December 5, 1968, facing the Boston Bruins, the club his brother had joined the previous season. Although Phil put two pucks past him into the net, Tony acquitted himself admirably in a 2–2 draw. In spite of posting two shutouts in the next dozen games he played for Montreal, he was sent back to the minors when Rogie Vachon and Gump Worsley recovered from their injuries. When Worsley got hurt again in the playoffs, Esposito suited up as backup again and earned what would prove to be his only Stanley Cup ring.

"He makes fundamental errors one minute and a miraculous save the next," observed Montreal coach

Claude Ruel who, along with the rest of Montreal's brain trust, had dismissed Esposito as a valuable asset. They soon looked foolishly shortsighted.

The Habs left Esposito unprotected in the intra-league draft and he was scooped up by Chicago, where he spent the next 15 seasons. The standard goalie numbers — 1 and 30 — were already assigned, but Esposito, who had worn the unconventional 29 in Montreal (Ken Dryden later made it famous there) made the unusual request for number 35, which had never been worn by an NHL goalie. "I wanted something different," he later explained, "something to make me stand out and for people to notice." He quickly had his wish fulfilled.

By then age 26, Esposito was still officially a rookie in 1969–70 when he won the Calder Trophy, the Vezina, and a First All-Star Team berth. Additionally, he was runner-up for the Hart Trophy as the NHL's Most Valuable Player, an award that his brother Phil had won the previous season. Esposito took charge of the Black Hawks' net in training camp, and played 63 games of the 70-game schedule. His 15 shutouts that season remain the modern record, the only goalie to have posted more was George Hainsworth with 22 in 1928–29.

"Tony O" was the Vezina Trophy runner-up the following season (1970–71), and then shared it with teammate Gary Smith in 1971–72 with a league- and career-best 1.77 goals-against average. The following season, Esposito notched 10 more shutouts and shared the Vezina with Philadelphia's Bernie Parent. He backstopped the Hawks to the 1971 and 1973 Stanley Cup final and joined Team Canada for the 1972 Summit Series against the Soviet Union, posting two wins, a tie and one loss. He made the First All-Star Team again in 1972 and 1980, joining the Second Team in 1973 and 1974.

While Esposito's style was considered radical early in his career, he was even more innovative when it came to his equipment. In 1969, he fitted an elastic mesh between his pant legs, making a considerable impediment to pucks going through the five hole with a 12-inch by 6-inch web. The league quickly wrote a rule to ban his device, so Esposito added two- to three-inch rolls of foam inside each leg instead.

He designed a protective neckpiece to cover a spot often left bare by goalie armor in 1971 after taking a shot in the throat. Esposito was the first to add a cheater to his catching glove, effectively making the cuff of the glove as wide as the mitt on top — the prototype of the modern catcher. After he suffered a number of eye injuries from pucks and wayward sticks, he made significant improvements to mask design in 1974–75. He fitted a wire cage over the eyeholes of his mask and added a fiberglass extension to protect the top of his head, both important steps toward the standard mask of today.

For all his success, and obvious dedication to his profession, Esposito claimed he didn't truly enjoy the game. "It's a job," he said in 1972. "I have to do it. But it's tough. I don't like it. To be playing well as a goalkeeper, you have to be afraid. Not afraid that you'll get hurt, but afraid that they're going to score on you. Every time they come down the ice with that puck, I'm afraid the puck is going to go in." But Esposito's fear didn't prevent him from wanting to play as many games as possible. Although the two-goalie system was well entrenched around the league, in Chicago Esposito averaged more than 60 games a year until his final two seasons.

After residing in Chicago for over a decade, Esposito took out American citizenship in 1981 and received some grief from Canadians for backstopping the United States

team in the Canada Cup tournament that fall. Esposito had begun serving as president of the NHL Players' Association (NHLPA) after Ken Dryden retired in 1979, and he continued to work for the NHLPA as a consultant after he retired. Esposito helped negotiate a new collective bargaining agreement that prevented a labor disruption in 1982.

At 41, and the oldest player in the league, Esposito hung up his pads after the 1983–84 season. Despite not winning a Cup in Chicago, his teams never failed to make the playoffs, and his 76 career regular season shutouts were sixth highest at the time of his retirement; he remains tied at ninth spot today. Esposito entered the Hall of Fame in 1988, the same year the Hawks retired his number 35, which had long become a favorite number for young and aspiring goalies everywhere.

Career Stats

REGULAR SEASON

Season	Age	Team	Lg	GP	W	L	T	SO	GA	GAA	G	A	PTS	PIM
1968-69	25	Montreal Canadiens	NHL	13	5	4	4	2	34	2.73	0	0	0	0
1969-70	26	Chicago Black Hawks	NHL	63	38	17	8	15	136	2.17	0	2	2	2
1970-71	27	Chicago Black Hawks	NHL	57	35	14	6	6	126	2.27	0	1	1	4
1971-72	28	Chicago Black Hawks	NHL	48	31	10	6	9	82	1.77	0	1	1	2
1972-73	29	Chicago Black Hawks	NHL	56	32	17	7	4	140	2.51	0	2	2	0
1973-74	30	Chicago Black Hawks	NHL	70	34	14	21	10	141	2.04	0	1	1	0
1974-75	31	Chicago Black Hawks	NHL	71	34	30	7	6	193	2.74	0	1	1	11
1975-76	32	Chicago Black Hawks	NHL	68	30	23	13	4	198	2.97	0	1	1	2
1976-77	33	Chicago Black Hawks	NHL	69	25	36	8	2	234	3.45	0	2	2	6
1977-78	34	Chicago Black Hawks	NHL	64	28	22	14	5	168	2.63	0	4	4	0
1978-79	35	Chicago Black Hawks	NHL	63	24	28	11	4	206	3.27	0	1	1	2
1979-80	36	Chicago Black Hawks	NHL	69	31	22	16	6	205	2.97	0	1	1	2
1980-81	37	Chicago Black Hawks	NHL	66	29	23	14	0	246	3.75	0	3	3	0
1981-82	38	Chicago Black Hawks	NHL	52	19	25	8	1	231	4.52	0	2	2	0
1982-83	39	Chicago Black Hawks	NHL	39	23	11	5	1	135	3.46	0	0	0	0
1983-84	40	Chicago Black Hawks	NHL	18	5	10	3	1	88	4.82	0	3	3	0
NHL Career – 16 Seasons				886	423	306	151	76	2563	2.92	0	25	25	31

PLAYOFFS

Season	Age	Team	Lg	GP	W	L	T	SO	GA	GAA	G	A	PTS	PIM
1969-70	26	Chicago Black Hawks	NHL	8	4	4		0	27	3.38	0	0	0	0
1970-71	27	Chicago Black Hawks	NHL	18	11	7		2	42	2.19	0	0	0	0
1971-72	28	Chicago Black Hawks	NHL	5	2	3		0	16	3.20	0	0	0	0
1972-73	29	Chicago Black Hawks	NHL	15	10	5		1	46	3.08	0	0	0	0
1973-74	30	Chicago Black Hawks	NHL	10	6	4		2	28	2.88	0	0	0	0
1974-75	31	Chicago Black Hawks	NHL	8	3	5		0	34	4.32	0	0	0	0
1975-76	32	Chicago Black Hawks	NHL	4	0	4		0	13	3.25	0	0	0	0
1976-77	33	Chicago Black Hawks	NHL	2	0	2		0	6	3.00	0	0	0	0
1977-78	34	Chicago Black Hawks	NHL	4	0	4		0	19	4.52	0	0	0	0
1978-79	35	Chicago Black Hawks	NHL	4	0	4		0	14	3.46	0	0	0	0
1979-80	36	Chicago Black Hawks	NHL	6	3	3		0	14	2.25	0	0	0	0
1980-81	37	Chicago Black Hawks	NHL	3	0	3		0	15	4.19	0	0	0	0
1981-82	38	Chicago Black Hawks	NHL	7	3	3		1	16	2.52	0	0	0	0
1982-83	39	Chicago Black Hawks	NHL	5	3	2		0	18	3.47	0	0	0	0
NHL Career – 14 Seasons				99	45	53		6	308	3.07	0	0	0	0

Page 162: Tony Espositio collects himself after making a save against the Leafs.

Page 163: A close up of No. 35. Esposito was the first NHL goaltender to wear the number.

Page 164: Esposito in net for Team Canada during the 1972 Summit Series.

INDUCTED 2003

GRANT FUHR

Fuhr-ious Goaltending

GRANT FUHR HAD THE rare experience of hitting hockey's highest heights as a hometown hero. Born in Spruce Grove, Alberta, located just outside the city of Edmonton, he had the good fortune to be coached as a peewee by the legendary Glenn Hall, whose farm was only five miles away. Fuhr picked up Hall's butterfly style, which helped him get drafted in the first round by the Edmonton Oilers in the 1981 NHL entry draft after an auspicious two years of junior hockey with the Victoria Cougars.

Still a teenager, Fuhr played 48 games for the 1981–82 Oilers, posting a 28–5–14 record, finishing second to Billy Smith for the Vezina Trophy, and making the Second All-Star Team. Midseason, he became the youngest goalie to play in the NHL All-Star Game. Before the decade was out, he had earned five Stanley Cup rings with a star-laden but predominantly offensive-minded Edmonton club.

"We all knew he was great from the first day of camp," recalled Ron Low, a former Oiler goalie and coach. "A natural. Yet he had no style. Or, rather, his style was all styles. He would come out 15 feet to challenge the shot on one offensive rush. The next time he would be back in his crease. He could read the game so well. He anticipated the game. Grant was just … different. Different from anyone I'd ever seen."

"I rate him right up there among [the best] goalies of any era," said Glenn Hall, years after Fuhr had starred in the NHL. "He gave [Edmonton] the opportunity to play that run-and-gun style. Without a goalie like Fuhr, none of it works." Fuhr shared regular season duties with goaltender Andy Moog, but in 1983–84, he became the Oilers' go-to goalie in the playoffs. He tallied a record for netminders with 14 points in the regular season (all assists), then backstopped the Oilers to their first Cup win. The Oilers defended their crown the following season, were upset in the 1986 playoffs, but then won two more consecutive Stanley Cups (1987, 1988).

The 1987–88 campaign was undoubtedly Fuhr's personal best. He was a workhorse, guiding Canada to victory in the pre-season Canada Cup tournament, most notably against the last great team from the Soviet Union in a closely fought three-game final, then setting an NHL regular-season record by starting 75 games. Fuhr made the First All-Star Team, earned the Vezina Trophy as top goaltender and finished runner-up to Mario Lemieux for

the Hart Trophy as the league's Most Valuable Player.

Things began to unravel in Edmonton when team owner Peter Pocklington sold Wayne Gretzky to the Los Angeles Kings in the summer of 1988, the start of a fire sale. "Grant never gets excited," Gretzky had said in 1985. "He never gets mad. He never gets happy. His attitude to anything is just, 'Oh well.' He's like a relief pitcher. Nothing gets him down. Nothing gets him up. He's a hard guy to describe." But Fuhr was not himself by 1989, his play slipping due to what he later admitted was a longstanding drug problem. He was relegated to being a backup for Bill Ranford when the Oilers won a fifth Cup in 1990 and was suspended for 60 games in 1990–91 when his drug use became public. He successfully underwent treatment but was traded to Toronto in September 1991.

Fuhr seemed back on track with the Maple Leafs, and he was the league's highest paid netminder with a salary of $1.6 million, but he mentored young goalie Felix Potvin so successfully that, midway through the 1992–93 season, Toronto traded Fuhr to Buffalo. Again, an up-and-coming NHL star — Dominik Hasek — usurped his starting role.

The two shared the 1994 Jennings Trophy for the lowest team goals-against average, but the Sabres traded Fuhr to Los Angeles early in the 1994–95 campaign.

Fuhr's goals-against average was never his strong suit. "The only statistic that matters is winning," he said. Yet when his average ballooned to over four goals a game, and the wins were no longer coming, it appeared he was just playing out the string. Fuhr signed with the St. Louis Blues as a free agent in July 1995, but when he was sent home from training camp after arriving almost 25 pounds overweight, many thought his career was over. Fuhr, however, had more great hockey in him. He quickly took off much of the excess weight, returned to St. Louis, and went on to set a new NHL record with 79 starts — 76 in succession — in 1995–96. Unfortunately, a knee injury suffered in the playoffs against Toronto ended his season, and he was never quite the same again.

During his four-year stop in St. Louis (1995–96 to 1998–99) Fuhr's goals-against average had consistently stayed below 3.00 for the first time in his career, but he still looked back fondly at his days with the firewagon

Oilers. "The style of hockey we played was a lot of fun," he said. " A 7–4 or 7–3 game is a lot of fun to play in and it's exciting for the fans. When I got to St. Louis, the game had changed and I was putting up much better stats, but we weren't as successful a team as we should have been. I would much rather have the team success."

At 37, age and injuries started to take their toll. "You hear a lot of talk about the goalie who flops or goes down too much," Fuhr once said. "The problem is not going down; it's returning to your feet too slowly." Fuhr returned to Alberta in a trade, but this time joined the Calgary Flames, for his last NHL season. In 1999–2000, he notched his 400th career victory, becoming only the

sixth NHL goalie to hit that milestone. His final game was against the Oilers, in Edmonton, and although he lost the game, the Edmonton fans chanted his name throughout the game and gave him a number of standing ovations.

In 2003, in his first year of eligibility, Fuhr was inducted to the Hockey Hall of Fame. "Being a black athlete going into the Hall of Fame is obviously a special honor," he told the *Philadelphia Enquirer*, "especially in hockey, being the first one — but the reason you get into the Hall of Fame is for what you have accomplished on the ice, and I probably take the most pride in that." That same year Oiler fans got to cheer for their acrobatic netminder one last time as his No. 31 was raised to the rafters.

Career Stats

REGULAR SEASON

Season	Age	Team	Lg	GP	W	L	T	SO	GA	GAA	G	A	PTS	PIM
1981–82	19	Edmonton Oilers	NHL	48	28	5	14	0	157	3.31	0	0	0	0
1982–83	20	Edmonton Oilers	NHL	32	13	12	5	0	129	4.29	0	0	0	6
1983–84	21	Edmonton Oilers	NHL	45	30	10	4	1	171	3.91	0	14	14	6
1984–85	22	Edmonton Oilers	NHL	46	26	8	7	1	165	3.87	0	3	3	6
1985–86	23	Edmonton Oilers	NHL	40	29	8	0	0	143	3.93	0	2	2	0
1986–87	24	Edmonton Oilers	NHL	44	22	13	3	0	137	3.44	0	2	2	6
1987–88	25	Edmonton Oilers	NHL	75	40	24	9	4	246	3.43	0	8	8	16
1988–89	26	Edmonton Oilers	NHL	59	23	26	6	1	213	3.83	0	1	1	6
1989–90	27	Edmonton Oilers	NHL	21	9	7	3	1	70	3.89	0	0	0	2
1990–91	28	Edmonton Oilers	NHL	13	6	4	3	1	39	3.01	0	0	0	0
1991–92	29	Toronto Maple Leafs	NHL	66	25	33	5	2	230	3.66	0	1	1	4
1992–93	30	Toronto Maple Leafs	NHL	29	13	9	4	1	87	3.14	0	0	0	0
1992–93	30	Buffalo Sabres	NHL	29	11	15	2	0	98	3.47	0	0	0	10
1993–94	31	Buffalo Sabres	NHL	32	13	12	3	2	106	3.68	0	4	4	16
1994–95	32	Buffalo Sabres	NHL	3	1	2	0	0	12	4.00	0	0	0	0
1994–95	32	Los Angeles Kings	NHL	14	1	7	3	0	47	4.04	0	0	0	2
1995–96	33	St. Louis Blues	NHL	79	30	28	16	3	209	2.87	0	1	1	8
1996–97	34	St. Louis Blues	NHL	73	33	27	11	3	193	2.72	0	2	2	6
1997–98	35	St. Louis Blues	NHL	58	29	21	6	3	138	2.53	0	2	2	6
1998–99	36	St. Louis Blues	NHL	39	16	11	8	2	89	2.44	0	0	0	12
1999–00	37	Calgary Flames	NHL	23	5	13	2	0	77	3.83	0	0	0	2
NHL Career – 19 Seasons				868	403	295	114	25	2756	3.38	0	40	40	114

PLAYOFFS

Season	Age	Team	Lg	GP	W	L	T	SO	GA	GAA	G	A	PTS	PIM
1981–82	19	Edmonton Oilers	NHL	5	2	3		0	26	5.05	0	1	1	0
1982–83	20	Edmonton Oilers	NHL	1	0	0		0	0	0.00	0	0	0	0
1983–84	21	Edmonton Oilers	NHL	16	11	4		1	44	2.99	0	3	3	4
1984–85	22	Edmonton Oilers	NHL	18	15	3		0	55	3.10	0	3	3	2
1985–86	23	Edmonton Oilers	NHL	9	5	4		0	28	3.11	0	1	1	0
1986–87	24	Edmonton Oilers	NHL	19	14	5		0	47	2.46	0	1	1	0
1987–88	25	Edmonton Oilers	NHL	19	16	2		0	55	2.90	0	1	1	6
1988–89	26	Edmonton Oilers	NHL	7	3	4		1	24	3.45	0	0	0	0
1990–91	28	Edmonton Oilers	NHL	17	8	7		0	51	3.00	0	2	2	2
1992–93	30	Buffalo Sabres	NHL	8	3	4		1	27	3.42	0	0	0	2
1995–96	33	St. Louis Blues	NHL	2	1	0		0	1	0.87	0	0	0	0
1996–97	34	St. Louis Blues	NHL	6	2	4		2	13	2.18	0	0	0	4
1997–98	35	St. Louis Blues	NHL	10	6	4		0	28	2.73	0	1	1	2
1998–99	36	St. Louis Blues	NHL	13	6	6		1	31	2.35	0	1	1	2
NHL Career – 14 Seasons				150	92	50		6	430	2.92	0	14	14	24

Page 166: Grant Fuhr tracks the puck despite the pile up of Edmonton and New Jersey players in his crease during his Cup years in Edmonton.

Page 167: Fuhr as a St. Louis Blue. Despite not much team success, Fuhr posted his best goals-against average while wearing the blue note.

Page 168: Fuhr does the splits as a Toronto Maple Leaf. Fuhr's greatest strengths as a goaltender was his lightning-quick reflexes, flexibility and acrobatic style.

EDDIE

GIACOMIN

Ready, Steady, Eddie

ALTHOUGH HE HASN'T played NHL hockey for over 30 years, New York Ranger fans can still be heard to chant "Eddie! Eddie! Eddie!" — a tradition in honor of Ed Giacomin. His success and the exciting manner in which he executed his game earned him everlasting affection, although that was never expressed in so heartfelt a way until he was with an opposing club.

Early in the 1975–76 season, Giacomin got off to a terrible start with New York, posting a 4.74 goals-against average, with three losses and a tie in his first four games. The Rangers had a new general manager in John Ferguson that season, and he decided that Giacomin's 10-year reign was over. The Ranger veteran was both saddened and

embarrassed when he was claimed on waivers by Detroit. "I remember having such an empty feeling," he recalled. "I had given 10 years of my life to that team and the worst part about it was there was nobody around. My teammates were on their way to Montreal. And here I am in this empty parking lot walking to my car. I had visions of walking straight into the bay."

On November 2, 1975, two days after becoming a Red Wing, he made a quick return to New York. Giacomin feared the reaction the fans might have upon seeing him in an opponent's uniform, and his family didn't dare attend the game. But the fans had been almost as upset as their star goaltender at the turn of events. The crowd's continual roar of "Eddie!" began when they drowned out the national anthem, and he received numerous prolonged standing ovations throughout the game. "I've never been an emotional man, but I couldn't hold back the tears tonight," said Giacomin in a post-game interview. "When

the people started cheering me at the beginning, the tears came down my face. A couple of times, I thought I would collapse from the emotion." He sparkled, however, in facing 46 shots in a 6–4 victory. The fans booed the Ranger goals, and one former teammate apologized for scoring.

Giacomin's career in New York did not begin with immediate success. He served a six-season minor-league apprenticeship before getting his first NHL shot. In 1958–59, the Washington Eagles of the Eastern Amateur Hockey League had called upon Sudbury Wolves' backup goalkeeper, Rollie Giacomin, to play the final four games of their season. Rollie didn't want to leave the Wolves of the Northern Ontario Hockey Association, so instead he sent his brother Eddie, five years his junior. Giacomin won all four games for the Eagles and earned a spot on the team for the next season. The Providence Reds of the American Hockey League purchased the rights to Giacomin in 1960, and once there, Giacomin caught the eye of a Rangers' scout from the area.

"The Reds were a last place team most of the time I was with them," said Giacomin, recalling his five years on Rhode Island, "but this was a blessing in disguise. I saw a lot of rubber and learned how to play goal." In 1965–66, he began the season with the New York Rangers, but a rocky start led to another two-week stint in the AHL. When Giacomin returned, everything fell into place, and he was in the NHL for good.

Almost perennial also-rans in those days, the Rangers didn't fare well in Giacomin's rookie season. "I was so excited," he later recalled. "I was 26, and I didn't think I was ever going to make it to the NHL. I forgot that I was there to stop pucks." But in 1966–67, Giacomin led the league with 68 games played, 9 shutouts and 30 wins, and he was elected to the First All-Star Team. The Rangers made the playoffs for the first time in five years, and never missed the post-season again until they released Giacomin in 1975–76.

Unmasked until 1970 ("I do think you see the puck

better without a mask," he stated that year. "I tried [Jacques] Plante's newfangled creation for a while, but I don't like it"), Giacomin played a fearless style, wandering far from his crease, sprawling acrobatically with great success and snapping crisp passes to teammates. "I hear Chuck Rayner of the old Rangers used to come right up and take part in the power play in the last minute of the game," he laughed in 1971, admitting he would love to score a goal. "Unfortunately, the rules no longer let goalies go past the center-ice line. Maybe I should have been a forward!" He actually hit the opposition's goal post with one long shot, and he was the first NHL goalie to record two assists in one game.

He was the league's busiest netminder for several seasons when with the Rangers, leading the league in games played while making the 1968, 1969 and 1970 Second All-Star Teams. When the game of No. 2 goaltender, Gilles Villemure, came into form, he proved the perfect goalten-

ding partner. The two shared the 1970–71 Vezina Trophy, while Giacomin was named to the First All-Star Team with a league-leading 8 shutouts in 45 games. He backstopped the Rangers to the 1972 Stanley Cup final, pushing Bobby Orr and the Boston Bruins to six games. Giacomin helped vanquish Boston the following season, but never got past the semifinal, and finished his career without a Cup ring.

The Wings failed to make the playoffs in 1975–76, and Giacomin played 29 games that season, relegated to a backup role for netminder Jim Rutherford. His average rose to 3.58 in 1976–77, the team missed the post-season again, and Giacomin quit after playing only nine games the following season. "My biggest thrill would have been winning the Stanley Cup," he said at his entry into the Hall of Fame in 1987, "but an individual can get no greater honor than this." A year and a half later, the Rangers bestowed further tribute, making Giacomin's number one only the second sweater ever retired by the club.

Career Stats

REGULAR SEASON

Season	Age	Team	Lg	GP	W	L	T	SO	GA	GAA	G	A	PTS	PIM
1965–66	26	New York Rangers	NHL	35	8	20	6	0	125	3.68	0	0	0	8
1966–67	27	New York Rangers	NHL	68	30	27	11	9	173	2.61	0	0	0	8
1967–68	28	New York Rangers	NHL	66	36	20	10	8	160	2.44	0	0	0	4
1968–69	29	New York Rangers	NHL	70	37	23	7	7	175	2.55	0	0	0	2
1969–70	30	New York Rangers	NHL	70	35	21	14	6	163	2.36	0	2	2	2
1970–71	31	New York Rangers	NHL	45	27	10	7	8	95	2.16	0	0	0	4
1971–72	32	New York Rangers	NHL	44	24	10	9	1	115	2.70	0	3	3	4
1972–73	33	New York Rangers	NHL	43	26	11	6	4	125	2.91	0	2	2	6
1973–74	34	New York Rangers	NHL	56	30	15	10	5	168	3.07	0	1	1	4
1974–75	35	New York Rangers	NHL	37	13	12	8	1	120	3.48	0	0	0	20
1975–76	36	New York Rangers	NHL	4	0	3	1	0	19	4.75	0	0	0	0
1975–76	36	Detroit Red Wings	NHL	29	12	14	3	2	100	3.45	0	0	0	0
1976–77	37	Detroit Red Wings	NHL	33	8	18	3	3	107	3.58	0	1	1	4
1977–78	38	Detroit Red Wings	NHL	9	3	5	1	0	27	3.14	0	0	0	0
NHL Career – 13 Seasons				609	289	209	96	54	1672	2.82	0	9	9	66

PLAYOFFS

Season	Age	Team	Lg	GP	W	L	T	SO	GA	GAA	G	A	PTS	PIM
1966–67	27	New York Rangers	NHL	4	0	4		0	14	3.41	0	0	0	0
1967–68	28	New York Rangers	NHL	6	2	4		0	18	3.00	0	0	0	0
1968–69	29	New York Rangers	NHL	3	0	3		0	10	3.33	0	0	0	5
1969–70	30	New York Rangers	NHL	5	2	3		0	19	4.07	0	0	0	0
1970–71	31	New York Rangers	NHL	12	7	5		0	28	2.21	0	0	0	2
1971–72	32	New York Rangers	NHL	10	6	4		0	27	2.70	0	0	0	2
1972–73	33	New York Rangers	NHL	10	5	4		1	23	2.56	0	0	0	4
1973–74	34	New York Rangers	NHL	13	7	6		0	37	2.82	0	0	0	6
1974–75	35	New York Rangers	NHL	2	0	2		0	4	2.79	0	0	0	4
NHL Career – 9 Seasons				65	29	35		1	180	2.81	0	0	0	23

Page 170: Ed Giacomin shuts the door on the Leafs.

Page 171: A young mask-less Giacomin in the Ranger net. Giacomin played 10 seasons on Broadway before he was unceremoniously dumped by the Rangers in 1975.

Page 172: Giacomin, in his later years with the Rangers, reluctantly took to wearing a mask, citing poor vision as the main deterrent.

INDUCTED 1984

BERNIE PARENT

Forever a Flyer

BERNIE PARENT BROKE into the NHL straight out of junior hockey, landing in Boston for the final two years of the Original Six era. With only brief stints in the minors with the Oklahoma City Blazers, Parent had an unimpressive 15–32–5 combined win–loss–tie record as a Bruin. Boston management chose to leave Parent unprotected in the league's first expansion draft in June 1967, and the Philadelphia Flyers selected him to share goaltending duties with Doug Favell, another goaltender plucked from the Bruins.

Parent and Favell were partners for the better part of four seasons, and enjoyed a modicum of success. The Flyers won the 1967–68 divisional championship, and Parent established himself as a strong, but not dominant, goaltender, shouldering the majority of the work in the Philadelphia net. So he was genuinely shocked when

he was traded in February 1971. "I heard the words and opened my mouth to say something but nothing came out," recalled Parent, who got the news from Flyers' general manager Keith Allen. "I couldn't speak."

Before Parent learned to skate, he played a lot of goal in the street while growing up in Montreal in the 1950s. Naturally, he idolized the Canadiens' star netminder Jacques Plante. Therefore, there was a silver lining in the trade that sent Parent to the Toronto Maple Leafs. Plante, by then a 42-year-old veteran, had joined the Leafs earlier that season, and he helped Parent take a more systematic approach to goaltending.

"There was no one in the world quite like Plante," noted Parent. "I learned more from him in two years with the Leafs than I did in all my other hockey days. He taught me a great deal about playing goal both on the ice and in my head off the ice. He taught me to be aggressive around

the goal and take an active part in play instead of waiting for things to happen. He showed me how I kept putting myself off balance by placing my weight on my left leg instead of on my stick side. He taught me how to steer shots off into the corner instead of letting them rebound in front of me. That old guy made a good goalie out of me."

With Plante's tutelage, and more NHL experience under his belt, Parent was emerging as a top NHL talent when the World Hockey Association was birthed in 1972. He was drafted and signed by the Miami Screaming Eagles, who folded before even building an arena to play in. The WHA's Philadephia Blazers quickly picked up Parent's rights, and he played the 1972–73 season back in his adopted hometown. Disenchanted having to face an excessive barrage of pucks, and paychecks that sometimes bounced, Parent expressed a strong interest in returning to the NHL, but with the Flyers rather than Toronto, which held his rights.

Toronto management agreed, reluctantly, and traded Parent back to the Flyers in May 1973, and he immediately

fashioned back-to-back Stanley Cup winning seasons. "When Parent is out there," said Philadelphia coach Fred Shero, "we know we can win games that we have no business winning."

With 73 starts in a 78-game season in 1973–74, Parent tallied 47 wins — a record that stood until Marty Brodeur notched 48 in 2006–07. (Parent still retains the record for "most regulation time wins" as he posted a dozen ties that season, without the benefit of overtime or shootouts.) He also earned a league-best and career-high dozen shutouts, guiding Philadelphia to first place in the West Division while compiling a 1.89 goals-against average. Parent won the Vezina Trophy (in a tie with Chicago's Tony Esposito) and was selected to the First All-Star Team. In the play-offs, he won the Conn Smythe Trophy as playoff MVP in leading the Flyers to victory over Bobby Orr and the Boston Bruins, winning the sixth and deciding game of the final with a 1–0 shutout.

"Only the Lord saves more than Bernie Parent" became a popular bumper sticker in Philadelphia, and

Parent's 1974–75 campaign finished in almost identical fashion to the previous one. He posted 12 shutouts again (with four more in the playoffs), retained ownership of the Vezina with a league-best 2.03 goals-against average, and made the First All-Star Team. He then earned his second consecutive Conn Smythe Trophy while helping the Flyers successfully defend the Stanley Cup, punctuating another season for the ages with a 2–0 shutout against the Buffalo Sabres in the deciding sixth game of the final. After the game, Parent was reluctant to pose with the Smythe, a personal rather than team award, a second time. "If you want to take a picture of me with a trophy," he said, "take me with the Stanley Cup. That's what this game is about."

Parent lost much of the following season due to a neck injury, and the Flyers were without him when the Montreal Canadiens and star goalie Ken Dryden swept them from the 1976 Cup final. Parent played the majority of the Flyers' games over the next three seasons, and led the league with seven shutouts in 1977–78, before his career came to a sudden halt.

On February 17, 1979, during a goalmouth scramble, an errant stick hit Parent in his right eye. A sympathetic reaction in his other eye had him lying in a hospital bed for two weeks, completely blind. "The doctors were honest with me and told me they could do very little to restore my sight," recalled Parent. "Ninety-five percent of the damage could be repaired only by my body's ability to heal itself. I was fearful, but I prayed and hoped for the best, and one morning, I saw a little bit of light."

His vision slowly returned, but Parent was left with permanent damage to his depth perception and his ability to focus. He was forced to retire from hockey at the age of 34. The Flyers retired his No. 1 sweater in the first game of the following season, and he entered the Hockey Hall of Fame in 1984. As Philadelphia's goaltending coach, Parent helped Pelle Lindbergh to a Vezina Trophy winning season in 1984–85 and Ron Hextall to the same in 1986–87.

Career Stats

REGULAR SEASON

Season	Age	Team	Lg	GP	W	L	T	SO	GA	GAA	G	A	PTS	PIM
1965-66	20	Boston Bruins	NHL	39	11	20	3	1	128	3.69	0	0	0	4
1966-67	21	Boston Bruins	NHL	18	4	12	2	0	62	3.64	0	0	0	2
1967-68	22	Philadelphia Flyers	NHL	38	16	17	5	4	93	2.48	0	1	1	23
1968-69	23	Philadelphia Flyers	NHL	58	17	23	16	1	151	2.69	0	0	0	4
1969-70	24	Philadelphia Flyers	NHL	62	13	29	20	3	171	2.79	0	3	3	14
1970-71	25	Philadelphia Flyers	NHL	30	9	12	6	2	73	2.76	0	2	2	5
1970-71	25	Toronto Maple Leafs	NHL	18	7	7	3	0	46	2.65	0	0	0	0
1971-72	26	Toronto Maple Leafs	NHL	47	17	18	9	3	116	2.56	0	1	1	6
1972-73	27	Philadelphia Blazers	WHA	63	33	28	0	2	220	3.61	0	1	1	36
1973-74	28	Philadelphia Flyers	NHL	73	47	13	12	12	136	1.89	0	3	3	24
1974-75	29	Philadelphia Flyers	NHL	68	44	14	10	12	137	2.03	0	0	0	16
1975-76	30	Philadelphia Flyers	NHL	11	6	2	3	0	24	2.34	0	0	0	2
1976-77	31	Philadelphia Flyers	NHL	61	35	13	12	5	159	2.71	0	0	0	0
1977-78	32	Philadelphia Flyers	NHL	49	29	6	13	7	108	2.22	0	0	0	4
1978-79	33	Philadelphia Flyers	NHL	36	16	12	7	4	89	2.70	0	2	2	8
Career – 14 Seasons				671	304	226	121	56	1713	2.55	0	13	13	148

PLAYOFFS

Season	Age	Team	Lg	GP	W	L	T	SO	GA	GAA	G	A	PTS	PIM
1967-68	22	Philadelphia Flyers	NHL	5	2	3		0	8	1.35	0	0	0	0
1968-69	23	Philadelphia Flyers	NHL	3	0	3		0	12	4.00	0	0	0	0
1970-71	25	Toronto Maple Leafs	NHL	4	2	2		0	9	2.30	0	0	0	0
1971-72	26	Toronto Maple Leafs	NHL	4	1	3		0	13	3.21	0	0	0	0
1972-73	27	Philadelphia Blazers	WHA	1	0	1		0	3	2.57	0	0	0	0
1973-74	27	Philadelphia Flyers	NHL	17	12	5		2	35	2.02	0	0	0	4
1974-75	29	Philadelphia Flyers	NHL	15	10	5		4	29	1.89	0	0	0	0
1975-76	30	Philadelphia Flyers	NHL	8	4	4		0	27	3.38	0	0	0	0
1976-77	31	Philadelphia Flyers	NHL	3	0	3		0	8	3.90	0	0	0	0
1977-78	32	Philadelphia Flyers	NHL	12	7	5		0	33	2.74	0	0	0	0
Career – 10 Seasons				72	38	34		6	177	2.46	0	0	0	4

Page 174: Parent tracks a puck to his blocker-side post in his early years with Philadelphia, wearing the unfamiliar No. 30 and pretzel-style mask.

Page 175: Parent in his more familiar No.1 and white mask in his second stint with the Flyers, 1973–74 to 1978–79.

Page 176: Parent in the early 1970s with Toronto where he was under the tutelage of his childhood idol, Jacques Plante.

INDUCTED 2006

PATRICK
ROY

Saint Patrick

ALTHOUGH HE WAS as idiosyncratic and eccentric as any man who has donned the pads in the National Hockey League, Patrick Roy developed a style that gave rise to a new breed of goaltender emerging from the province of Quebec and copied around the world.

Refining the butterfly style and blending it with standup-style elements proved wonderfully effective and Roy hung up his skates as the NHL's goaltending record holder in a multitude of categories, including games (1,029), wins (551) and playoff wins (151). "I was extremely comfortable when I retired," said Roy. "I emptied the tank." Although Martin Brodeur has bettered some of Roy's achievements as he continues an assault on the record books, "St. Patrick" made an indelible mark on goaltending history.

Roy played his junior hockey for the Granby Bisons in Quebec, and was drafted 51st overall by the Montreal Canadiens in the 1984 NHL entry draft. Ironically, Roy had grown up hating the Habs, as he was a fan of Montreal's provincial rival, the Quebec Nordiques. Roy was called up to Montreal to serve as backup for one game midway through his last junior season (1984–85), and notched his first NHL win when he entered a tied game in the third period and held the fort for the remaining time as Montreal took the lead. He returned to his junior team, but when Granby missed the playoffs, he got called

up to Montreal's AHL club. Roy starred in helping the Sherbrooke Canadiens win the 1985 Calder Cup. Playoff successes would prove to be the highlights of his career.

With only 20 minutes of NHL experience, Roy was the unlikely, but successful, candidate to win a full-time NHL job when he attended his first professional training camp. Goaltending coach François Allaire found Roy to be the perfect pupil. He cured Roy's tendency to dive for the puck (head coach Jacques Lemaire told him he "needed a mattress and a pillow" for all the time he spent lying on the ice, recalled Roy), and soon had the young puckstopper moving side-to-side on his knees by pushing off on his toes, adding a two-pad slide and working on reducing rebounds and using his blocker more effectively. With Roy still rather ungainly in net, yet stopping most of the pucks, Montreal made an improbable run to Stanley Cup victory in 1985–86. Roy, only 20 years old, was awarded the Conn Smythe Trophy.

Although the Canadiens team struggled at times over the next six seasons, Roy was firmly entrenched as one of the league's elite goalies. With Brian Hayward as his partner, Roy shared the Jennings Trophy (for lowest goals-against) for the next three seasons, and won it solo for his work in 1991–92. He was named to the NHL First All-Star Team in 1989, 1990 and 1992, and the Second Team in 1988 and 1991, and won the Vezina Trophy as the league's top netminder in 1989, 1990 and 1992.

Roy superstitiously never skated on the blue lines, hopping over them carefully, and his frequent craning of his neck and "talking to his goalposts" looked to some like nervous habits. He was, in truth, meticulous in preparing himself mentally for the challenge at hand. "I really like to look back on goals I gave up against that team in past games," he explained in 1996. "In reviewing the goal, I try to understand what I could have done to stop the puck. If there is a question about my positioning or how I reacted, I imagine the situation changed and I'm making the save. In my visualizations, I'm focusing mostly on myself and what I'm going to do, but sometimes, I focus on specific players on the other team. Players like Mario Lemieux and Wayne Gretzky usually have an impact on the game, so I'll

see myself facing them and making some saves. Just before the game, I like to look at the net and imagine the goalposts shrinking, the net grown smaller."

By 1993, only Roy and captain Guy Carbonneau remained from Montreal's 1986 Cup-winning team. The Canadiens finished fourth in their conference over the regular season, but Roy became almost unbeatable in the playoffs. He lost only four times against 16 wins, including 10 consecutive overtime victories. Roy was in such a "zone" in the Stanley Cup final against Wayne Gretzky's Los Angeles Kings, he even gave a cocky wink to L.A.'s Tomas Sandstrom after continually thwarting the Finnish sniper. "I knew he wasn't going to beat me," said Roy, and the moment, caught by a TV camera, became a defining one for Roy. He won his second Conn Smythe Trophy when the Habs defeated the Kings in five games.

Roy's career took a shocking turn on December 2, 1995. At home facing the Detroit Red Wings, Montreal played its worst home game in franchise history, losing 12–1. The crowd jeered Roy, who was kept in by coach Mario Tremblay for nine of the goals. When he was pulled midway through the second period, Roy stormed over to team president Ronald Corey and publicly announced he had played his final game for the club. General Manager Réjean Houle was forced to trade Roy, and dealt him to the Colorado Avalanche (the newly transplanted Quebec Nordiques).

A new Roy era began immediately. "I felt that with the offense that was on that team that we had a good chance to win the Stanley Cup," said Roy. "I knew the talent that was on that team and I was excited about the challenge. It was a perfect situation for me." The Avalanche were a team on the rise, and with Roy backstopping the high-powered offense, they swept the Florida Panthers in the 1996 Stanley Cup final.

Roy won the 2000–01 Jennings Trophy on his way to another Stanley Cup ring and a third Conn Smythe trophy. He was named to the 2002 First All-Star Team, but left the game on his own terms while still in top form after the 2002–03 season. The Avalanche retired his No. 33 the following season, and he entered the Hall of Fame in 2006, the first year he was eligible.

Proving "time heals all wounds," the Montreal Canadiens retired his number in 2008. "Looking back, I know I had great years with the Canadiens," said Roy. "I think we brought joy to Habs' fans and even probably surprised them somewhat with the two Cups we won. That's what I want people in Montreal to remember."

Career Stats

REGULAR SEASON

Season	Age	Team	Lg	GP	W	L	T	SO	GA	GAA	G	A	PTS	PIM
1984-85	19	Montreal Canadiens	NHL	1	1	0	0	0	0	0.00	0	0	0	0
1985-86	20	Montreal Canadiens	NHL	47	23	18	3	1	148	3.35	0	3	3	4
1986-87	21	Montreal Canadiens	NHL	46	22	16	6	1	131	2.93	0	1	1	8
1987-88	22	Montreal Canadiens	NHL	45	23	12	9	3	125	2.90	0	2	2	14
1988-89	23	Montreal Canadiens	NHL	48	33	5	6	4	113	2.47	0	6	6	2
1989-90	24	Montreal Canadiens	NHL	54	31	16	5	3	134	2.53	0	5	5	0
1990-91	25	Montreal Canadiens	NHL	48	25	15	6	1	128	2.71	0	2	2	6
1991-92	26	Montreal Canadiens	NHL	67	36	22	8	5	155	2.36	0	5	5	4
1992-93	27	Montreal Canadiens	NHL	62	31	25	5	2	192	3.20	0	2	2	16
1993-94	28	Montreal Canadiens	NHL	68	35	17	11	7	161	2.50	0	1	1	30
1994-95	29	Montreal Canadiens	NHL	43	17	20	6	1	127	2.97	0	1	1	20
1995-96	30	Montreal Canadiens	NHL	22	12	9	1	1	62	2.95	0	0	0	6
1995-96	30	Colorado Avalanche	NHL	39	22	15	1	1	103	2.68	0	0	0	4
1996-97	31	Colorado Avalanche	NHL	62	38	15	7	7	143	2.32	0	1	1	15
1997-98	32	Colorado Avalanche	NHL	65	31	19	13	4	153	2.39	0	3	3	39
1998-99	33	Colorado Avalanche	NHL	61	32	19	8	5	139	2.29	0	2	2	28
1999-00	34	Colorado Avalanche	NHL	63	32	21	8	2	141	2.28	0	3	3	10
2000-01	35	Colorado Avalanche	NHL	62	40	13	7	4	132	2.21	0	5	5	10
2001-02	36	Colorado Avalanche	NHL	63	32	23	8	9	122	1.94	0	3	3	26
2002-03	37	Colorado Avalanche	NHL	63	35	15	13	5	137	2.18	0	0	0	20
NHL Career – 19 Seasons				1029	551	315	131	66	2546	2.54	0	45	45	262

PLAYOFFS

Season	Age	Team	Lg	GP	W	L	T	SO	GA	GAA	G	A	PTS	PIM
1985-86	20	Montreal Canadiens	NHL	20	15	5		1	39	1.92	0	0	0	10
1986-87	21	Montreal Canadiens	NHL	6	4	2		0	22	4.00	0	0	0	0
1987-88	22	Montreal Canadiens	NHL	8	3	4		0	24	3.35	0	0	0	0
1988-89	23	Montreal Canadiens	NHL	19	13	6		2	42	2.09	0	2	2	16
1989-90	24	Montreal Canadiens	NHL	11	5	6		1	26	2.43	0	1	1	0
1990-91	25	Montreal Canadiens	NHL	13	7	5		0	40	3.06	0	0	0	2
1991-92	26	Montreal Canadiens	NHL	11	4	7		1	30	2.62	0	0	0	2
1992-93	27	Montreal Canadiens	NHL	20	16	4		0	46	2.13	0	1	1	4
1993-94	28	Montreal Canadiens	NHL	6	3	3		0	16	2.56	0	0	0	0
1995-96	30	Colorado Avalanche	NHL	22	16	6		3	51	2.10	0	0	0	0
1996-97	31	Colorado Avalanche	NHL	17	10	7		3	38	2.21	0	0	0	12
1997-98	32	Colorado Avalanche	NHL	7	3	4		0	18	2.51	0	1	1	0
1998-99	33	Colorado Avalanche	NHL	19	11	8		1	52	2.66	0	2	2	4
1999-00	34	Colorado Avalanche	NHL	17	11	6		3	31	1.79	0	1	1	4
2000-01	35	Colorado Avalanche	NHL	23	16	7		4	41	1.70	0	1	1	0
2001-02	36	Colorado Avalanche	NHL	21	11	10		3	52	2.51	0	2	2	0
2002-03	37	Colorado Avalanche	NHL	7	3	4		1	16	2.27	0	0	0	0
NHL Career – 17 Seasons				247	151	94		23	584	2.30	0	11	11	54

Page 178: Patrick Roy, early in his time with Colorado, blocks an Andreas Dackell attempt from in close.

Page 179: Roy in the early-1990s with the Montreal Canadiens, where he kept the crease in parts of 12 seasons and earned two Stanley Cups.

Page 180: Roy the rookie stumps the Flames in the 1986 Stanley Cup final. Roy helped Montreal to a Cup win and earned the Conn Smythe.

INDUCTED 1993

BILLY
SMITH

Battlin' Billy

BILLY SMITH'S COMPETITIVE streak was a mile wide. He was known to forsake the ritual of shaking hands with the opposition after a playoff defeat and he regularly lambasted the referee and even his own teammates at times. But Smith picked up his nickname "Battlin' Billy" for more than verbal assaults. He frequently demonstrated his willingness to wield his stick like a scythe to rid his crease of encroaching forwards, and once received a six-game suspension for breaking an opponent's jaw and cheekbone.

"I just try to give myself a little working room," he once explained. "But if a guy bothers me, then I retaliate." As a rookie, Smith set a record for penalty minutes in a season (42) by a goalie, and once broke three of his sticks on the ankles of Buffalo players in one period. He also fought some of the league's toughest forwards and, by the time he retired, he had accumulated 489 penalty minutes in the regular season and 78 in the playoffs.

The Islanders experienced several difficult years but, primarily through judicious drafting, eventually assembled a team for the ages. Smith, who got his first NHL starts for Los Angeles — playing five games for the Kings in 1971–72 — was drafted to Long Island for the 1972–73 season when the NHL expanded to 16 teams. He started sharing

duties with Glenn "Chico" Resch in 1974–75, when they backstopped the Isles into the playoffs for the first time. The partnership lasted for seven seasons, and Smith was content to watch half the games from the bench. "You can't do your job and keep an eye on the other guy," noted Smith, "so the most help you can give another goalie is to get along as partners." Resch, gregarious and colorful, seemed to outsiders more the leader than the terse, gruff Smith, but when the playoffs rolled around, New York coach Al Arbour increasingly leaned on Smith.

Smith played in only one All-Star Game, in 1978, and was voted Most Valuable Player, an unusual feat in what is usually a high-scoring goal-fest. In later years, Smith identified this time period, in his late twenties, as when he hit his peak. "I was comfortable and had my game under control," he said. "When I was younger, I was feistier and tried to do too much. A lot of times when I was poking

guys or trying to push them out of my crease, I'd be scored on. I couldn't take control of my opponent and stop the puck at the same time."

Smith made history on November 28, 1979, when he became the first NHL netminder to be credited with a goal. The Colorado Rockies pulled their goalie during a delayed penalty call, and when a pass between two Rockies went astray and inadvertently landed in the Colorado net, Smith's name was put on the score sheet as the last Islander to touch the puck — he had taken a shot off his chest.

The 1979–80 season became even more memorable when the Islanders won their first of four consecutive Stanley Cups. "Just to get out of our own division was always a battle," recalled Smith. "Many series went to seven games. The first and the fourth Stanley Cups were probably the most satisfying. The first was special because we didn't know yet if we were capable of winning." The Islanders beat the Philadelphia Flyers in the final, although

the Flyers had finished the regular season 25 points ahead of them in the standings.

"I think we lost a couple of Stanley Cups before we won the first one because we just didn't know what it took," said Smith. "We caught a couple of teams sleeping right at the beginning and then in the end against Philly, we scored in overtime in the sixth game. I'll predict today that if we had lost that game on Long Island, we would have had our hands more than full in Philadelphia. We would have been pretty shaken. But we had a good team, we had a good system, and we stuck with it even in overtime, and we got a break at the right time."

Smith and the Isles finished atop the league in 1980–81, and successfully defended the Cup, but the team was at its most powerful in the 1981–82 season. Led by forwards Mike Bossy and Bryan Trottier, defenseman Denis Potvin, and backed by Smith (Resch was traded in March 1981), the team finished high atop the league with 118 points.

Bossy and Trottier were among the top five scorers, and Smith was named to the First All-Star Team and won the Vezina Trophy, awarded for the first time to the league's best goalie as determined by the NHL's general managers. They swept the Vancouver Canucks in the Stanley Cup final, and Smith had his third ring.

In 1982–83, Smith shared the Jennings Trophy with his new partner Roland Melanson, for the league's lowest goals-against average. For Smith, the Islanders' fourth consecutive Cup win was all the sweeter for the "hype" over the high-flying Wayne Gretzky and the Edmonton Oilers, their opponent in the Stanley Cup final. "The Islanders were three-time champions but got little respect," said Smith, who managed to stop Gretzky from scoring in four straight games, and allowed only six goals in total in the final. "We won the first game against Edmonton 2–0,

probably the finest game I ever played. Even though the series ended in four games, it was far from a sweep. Every game was do-or-die, and it was great hockey. To top things off for me personally, I also won the Conn Smythe award."

In 1983–84, the Islanders finished tied for first in their conference, and Smith had the satisfaction of becoming the league's all-time playoff-win leader with 81 victories, passing Ken Dryden on April 28, 1984 (Patrick Roy is the current holder of the record with 151 wins). The Islanders' dynastic reign came to an end three weeks later, however, when the Oilers beat them in the final.

Billy Smith retired after the 1988–89 season, the last of the original Islanders. He turned to coaching goalies, first for the Islanders and later for the Florida Panthers. Smith's No. 31 was retired on Long Island in 1993, the same year he entered the Hall of Fame.

Career Stats

REGULAR SEASON

Season	Age	Team	Lg	GP	W	L	T	SO	GA	GAA	G	A	PTS	PIM
1971–72	21	Los Angeles Kings	NHL	5	1	3	1	0	23	4.60	0	0	0	5
1972–73	22	New York Islanders	NHL	37	7	24	3	0	147	4.16	0	0	0	42
1973–74	23	New York Islanders	NHL	46	9	23	12	0	134	3.07	0	0	0	11
1974–75	24	New York Islanders	NHL	58	21	18	17	3	156	2.78	0	0	0	21
1975–76	25	New York Islanders	NHL	39	19	10	9	3	98	2.61	0	1	1	10
1976–77	26	New York Islanders	NHL	36	21	8	6	2	87	2.50	0	1	1	12
1977–78	27	New York Islanders	NHL	38	20	8	8	2	95	2.65	0	0	0	35
1978–79	28	New York Islanders	NHL	40	25	8	4	1	108	2.87	0	2	2	54
1979–80	29	New York Islanders	NHL	38	15	14	7	2	104	2.95	1	0	1	39
1980–81	30	New York Islanders	NHL	41	22	10	8	2	129	3.28	0	0	0	33
1981–82	31	New York Islanders	NHL	46	32	9	4	0	133	2.97	0	1	1	24
1982–83	32	New York Islanders	NHL	41	18	14	7	1	112	2.87	0	0	0	41
1983–84	33	New York Islanders	NHL	42	23	13	2	2	130	3.42	0	2	2	23
1984–85	34	New York Islanders	NHL	37	18	14	3	0	133	3.82	0	0	0	25
1985–86	35	New York Islanders	NHL	41	20	14	4	1	143	3.72	0	3	3	49
1986–87	36	New York Islanders	NHL	40	14	18	5	1	132	3.52	0	2	2	37
1987–88	37	New York Islanders	NHL	38	17	14	5	2	113	3.22	0	0	0	20
1988–89	38	New York Islanders	NHL	17	3	11	0	0	54	4.44	0	0	0	8
NHL Career – 18 Seasons				680	305	233	105	22	2031	3.17	1	12	13	489

PLAYOFFS

Season	Age	Team	Lg	GP	W	L	T	SO	GA	GAA	G	A	PTS	PIM
1974–75	24	New York Islanders	NHL	6	1	4		0	23	4.14	0	0	0	6
1975–76	25	New York Islanders	NHL	8	4	3		0	21	2.88	0	0	0	11
1976–77	26	New York Islanders	NHL	10	7	3		0	27	2.79	0	0	0	8
1977–78	27	New York Islanders	NHL	1	0	0		0	1	1.28	0	0	0	9
1978–79	28	New York Islanders	NHL	5	4	1		1	10	1.90	0	0	0	4
1979–80	29	New York Islanders	NHL	20	15	4		1	56	2.80	0	0	0	11
1980–81	30	New York Islanders	NHL	17	14	3		0	42	2.54	0	1	1	2
1981–82	31	New York Islanders	NHL	18	15	3		1	47	2.52	0	0	0	6
1982–83	32	New York Islanders	NHL	17	13	3		2	43	2.68	0	1	1	9
1983–84	33	New York Islanders	NHL	21	12	8		0	54	2.72	0	0	0	17
1984–85	34	New York Islanders	NHL	6	3	3		0	19	3.33	0	0	0	6
1985–86	35	New York Islanders	NHL	1	0	1		0	4	4.00	0	0	0	0
1986–87	36	New York Islanders	NHL	2	0	0		0	1	0.90	0	0	0	0
NHL Career – 13 Seasons				132	88	36		5	348	2.73	0	2	2	89

Page 182: Billy Smith, with an early helmet-and-cage style mask, protects the Islander net.

Page 183: A young Smith signals to the referee that the puck is stuck on the back of the net in a game against Toronto.

Page 184: Smith moves to clear the puck away from Bernie Federko.

VLADISLAV
TRETIAK

The Soviet Superstar

V LADISLAV TRETIAK WAS the first Russian player inducted into the Hockey Hall of Fame. He is also one of very few members who never played on a professional North American team. His star has risen a long way from being the "weak link" North American observers expected when Team Canada met the Soviet Union in the September 1972 Summit Series.

1972 was the first time Canada's best players, all NHLers, had played against the powerhouse Soviets, who had long dominated international hockey. Canadian scouts had dismissed the 20-year-old Tretiak as a concern, based upon an exhibition match they watched between the Soviet National Team and the Red Army club. Tretiak looked rather hapless in that Moscow game, letting in nine goals. It turned out later that Tretiak had other things on his mind that night. "I was getting married the next morning," he revealed later. "I couldn't concentrate on the game."

Anticipating a brutal routing of the young netminder, Jacques Plante, perhaps the most analytical goaltending expert of the day, who literally had a book on the NHL's premier shooters, took pity on Tretiak. "Jacques Plante came into our room with an interpreter and amazed us

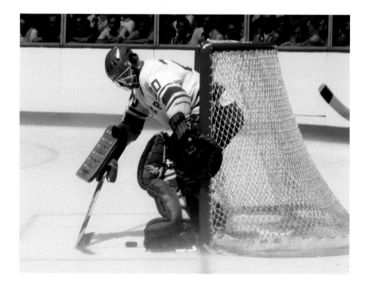

by sitting with me and explaining in detail how I should play against the likes of [Frank] Mahovlich, [Phil] Esposito, [Yvan] Cournoyer and [Paul] Henderson," said Tretiak, who added his gratitude to Plante, "[His] suggestions helped me very much." By the time the eight-game series was over, with Canada squeaking out a victory in the last minute, Canada's scoring hero Henderson was likening Tretiak to the legendary Terry Sawchuk. And no one scoffed.

Tretiak was first tutored by the legendary Soviet coach Anatoly Tarasov as a 15-year old, when he filled in as a fourth goaltender with the Central Red Army team, in order to make practices "more efficient." After he backstopped his junior team to the European Junior Championships title the following year, he was made a permanent Red Army member. "He wanted me to feel that each puck in my net was a personal defeat," recalled Tretiak. "I will never forget Tarasov's lessons. Now,

looking back after many years, I clearly understand that he was not only teaching us hockey, he was teaching us life."

Tretiak got his first Olympic experience in 1972, when he collected his first Olympic gold medal. Before he was done, he had fashioned a remarkable 1.78 goals-against average over 98 international games, won three Olympic gold medals and a silver, and backstopped the Soviets to 10 World Championships and 9 European titles. From 1971 to 1984, he was the Soviet league's First All-Star goalie. Ostensibly an amateur player and a Central Red Army member, he guided the Red Army team to 13 league titles while capturing the MVP honors five times. He was awarded the Order of Lenin for his service to his country in 1978, and won the coveted Golden Hockey Stick as the outstanding player in all of Europe in 1981, 1982 and 1983.

In addition to his "amateur" successes, Tretiak habitually played his very best during exhibition games against professionals. In 1972, Team Canada members had to be NHL players, leading to the controversial decision not to

include superstar Bobby Hull on the team after he signed to play in the new World Hockey Association (WHA). In 1974, the WHA fielded its own team in the Summit '74 series. This time, despite Hull's seven goals over the eight-game series, Tretiak and the Soviets prevailed with four wins, a loss and three ties.

The Red Army club and the Soviet Wings (the Soviet Union's top teams) faced some of the NHL's best in the 1975–76 "Super Series." In a performance that many still hail as the greatest goaltending performance of all time, Tretiak held the powerhouse Montreal Canadiens to a 3–3 draw on New Year's Eve, despite having his team badly outplayed and outshot 38–13. "The Montreal game made a lasting impression on us," said Tretiak years later. "As far as I'm concerned, this is what the game of hockey is all about — fast, full of combinations, rough but not rude, with an exciting plot. Every little detail of that excellent night in Montreal comes back to me. I would love to play it all over again."

At the 1980 Olympics in Lake Placid, the United States scored a surprising goal with one second left in the first period of a critical game against the Soviets, and coach Viktor Tikhonov immediately pulled Tretiak in anger. Many speculate that move was critical to the American's "Miracle on Ice" victory that day, and Tikhonov later rued the decision as "the biggest mistake of my career."

The Montreal Canadiens made a surprising choice in the 1983 entry draft, selecting Tretiak as a long-shot with their ninth pick. Despite Tretiak's interest and many discussions with Soviet officials, permissions could not be arranged, and Tretiak never did play in the NHL. "I would have loved to play in the Forum," Tretiak admitted years later, when the Iron Curtain had fallen and Russian and Eastern European players could freely emigrate. "I was hoping to one day play in the NHL ... even for just one season. I regret not having the chance."

Tretiak retired from active play on a high note in 1984, after shutting out Czechoslovakia 2–0 to win Olympic gold in Sarajevo. "I left because I was very tired," he explained later. "Backup goalies came and went, as did three generations of forwards and defensemen, but through four Olympic Games, all the important ones with the professionals, all the World Championships, all the Izvestia tournaments, it was I who played in the net." The actual close of his career came at the end of the Izvestia tournament in December 1984. He participated in a special All-Star Game between the USSR and the other European players who had taken part in the Izvestia games. The contest ended with a huge ovation for the tearful Tretiak as he said his goodbyes.

Tretiak was voted to the Hockey Hall of Fame in 1989. About a year later, he landed his first NHL job — a goaltending coach for the Chicago Blackhawks. He mentored a generation of goalies, including Ed Belfour, one of a number of NHL goalies who donned Tretiak's No. 20 to honor him. Tretiak was named head of the Russian Ice Hockey Federation in 2006 and served as general manager of Russia's 2010 Olympic team.

Career Stats

REGULAR SEASON											
Season	Age	Team	Lg	GP	W	L	T	SO	GA	GAA
1968–69	16	CSKA Moscow	USSR	3					2	0.67
1969–70	17	CSKA Moscow	USSR	34					76	2.24
1970–71	18	CSKA Moscow	USSR	40					81	2.03
1971–72	19	CSKA Moscow	USSR	30					78	2.60
1972–73	20	CSKA Moscow	USSR	30					80	2.67
1973–74	21	CSKA Moscow	USSR	27					94	3.48
1974–75	22	CSKA Moscow	USSR	35					104	2.97
1975–76	23	CSKA Moscow	USSR	33					100	3.03
1976–77	24	CSKA Moscow	USSR	35					98	2.80
1977–78	25	CSKA Moscow	USSR	29					72	2.48
1978–79	26	CSKA Moscow	USSR	40					111	2.78
1979–80	27	CSKA Moscow	USSR	36					85	2.36
1980–81	28	CSKA Moscow	USSR	18					32	1.78
1981–82	29	CSKA Moscow	USSR	41	34	4	3	6	65	1.59
1982–83	30	CSKA Moscow	USSR	29	25	3	1	6	40	1.38
1983–84	31	CSKA Moscow	USSR	22	22	0	0	4	40	1.82
Career – 16 Seasons				482	81	7	4	16	1158	2.40

Page 186: Vladislav Tretiak looks to smother the puck during Game 1 of the 1972 Summit Series, a 7–3 Soviet win.

Page 187: Tretiak faces the speedy Yvan Cournoyer during Game 2 of the Summit Series, in Toronto.

Page 188: Tretiak blocks a Stan Mikita drive in Game 2. Tretiak backed the Soviets to a 2–1–1 series lead in the four games in Canada.

GAME CHANGERS

BY BOB DUFF

FROM THE BIRTH of the game, it seems that the hockey world has been dead set against goaltenders. Their job, after all, is to spoil the fun — to prevent goals. No one pays admission to see a puckstopper. Goalies save shots. They don't sell tickets.

That's why, since hockey was first governed by rules, the makers of those rules have been most concerned with one agenda — finding ways to put more offense into the game. It has made the goaltender's lot in life less enjoyable and more demanding, but over the course of hockey history, there are netminders who have been willing to challenge the status quo, fight the system and unearth new methods to beat those who are trying to beat them.

Manon Rheaume's Team Canada jersey worn at the

1994 Women's World Championships.

PIONEERING PUCKSTOPPERS

In the early 1890s, goaltenders in Winnipeg began donning cricket pads for added protection on their legs and developing a wider base to the bottom half of their sticks in order to make it easier to parry pucks. Around the same time, Quebec netminder Frank Stocking discovered that by moving toward the shooter, he could use simple physics to take away the net. Stocking may have been the first goalie to employ playing the angles as an effective puckstopping tactic, but many other members of the goaltenders' union have since sought their own angle toward beating a system designed to prevent their success.

PEERLESS PERCY

Percy LeSueur could best be described as a thinking man's goaltender. A puckstopper in the pre-NHL days, LeSueur was one of the first goalies whose work not only altered the way the game was played between the pipes, but all over the ice.

"LeSueur was an innovator and pioneer of the game par excellence," noted hockey historian Bill Fitsell, when explaining LeSueur's nickname, "Peerless Percy." In net, LeSueur was always looking for ways to perform his puck-stopping duties in a much wiser fashion, once racing out of his net to bodycheck an onrushing forward and deprive him of the puck. He was also one of the early goaltenders capable of stickhandling the puck and leaving his net to help his teammates control possession of the disc. "He played with his head, his hands and his feet," reported the *Ottawa Free Press* in 1907. "He never throws the puck away and in the tightest corners, carries it to the back of his net and gives it to one of his forwards."

Among LeSueur's innovations were the goaltender's gauntlet gloves, which looked similar to regular players' gloves, but had a long padded area added to cover the goalie's arms up to just below the elbow and heavier padding in the hands. These became standard fare for pro goalies well into the 1920s. In 1909, he wrote a booklet entitled, *How To Play Hockey*, a 48-page handbook that outlined in detail the required elements to play all positions on the ice. He also patented the LeSueur goal net, which featured

a 17-inch top and 22-inch base. In 1920, it was adopted as the official net of the NHL and held forth as the net of choice in all major hockey leagues for nearly a decade.

After his playing days, LeSueur worked as an NHL referee and coached the NHL's Hamilton Tigers. He helped assemble the ownership group that brought the Detroit Cougars into the NHL in 1926 and managed arenas in Detroit and Syracuse in the U.S. and Windsor and Fort Erie in Canada. While coaching minor pro in Buffalo, he utilized players from the team during intermissions to help teach the intricacies of the game to fans who were new to hockey. He also wrote columns for the *Hamilton Spectator* and was one of the first reporters to tabulate shots on goal in his game summaries. He was a radio pioneer and one of the first hockey managers to introduce afternoon games as a way of attracting fans to the rink.

Detroit Red Wings Hall of Fame broadcaster Budd Lynch, who broke into radio working with LeSueur in Hamilton in the 1930s, put it best: "Percy was a man who was ahead of his time."

PRAYING BENNY

Early rules around stopping the puck were simple and straightforward and, in relation to the modern game, extremely Draconian. The first Ontario Hockey Association rules, established November 27, 1890, succinctly covered the restrictions placed upon the netminder. "The goalkeeper must not, during play, lie, sit or kneel on the ice," it read. "He may when in goal stop the puck with his hands but shall not throw it or hold it. Offenders may be ruled off the ice."

In major-league hockey, these rules were strictly enforced, though hockey historian Garth Vaughan uncovered evidence that the Coloured Hockey League of the Canadian maritime provinces permitted goalies to leave their feet to make a save around the turn of the 20th century.

The Pacific Coast Hockey Association, the major-league rival to the NHL, was the first of the big leagues to give goalies a break. They did away with the restrictive rule in 1913 and league co-founder Lester Patrick, who dabbled in goal throughout his career, found the flap over

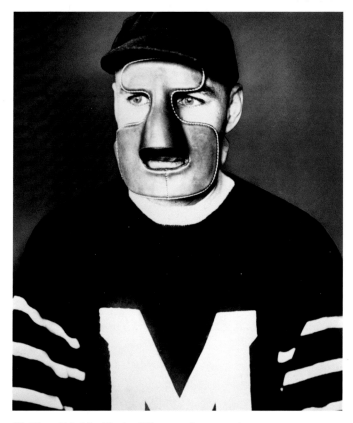

Clint Benedict of the Montreal Maroons shown wearing an
alternate version of the mask pictured on page 14.

flopping to be ridiculous. "A goalkeeper should be allowed
to make any move he wants, just like the rest of us,"
Patrick explained in Eric Whitehead's book, *The Patricks:
Hockey's Royal Family.* "He should be allowed to make the
most of his physical abilities."

That's exactly how Clint Benedict viewed the situation. Goaltender for the Ottawa Senators of the National
Hockey Association, forerunner to the NHL, Benedict
believed he should be allowed to flop and dive in the path
of pucks, which cost NHA goaltenders a two-dollar fine
for each offense.

Benedict, always a guy who'd tightrope the line
between the laws of the game and his own assessment
of what the rules should be, was willing to challenge
authority. "What you had to be is sneaky," he explained in
a 1976 interview with *Hockey Digest.* "You'd make a move,
fake losing your balance or footing, and put the officials on
the spot. Did I fall down, or did I intentionally go down?"

It was a perplexing problem for game officials and
critics of Benedict's style, who labeled him "Praying
Benny" and "Tumbling Clint" for his antics between the

pipes. The no-flopping zone in front of the net continued to be in vogue as the NHL was founded in 1917, and
Benedict continued to be a rebel with a cause. A strapping
six-footer in an era when most goaltenders were smaller
fellows, Benedict was capable of covering much of the net
even when on his knees.

Frustrated referees turned to NHL president Frank
Calder for help, and on January 9, 1918, Calder implemented the first major rule change in NHL history,
permitting goalies to fall in the path of shots. Queried by
a *Montreal Star* reporter as to whether he was going to
allow goalies to take the fall, Calder's answer created a bit
of hockey jargon that continues to be popular today: "In
the future, [goalkeepers] can fall on their knees or stand
on their heads, if they think they can stop the puck better
in that way than by standing on their feet."

JAKE THE SNAKE

It is Jacques Plante's legacy that he will forever be known
as the goalie who made the mask acceptable in hockey, but
truth be told, that's only one chapter among this pioneer's
legacy of innovation.

"He was an individual who portrayed his own style,"
former Montreal Canadiens teammate Dickie Moore told
the *Montreal Gazette.* "He wasn't a student of the game,
he was the professor, and he did it while he played, as well.
He changed the style of the game."

Consider that night in Chicago Stadium, during a
January 26, 1963, game between the Black Hawks and
Canadiens. Plante complained that the net that Chicago
defended for two of three periods was smaller than the one
he guarded for the Canadiens during those two frames.
Plante indicated he'd arrived at this conclusion because
he'd noticed that the crossbar didn't hit his back in the
same place it did while guarding the other net. Arena
workers measured the nets and found that Montreal's goal
was four feet high — the standard NHL rule — but the
Chicago net was only three feet, 10 inches in height.

"Even when he was off the ice, he was always thinking
of the game," said Hall of Fame goalie Glenn Hall, who
tended goal for Chicago in that game and who, in the

1968–69 season, teamed with Plante to win the Vezina Trophy with the St. Louis Blues.

Plante didn't find ways to bend the rules like many goaltenders. He lived in his own world, and while changing the way his position was played, forced rulemakers to adapt to his game.

One of his tactics was to roam far from his net, and if the Canadiens end was under siege, to immediately freeze the puck for a faceoff, no matter where it was located on the ice. The NHL frowned on this act and during the 1959–60 season instituted a rule prohibiting goalies from freezing pucks outside the goal crease. Hockey people referred to it as the Plante Rule, because he was the only NHL goalie of that era nimble enough on his skates to dart out and beat opposing players to the puck. "The other teams could have done the same thing as Jacques, but I guess nobody is as quick as Plante," Montreal coach Toe Blake complained when the rule was passed to limit Plante's abilities. "He can get away with things that other goalies can't."

Plante wasn't the first goalie to play the puck — Clint Benedict, Hugh Lehman and Charlie Rayner were among early netminders who were adept at this ploy — but Plante was the first goalie to roam behind the net to stop enemy shoot-ins, enabling his defensemen to set up counter-attacks.

"Possession of the puck is No. 1," Plante explained to *Toronto Star* columnist Jim Proudfoot. "That's all I'm doing, getting control until one of my teammates comes along."

Outsiders viewed Plante as quirky and offbeat, pointing out that among other things, he knitted his own socks and underwear. Even when he made his most common sense move and the one that saved face for generations of goaltenders — donning the mask for good — he dealt with ridicule.

Some viewed him as a coward, while others mocked his mask, viewing it as a fashion statement instead of a safety precaution.

"It looks like he's been hit in the face with a custard pie," Al Nickelson of *The Globe and Mail* wrote of Plante's first mask.

As was his custom, Plante ignored the naysayers and pointed out the obvious. "I already had four broken noses, a broken jaw, two broken cheekbones and almost 200 stitches in my head," he noted, countering his critics. "I didn't care how the mask looked."

Ever the studious one, Plante was asked to tend goal for the junior Montreal Canadiens in a December 15, 1965, exhibition game against the powerhouse Soviet national team. In preparation, Plante watched hours of the Russians in action, then stymied them in a 2–1 Montreal win. "My easiest game," he once explained. "In those days, all you had to do was study the Russians' passing plays and you'd know where the shots would come from."

Plante was one of the first hockey players to plan for the future, deferring much of the salary he earned late in his NHL career until well after he'd retired from the game. He helped tutor Soviet goalie Vladislav Tretiak on the nuances of NHL shooters prior the 1972 Canada-Russia Summit Series, and during the 1980s he worked as a goalie coach for the Philadelphia Flyers and St. Louis Blues, imparting his wisdom to a new generation of puckstoppers.

"It was like being able to go to a library and take out every book ever written about playing goal," said Rick Wamsley, a Blues goalie at the time.

THE BUTTERFLY EFFECT

He's recalled as the goaltender who threw up before — and sometimes during — every game. But Glenn Hall, "Mr. Goalie," should also be remembered as the goalie who threw a monkey wrench into conventional wisdom in terms of playing the position.

In the days when goaltending was primarily a stand-tall occupation, Hall opted to go down and lower himself below the bar. "Glenn Hall was the first goalie that I saw play what I call the spread eagle — the butterfly style," said fellow Hall of Famer Johnny Bower.

Ken Dryden, another Hall of Fame netminder, lists Hall as one of goaltending's true pioneers because he was the first to play the game with his face below the crossbar, and therefore risk self-preservation for effectiveness. "Glenn Hall was not only a great goaltender, he was an important goaltender," Dryden said.

Patrick Roy in the butterfly position.

As a junior goalie in Windsor, Ontario, Hall would travel across the Detroit River to watch the Red Wings and goaltender Terry Sawchuk in action. "I tried to copy his style, to use that low crouch which he played," Hall said. "I'd watch him and the league's other goalkeepers to see what they were doing right and where they had problems. It was an excellent learning experience."

Hall doesn't view himself as any sort of innovative genius, merely a guy who was the first to see a new way of stopping the puck. "It was a natural progression of goal-keeping," Hall said. "In the pre-mask days, goalies would stack their pads and keep their head away from the puck. With the butterfly, you could drop, but still keep your head up so you don't get hit. Critics said I couldn't do it and shouldn't do it, but they didn't know what they were talking about."

Glenn Hall laid out the butterfly blueprint and just two seasons after he left Chicago for St. Louis, Tony Esposito, another Black Hawks goaltender, came along to further refine the new style of puckstopping.

"We both were agile and had quickness," Esposito said of comparisons between him and Hall. "He was the beginning of the change of goaltending style."

When Esposito posted a modern-day NHL-record 15 shutouts for the Black Hawks during the 1969–70 season, it was a safe bet that the butterfly style — where the goaltender played with his legs splayed out into an inverted "V" — was here to stay.

"Aggressive goaltending," is how Esposito described his version of the butterfly. "Attacking the puck." With his lightning-quick reflexes and incredible agility, Esposito could be down to make a save and back up and in position before a shooter had time to corral the rebound. "I didn't like the stand-up style, because I felt you got caught out of position too much," Esposito explained. "There is nothing wrong with going down to stop a shot."

As Esposito's career was winding down in 1984, his way to play was about to become accepted as the most effective brand of goalkeeping.

Developments in modern equipment that offered vast improvements in both weight and protection for goalies made the butterfly style make sense. And a cocky young puckstopper from Quebec was about to take the game by storm and in the process, change the way goaltending was viewed forever. Patrick Roy was about to become the monarch of the butterfly.

He possessed all the tools to make it happen. Roy was big, athletic and supremely confident. Challenging the status quo, reinventing the way people thought about stopping the puck, that sort of audacity was right up his alley. "With his butterfly style, Roy created moves and changed the way goalies play the game," former NHL goalie and current St. Louis Blues president John Davidson said.

The genesis of a generation of Quebec-based butterfly aficionados began in the spring of 1984, when Roy was introduced to goalie guru François Allaire.

"I first met François when I was on my last junior year," Roy recalled. "What happened is the Granby Bison at the time were out of the playoffs, and [the Montreal Canadiens] decided to send me to practice with Sherbrooke [Montreal's American Hockey League farm club]. We started practicing, and then I felt François really liked the way I was playing."

In Roy, Allaire saw the perfect specimen to implement

his new way of approaching the art of puckstopping: playing percentages. Allaire was of the opinion that the most effective way to stop the puck was to rely on technique and discipline and to take away the bottom third of the net, where his studies had proven that the majority of goals were scored. And Roy was a goalie who laid on the ice so much that Montreal coach Jacques Lemaire once joked that Roy should keep a "mattress and a pillow" in his crease.

"When I saw Patrick for the first time, we matched together right away," Allaire recalled. "He was a tall and skinny kid who was going down all the time. He wasn't exactly going down at the right time and the right place, but he was going down, and he was stopping pucks more than anybody else."

Roy and Allaire helped guide Sherbrooke to the AHL title in 1985, and the next spring, the NHL rookie Roy backstopped the Habs to the Stanley Cup. And as the duo continued to refine the new style, it became widely accepted that this was the way forward for all goalies. The butterfly was here to stay.

When credit for changing the game is doled out to Roy, he deflects it to Allaire as adroitly as he turned aside shots: "François deserves a lot of credit for the way I played, especially on the butterfly," Roy says. "There were a lot of people that were saying I changed the style of goalies, but I think François was a big part of it."

THIRD DEFENSEMEN

For much of the NHL's first 50 seasons, goaltenders were forbidden to pass the puck to teammates — originally by the rules of the game, and later, by coaches fearful of the collateral damage capable of being committed by puckhandling netminders. That began to change in the 1950s, when Montreal's Jacques Plante would regularly venture from his net to get the puck for his defensemen. By the mid-1960s, other solid puckhandling goalies such as Ed Giacomin and Gary Smith emerged, but it wasn't really until a rebel with a cause emerged in the 1980s in the City of Brotherly Love that goalies handling the puck became an accepted notion in the game.

Outside of Philadelphia, he'll be forever known as one

Martin Brodeur, always a threat with the puck, prepares to move the puck up ice.

of hockey's ultimate villains. True, Ron Hextall sometimes used his stick in nefarious ways to handle intruders to his crease, but his true contribution to hockey was the way he handled the puck with his lumber. Better than any goalie before him. He possessed a harder wrist shot than some of his Flyer teammates, and could snap off a pass with such velocity that players occasionally couldn't corral it. Hextall utilized his powerful shot to twice score into empty nets during his career — once during the Stanley Cup playoffs. He was the first NHL goalie to shoot the puck the length of the ice and score a goal.

"I knew I was going to get one sooner or later, but I didn't work on scoring goals," Hextall said. "Face it. My job was to stop pucks. But if I could help the team out in other ways, like moving the puck up the ice quickly, I'd do it."

It may have been matter-of-fact to him, but his puck skills were a matter of much discussion in hockey circles. "It was stuff we hadn't seen before from a goaltender," noted former NHL player Peter McNab.

Hextall's defensemen, accustomed to coming back to the defensive zone to begin a breakout pattern, soon learned that with Hextall in net they could peel back up the boards and wait for an outlet pass from their goalie.

Mike Keenan, who coached the puckhandling goalie in Philadelphia, felt Hextall definitively changed the way the position was played. "Ron is bringing out something more, an extra dimension, than was thought to exist there in the first place," Keenan said when Hextall reached the NHL in 1987. "Change is an evolutionary process that's added to over time. It doesn't happen overnight. He'll touch the imaginations of youngsters watching him play and in a few years, one of those youngsters will come along and add to that dimension."

New Jersey Devils netminder Martin Brodeur, who arrived on the scene while Hextall was still in mid-career, was one of those youngsters who took what Hextall began and built onto the foundation.

"Brodeur handles the puck the same way Hextall did," Hall of Fame goalie Johnny Bower said, drawing comparisons to the former Flyer, who, like Brodeur, scored twice during his NHL career. "He gets it and gets it out of the zone before the other team has a chance to attack. He has great vision. He always seems to know where his wingers are up the ice and he gets the puck to them."

In fact, Brodeur became so adept at handling the puck, the NHL changed the rules to prohibit his skill. In 2005, the league instituted the trapezoid — an area behind the net delineated by two diagonal lines that start at the goal line just outside each post and run diagonally out to the boards — and prohibited goaltenders from handling the puck behind the goal line anywhere but inside that area.

Brodeur took the move to be a personal vendetta against strong puckhandling goaltenders such as himself, Marty Turco of the Dallas Stars and Rick DiPietro of the New York Islanders.

"I really don't understand the logic of taking away a talent that only a handful of goalies around the league really have," Brodeur said. "All the general managers who didn't have good puck-handling goalies voted this rule in, I'm sure. I think it's ridiculous. It takes away from the few goalies who do it."

Despite the trapezoid, puckhandling goaltenders have found ways to get to pucks before they are in restricted areas in order to help their team. And thanks to Hextall and Brodeur, puckhandling skill is one more prerequisite NHL clubs are looking for when scouting the goaltenders of the future.

RISE OF THE GOALIE GURU

When Hall of Famer Gump Worsley was traded by the New York Rangers to the Montreal Canadiens in the summer of 1963, he was immediately excited by the prospect of playing for legendary coach Toe Blake, figuring that now, he'd really gain some insight into playing goal from a brilliant hockey mind.

Much to Worsley's chagrin, Blake informed him he knew nothing about the position.

Got a problem? Figure it out yourself. This was the goaltender's lot in life well into the 1980s, before goalie-specific coaches became standard parts of an NHL staff.

"I never had a goalie coach until I was 26," noted Vancouver Canucks goalie coach and former NHL netminder Roland Melanson. "With the money that is invested in the game and the significance of the position in relation to team success, you would think every team would have been willing to do as much as possible to improve their goaltending. From minor hockey right up to pro, it was one of the most neglected areas in the game."

Phoenix Coyotes goalie coach Sean Burke, also a former NHL goaltender, sees a difference between Ilya Bryzgalov, his top student, and what he learned as a pro. "Technically, he's better than I was," Burke said. "He's come from that age group where they've worked on that technical game from the time they started. He's had a goalie coach all along."

While there is no registry or official governing body overseeing goalie camps, clinics and schools in Canada or the United States, a simple Internet search gives a good indication of how prevalent the idea of specialized goaltender training is. A 2010 Google search of "goalie schools" in Canada revealed 456,000 hits, and the same search criteria in the United States resulted in 311,000 hits. Not hardcore data, but a sure sign that there is great interest in puckstopping philosophies — three decades ago, finding a goalie-specific school would have been as likely as locating a California Golden Seals fan club.

Today, every goalie at virtually all levels of the game has a former goaltender he can turn to for advice and support. "Having a guy to talk to is good for a goalie," Detroit Red Wings netminder Chris Osgood said. "There are things that only a goalie would know and can pick out that will sharpen up your game and make you feel ready to play."

The relationship between a goalie coach and his netminders is one that can only be understood by those brave enough to strap on the gear and step in the path of vulcanized rubber missiles. "It's always nice to have someone who understands the position and who understands you when you have a bad game," San Jose Sharks goalie Evgeni Nabokov said.

Most early goalie coaches were merely ex-NHL netminders who offered a shoulder and a sounding board to their students. Today's instructors are high-tech experts who pay extreme attention to detail. Among the leaders in this department are the Allaire brothers, François and Benoit, who burst onto the scene in the mid-1980s, preaching revolutionary puckstopping methods. François, a goaltender at Sherbrooke University in the 1970s, traveled the world studying goaltending methods, and read over 200 books on the subject before opening his first goalies-only school just outside Montreal in 1978, with a handful of students. Today, he runs schools on three continents and lists hundreds of disciples to his teachings.

"I didn't know where I was going, but I got good success right away," said François Allaire, who was Patrick Roy's first goalie coach in the pros. "The goalies at that time, the information was so thin and so dry that I think that our guys got more information than anybody else, and we were ahead of the business."

The Allaire system of netminding is all about playing the percentages, a style as simple as it is successful. Its theories are built around sound positional play and steadfast dedication to discipline. Key components in its implementation involve staying square to the shooter at all times and, when going down to the ice, bringing the knees

together under the body and the feet of each leg out toward each post in order to take away the bottom part of the net.

"It's a technique that's simple to use, a foundation that I stay with whenever things go wrong or go right," said Toronto Maple Leafs goalie Jean-Sébastien Giguère, who first studied under François Allaire while with the Anaheim Ducks, and is again under his tutelage in Toronto. "He just brought my game back to a very simple way of playing. François gave me confidence by giving me tools in my bag to work with. He gave me a foundation to use."

INTERNATIONAL GAME CHANGERS

There was a time when European netminders were about as sought after as import cars on North American soil. With the wider ice surfaces of European rinks and the emphasis on lateral puck movement, netminders across the pond tended to stay back in the crease, understanding that to play the angles in such a style of hockey would too easily take them out of position on a quick passing play.

It was the polar opposite of the way NHL goalies were taught to foil shooters in their smaller arenas, so the thinking was that a European goaltender could never survive against NHL shooters.

That thinking began to change with the performance of Soviet goalie Vladislav Tretiak against Team Canada in the 1972 Summit Series. With further expansion to the NHL, by the late 1970s, European goalies were slowly beginning to make their way across the Atlantic Ocean. They became more prevalent in the 1980s, and today, some of the elite puckstoppers in the NHL own a European birth certificate.

THE MAGICIAN

Often overlooked when listing the greatest European netminders, there are those who believe Czech star Jiri Holecek — who shone internationally in the late 1960s and through the 70s — was not only the best goalie of his era, he may very well have been ahead of his time in terms of his style of play. Many would also list him ahead of Hall of Famer Vladislav Tretiak as the best goaltender who never played in the NHL.

Jiri Holecek makes a kick save.

Holecek stood 5-foot-11, which was large for a goalie of his era, and played an unorthodox style between the posts that was quite similar to the modern butterfly. He was a student of the game equipped with tremendous anticipation skills, lightning-fast reflexes and strong legs that he'd spread across the goal line from post to post and take away the lower half of the net.

In his homeland where he represented his country a record 164 times in international play, Holecek was known as "Kouzelnik" (The Magician) due to his acrobatics in goal. He saved some of his best work for games against the rival Soviet Union, adjusting his style somewhat to deal with the slick Russian stickhandlers. "I usually liked to skate out a bit to face the shooters, but against [the Russians] I stood on the goal line," Holecek told author Joe Pelletier. "Trying to skate out of your crease to cut the angles against the Russians would have been suicide."

After retiring in 1982, Holecek became a goalie coach and one of his first pupils was Dominik Hasek, in whose game it's easy to see similarities to Holecek's technique.

Many European hockey historians believe that if Holecek had been exposed to a North American audience as frequently as Tretiak was, he'd have been the goalie pursued by NHL teams. And some feel that if Holecek had been in goal for the Soviets in 1972, they'd have defeated the NHL stars.

TRETIAK THE GREAT

There are two schools of thought when it comes to Vladislav Tretiak, the legendary goaltender for the Soviet Union's powerhouse squads of the 1970s and early 1980s.

Some view him as one of hockey's absolute best puck-stoppers. "Tretiak is a legend no matter what country you come from," Ottawa Senators Russian defenseman Sergei Gonchar said. "Everybody in the world knows how unbelievable he was for Team Russia. He was one of the best ever. When he walks the streets of Montreal, everyone recognizes him. That's how great he was."

Still, others see him as being fortunate enough to play behind one of hockey's greatest juggernauts.

One factor is certain — before Tretiak's handling of Team Canada's powerful scorers in the 1972 Summit Series, European netminders were seen as inferior to their North American counterparts. "Before the series began, we were told Vladislav Tretiak was a poor goaltender, that we'd win all eight games," Bobby Orr recalled.

The netminder remembered the low opinion the NHLers held of him and his teammates. "Before the [first] game, Team Canada didn't even acknowledge we were there," Tretiak said. "They didn't say hello to us. They didn't even look at us. Each Canadian player said, 'Oh, Russians have no good players. There's no possible way they can play with us. Maybe we'll score 12 goals.'"

Tretiak and company changed that line of thinking, as the Soviets posted a 7–3 win.

"After the game, the next morning, Canadian players were coming up to us and saying, 'Oh, hello. Hello, buddy,'" Tretiak said.

As big as the 1972 series was, Tretiak described his sensational 35-save performance in a 3–3 tie with the Montreal Canadiens on New Year's Eve, 1975, as "my best game ever."

Others disagree. "The final of the 1981 Canada Cup," suggested former Russian teammate Igor Larionov, recalling one of the many great nights Tretiak had in goal for the former Soviet Union in an 8–1 rout of Canada. "We were outshot 20–3 in the first period and we were ahead. This was the best game I have ever seen a goaltender play."

Tretiak also came close to making history as the first Soviet player to skate in the NHL. The Canadiens drafted him in 1983, with hopes of bringing him to the NHL after the 1984 Sarajevo Winter Olympics, but the Soviets would hear none of it. "Nobody ever officially asked me if I wanted to play for the Canadiens," Tretiak recalled. "But I know that unofficially there were talks. It might have been interesting. I was born too early."

His prominence in the former Soviet Union was unquestioned. One day, while then-Soviet president Leonid Brezhnev was riding through Moscow in his limousine, shades drawn, he spotted Tretiak walking down the street. Brezhnev rolled down his window and had his driver slow the car so he could call out and wave to Tretiak.

THE LINDBERGH FLYER

In life, Pelle Lindbergh was remembered as much for his wit as for his sensational ability between the pipes. During warm-ups, he'd step aside and let low-scoring teammate Brad Marsh dent the twine, a way of teasing Marsh about his lack of a powerful shot. In his locker, he kept a miniature Swedish flag, a symbol of Lindbergh's homeland, but also an indication that the European goalie had arrived in the NHL to stay.

Before Lindbergh, there were a handful of Swedish goaltenders that tested North American waters. Kjell Svensson became the first European-trained goalie to suit up for an NHL team when he played for the Toronto Maple Leafs in pre-season action in 1963. Svensson fared well enough to be offered a spot on Toronto's AHL affiliate, the Rochester Americans. Ultimately, he opted to return home instead, helping Sweden skate to a silver medal at the 1964 Winter Olympic Games in Innsbruck. A decade later, other Swedes followed Svensson's lead. In the mid-1970s, Christer Abrahamsson and Leif Holmqvist played

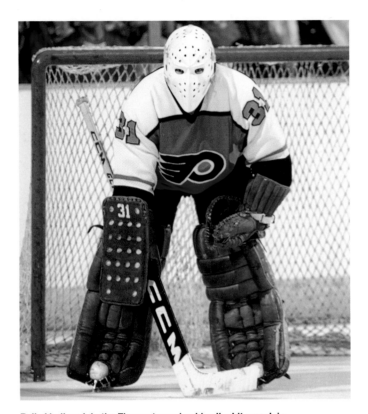

Pelle Lindbergh in the Flyer net wearing his all-white mask in homage to former Flyer great and goaltending coach, Bernie Parent.

in the World Hockey Association, and Goran Hogosta (New York Islanders) and Hardy Astrom (New York Rangers) joined NHL clubs. Hogosta and Astrom struggled to make the grade as regular NHL puckstoppers, and Astrom became the subject of many of Don Cherry's tales about the woeful Colorado Rockies he coached in 1979–80.

Lindbergh, though, was the real deal. During the 1984–85 campaign, Lindbergh, who wore an all-white mask to pay homage to legendary Flyer goalie Bernie Parent (his childhood hero), backstopped the Philadelphia Flyers to the Stanley Cup final. He played 65 games that season and won the Vezina Trophy, marking the first time the award had been earned by a European goalie. The future seemed unlimited for this budding star.

"I hadn't played with a foreign player before," former Flyers defenseman Doug Crossman recalled to the *Philadelphia Inquirer*. "The thing Pelle had was what a lot of them have — innocence. He had innocent ways of saying things, and he'd make us laugh. But when the game started, I'd look back there and see him do amazing things. He was some kind of goaltender."

By November 1986, Lindbergh was dead, killed in a car accident, a budding career cut down at the age of 26. No Flyer has worn No. 31, Lindbergh's number, since his death.

"He was the best goalie in hockey and there's no doubt he won a lot of games for us," former Flyers forward Tim Kerr said.

Though his star shone but briefly on the big stage, Lindbergh's legacy was that he'd accomplished a major feat, proving that a European-trained goaltender could be an NHL star.

THE DOMINATOR

As a youngster, he marveled at the way No. 9 performed on the ice, was awed by how he completely dominated play, and continued to dominate from his teenage years and for decades to come. Jiri Fischer could have easily been talking about Maurice Richard or Gordie Howe, a pair of No. 9s many grew up idolizing, but his No. 9 performed closer to home.

That's because Fischer's hero was — and is — Dominik Hasek, his former Detroit Red Wings teammate.

"When I was a little kid, even before I started playing hockey, I remember watching him playing for Pardubice [in the Czech League]," Fischer said. "He was only 17 and was wearing No. 9 on his jersey, but he was already the No. 1 goalie in Czechoslovakia."

In the Czech Republic, Hasek is held in the highest regard. "He is our Michael Jordan," Fischer explained. "Our Muhammad Ali."

"I don't think anyone in sport from our country has accomplished as much. He's put our little country on the map."

Coming to North America in 1990 at the age of 25, Hasek also put the NHL on notice that modern schools of thought toward puckstopping were going to have to undergo a paradigm shift. Trying to pinpoint Hasek's style, to get a book on him, was like trying to score on him — virtually impossible. He was the Picasso of the goal crease. Part butterfly, part Baryshnikov, part Gumby, nobody did it like him.

Dominik Hasek takes a breather during the 1994–95 campaign, his second of six straight seasons leading the league in save percentage.

Then. Or now.

He'd lay his body across the goal line. Race to the blueline to poke a puck away from an onrushing forward. Toss his stick aside and scoop up the puck with the fingers of his blocker. Twist and turn to make seemingly impossible saves, as if he had a Slinky for a spine. He'd even work in practice at deliberately turning aside shots with his forehead, like a soccer player heading a ball.

"Hasek came along and created his own moves," St. Louis Blues president and former NHL goalie John Davidson said.

"He was a goaltender without a style," added Hall of Fame netminder Johnny Bower.

And yet it was a style that worked better than anyone else of his era. Hasek owned the Vezina Trophy, winning it six times, and remains the only NHL goalie to twice win the Hart Trophy as league MVP.

It may have been difficult to pinpoint Hasek's method of puckstopping, but perfection was the goal of this goalie. "Dominik Hasek's work habits are legendary," Detroit Red

Wings goalie coach Jim Bedard said. "He never gave up, just battled, battled, battled. That's why he made great saves, because he knew he could make the third save if he had to. Good wasn't good enough for him. He had to be the best."

Hall of Famer Scotty Bowman, who coached Hasek in Detroit, compared him to another Hall of Fame innovator, Jacques Plante, who played for Bowman in St. Louis.

"They were different styles of goalies, but very similar in that they were both perfectionists, dedicated to fitness and determined to always find ways to improve," Bowman said. "They were definitely unique individuals, but both men played the game with a lot of confidence."

Asked to explain what inspired him, Hasek's answer wasn't complicated, even if the task he asked of himself was.

"Hockey is supposed to be fun," Hasek explained. "For me, fun is stopping all the shots."

WOMEN OF INFLUENCE

Pioneers push the boundaries. They break new ground. They tread where no one before has sought to go.

That was definitely the case with the inaugural group of female puckstoppers. Taming the best of the shooters their side of the game had to offer, they didn't settle for that level of dominance. Seeking to improve their own game, and in turn, also grow the quality of their own brand of hockey, these early women puckstopping elite crossed over and challenged the men to find a way to beat them.

LIGHTNING STRIKES

It doesn't matter to Manon Rheaume how or why she became the first woman to participate in an NHL game. It only matters that she did it, and that she succeeded at it.

The expansion team Tampa Bay Lightning gave Rheaume the start in goal for a September 23, 1992, exhibition game against the St. Louis Blues, making Rheaume the first female to play in the pro ranks. She allowed two goals on nine shots in her one period of work.

Years later, Lightning general manager Phil Esposito admitted he only signed Rheaume as a publicity stunt, but Rheaume saw it merely as a chance for her to prove she

belonged at that level of the game. "When I got invited to Tampa Bay, at that point, I didn't care why they invited me, Rheaume told the *Calgary Herald*. "I had an opportunity to play at the highest level possible." Rheaume said. "So many times, people said no to me because I was a girl. I thought, 'If they are saying yes to me because I'm a girl now, I'll do it.' I look back now and I'm happy I took that chance, because it changed my life."

To others in the women's game, it was what Rheaume, and other female goalies who played in men's leagues such as Erin Whitten, returned to their own brand of hockey that was most significant. "The visibility they got from playing in those men's leagues games was great for our sport," said U.S. defender Angela Ruggiero, a four-time Olympian. "They also brought a lot back to the women's game, raising the bar and challenging the shooters and forcing the women players to get better to be able to beat them. We all had to learn to shoot the puck better, because they were unbeatable back in the day."

Already the first female to play in the world-famous Quebec International Peewee Tournament, Rheaume delivered many other firsts for the women's game, starting November 26, 1991, when she replaced Jocelyn Thibault in goal for the Trois-Rivières Draveurs, becoming the first woman to play in a regular-season Quebec Major Junior Hockey League game.

"She was with our farm team, and she got called up for the game," recalled Pascal Rheaume, Manon's brother and a future NHLer who was his sister's teammate that night. "She was the backup goalie, but we were down 6–1, and Jocelyn Thibault got pulled and she went in. I was really nervous for her, but she did a great job."

On December 13, 1992, Manon became the first woman to play in a regular-season professional game when she appeared in the Atlanta Knights' 4–1 International Hockey League loss to Salt Lake City.

Pascal is one of the few NHL players who has a sister who is more famous in hockey, but he doesn't mind one bit. "I'll always be Manon's brother," he said. "But that's okay. She deserves the recognition. I'm really proud of all that she's accomplished."

The bond between brother and sister has been strengthened by their shared experiences in hockey. "I'm so impressed with what she's been able to do," Pascal said. "I didn't think she'd stick with hockey. I thought she would quit as she got older, but instead, she has gone out and accomplished things that no other woman has done."

A two-time women's world champion and an Olympic silver medalist in 1998, Manon Rheaume played 24 games in men's minor league action between 1992 and 1997 and suited up one more time for the International League's Flint Generals in 2009, but finds it difficult to view herself as a women's hockey pioneer.

"I wouldn't say that I'm the only one who helped promote the game," she said.

RAISING THE BAR

Like every kid donning a pair of skates, Erin Whitten's dream was to go as far as she could in hockey, and if that meant barging through doors that were previously closed, then so be it.

"I grew up playing boys' hockey and every boy growing up playing hockey wants to make it to the NHL," Whitten said. "For us, we didn't really have an opportunity to make it to the NHL, or so we thought.

"My goal was to keep playing and to figure out how I could get myself to stay in shape for national team hockey, and to also to see how far I could go and, I guess, how far teams would let me go. How far I could push the envelope.

"For me, it was really just the challenge to be in the sport that I loved and to continue on the path that I was hoping would take me to the Olympics."

Playing at the elite level of the women's game wasn't the deep challenge during Whitten's career that it is today, which was one reason she sought to improve herself by facing men on the ice.

"In 1992, for the next four or five years, there were a lot of women who I played with that kind of stayed consistent over that time," Whitten said. "I would say probably after the first five years or so, there was really a big jump when the college players got in, you could see the level going up and up and up. That's why I think I was fortunate

to be in as early as I was. There's times when I look at it today and I find myself wondering if I would make a team as compared to 10 or 15 years ago. New players come in each year and the freshmen look better than the seniors by halfway through the year. It's a tough road for a lot of the older players. It's so much of a challenge to make the Olympic team. The pool has grown so much.

"I think when I was playing, it was a much smaller group to pull from. Today, you've got college programs being run nationally, you've got players going up to play in the Canadian league. There are women who are jumping into the highest level they can to stay a part of it, but they're always fighting a battle with the younger players, who are stronger and have been training to be a Division I NCAA player since their freshman year in high school."

Whitten's résumé is littered with significant lists of firsts: the first woman to win a professional hockey game; the first woman to record a complete-game victory in the pros; the first U.S.-born female goaltender to play pro hockey; and the first woman to suit up for a game in the American, East Coast, Central and Colonial Hockey Leagues. But Whitten never viewed herself as a groundbreaker as much as she was simply looking to get a break.

"I was really just playing," Whitten said. "The accolades and the things that came along with it, the recognition for being the first at doing a couple of things, it wasn't anything I strove for. It was just something that happened along the way.

"I am very proud of what I accomplished. People gave me an opportunity and I was fortunate enough to be a part of it."

On October 30, 1993, Whitten backstopped the Toledo Storm to a 6–5 ECHL victory over Dayton, becoming the first woman to win a pro game.

"There were quite few key goalies from the early years who come to mind and Erin was definitely one of them," said Michele Amidon, former U.S. national team player and general manager of the 2010 U.S. women's Olympic team. "I was fortunate enough to be a teammate of Erin's. She was a standout goalie who was always tough to compete against, as an opponent, or in practice if she was on your team. She did a great job in the pros, playing with the boys. Now she's turned that into a career."

These days, Whitten is an assistant coach with the women's team at the University of New Hampshire.

"It's been a great experience," she said. "I don't think I ever thought I'd be having this experience. I never wanted to coach hockey. It wasn't my ultimate goal. I fell into it, but I'm fortunate that I did, because I really truly love coaching and teaching and being a part of these kids' lives for four years. You help to build something. It's nice to be able to pass along my knowledge and to learn a little more from them. It's great to have some sort of impact on their lives."

Many in the game would suggest Whitten had already accomplished that goal by playing as well as she did.

"People have said it before, so I guess I'm used to hearing it," Whitten said about the impact she's had on younger generations. "It's been so long since I've played, I don't know if it makes a difference anymore. It's a little odd at times.

"It's what I love to do. It's what I wanted to do."

KELLY'S A HERO

Kelly Dyer's path to between the pipes started out no differently than most young goalies. She was the younger sibling, and there was just one option open to her if she wanted to play with the big boys.

"I have a brother David, who is two years older than me," Dyer explained. "I was the youngest kid in the neighborhood and the only girl of the crew. So they said, 'Yeah, you can play with us. Get in the net.'"

Almost immediately, Dyer was a groundbreaking goaltender. "I was very fortunate," she said. "I played for Assabet Valley Girls Ice Hockey Program in Concord, Massachusetts. It's one of the original women's programs in the U.S. I think they started in 1977. They're super strong now. They had 310 girls last season."

In the high school ranks, Dyer earned the back-up spot on the boys team at Acton-Boxborough, playing behind No. 1 goalie Tom Barrasso, an idea which didn't sit well with the Barrasso family.

"They weren't overly friendly to me during that time," Dyer recalled. "The problem was that Mr. Barrasso kind of got it in his head that having a woman back-up for his son might hurt Tommy's chances of getting high-level recognition. He felt that if they have a girl back-up, people might think that the league's not very good. Of course, Tommy went right from high school to the Buffalo Sabres, so it didn't hurt him at all.

"I'm friendly with Tom Barrasso now, because we served on the USA Hockey athletic committee together. Actually, my husband hit it off with him great because they both love to hunt.

"It's pretty funny. Now we sit around and talk, but back then, he wouldn't speak to any of the little peon goalies. But just to have the opportunity to watch him practice and play every day. He was so amazing and so focused every day of practice and at games. It was pretty cool to have the exposure at that time to a kid who was so talented and so focused."

Dyer was part of history, tending goal for the United States in the 1990 World Championships, the first for women's hockey. "The 1990 World Championships were pivotal for everything moving forward in women's hockey," Dyer said. "That was the test event for the International Ice Hockey Federation to see if it would be approved for the Olympic Games. Just being part of that event makes you a pioneer, because it was the first ever."

Dyer played in the gold-medal game, which saw Canada defeat the United States 5–2 before 8,784 fans at the Ottawa Civic Centre. "I couldn't believe that so many people were so excited about women's hockey," recalled Dyer, named MVP of the event. "It was in Ottawa and the arena was sold out. It was the largest attendance to ever witness a women's hockey game when we played Canada in the final. The sound from the crowd was actually vibrating my body, because they were cheering so loudly. The energy in the building was so alive. You couldn't hear yourself talk to your teammates."

Like Manon Rheaume and Erin Whitten before her, Dyer eventually played pro hockey, suiting up for Jacksonville and West Palm Beach in the Sunshine Hockey League.

"It was out of necessity," Dyer said. "We had no other place to play. I'd already graduated college and was playing

Kelly Dyer makes a glove save against Canada in 1990 at the first ever Women's World Championships.

men's league, Senior A, on Sundays. You couldn't stay on the ice enough and be challenged enough with the options we had to stay competitive. With the national team, we'd be in camp two, three, four times a year and the world championships were just on even years."

Dyer's pro opportunity developed completely by chance. "I was asked to play in a summer pro league when the goalie didn't show up," she said. "That's where I met former Boston Bruins goalie Doug Keans. He was the one who invited me to a tryout with Jacksonville of the Sunshine Hockey League. It was kind of fun the way the whole thing turned out."

Dyer made more women's hockey history once she turned pro. She was the first woman to be traded by a professional team when Jacksonville shipped her to West Palm Beach midway through the 1993–94 season.

"I went away to a Christmas camp with the U.S. team and when I came back, I had been traded," Dyer recalled.

"At first, it was an awful feeling. Little did I know at the time it would be the best thing ever. West Palm Beach is beautiful. I was on the best team, with the best organization. Our owner was [former NHL defenseman] Bill Nyrop. Everything was first class. We were paid regularly. I got a free rental car. And then we went on to win the three Sunshine League championships while I was there — without any big contributions from me, I might add.

"We had this awesome goalie named Todd Bojcun. He was just phenomenal. The reason I got traded there was because he got hurt — strained his MCL. It was a nice way to enter a team, because I was actually needed. I came in under a legitimate situation, other than just being the female attraction. But as it turned out, they sold out my first five or six home starts, so Bill Nyrop was pleased about that."

Dyer retired following the 1995–96 season and went to work helping Louisville TPS Hockey Equipment develop female-specific hockey gear. "I still have my original pieces," Dyer said. "The line was first launched October 1, 1996. Cammi Granato, Lisa Brown-Miller, Erin Whitten and myself were the prototypes for the gear. We actually used their proportions for our sizes, large, medium, small. It was fun and gave me the ability to sign my friends to endorsement contracts."

Today, Dyer still works as an equipment rep with Brian's Goal Equipment and Cascade sports and reminisces about the spartan existence early women players like herself lived through. "Everything from the Olympics to what it's done for women's hockey programs for both USA Hockey and Hockey Canada in making a full commitment to both programs, it's pretty amazing," Dyer said of the advances in women's hockey, in terms of both depth and attention. "I remember back then, we got two cotton sweat suits and one jacket which was just a windbreaker. And we were so excited to receive those three items. And now, they've got inside travel suits, outside travel suits, training suits, pre-game suits. It's pretty funny how much they get now."

CRAZY LIKE A FOX

BY BRIAN HAYWARD

I **GREW UP IN TORONTO** at the height of the last Maple Leaf dynasty and, like most kids my age, I idolized the Toronto players. However, I rarely got to see the Leafs play live because tickets were too expensive. But one day, when I was eight years old, my father took me to watch the Leafs practice at Maple Leaf Gardens. That was my chance to collect autographs.

One of my idols was Leaf netminder Johnny Bower, and I can still recall how intimidated I was as I approached him to ask for his signature. It wasn't because I was particularly shy, or that I was in awe of an athlete I had heard so much about. It wasn't because he was unwelcoming, either. As a matter of fact, Bower was quite the opposite. He was all smiles, and he engaged each person in rather animated conversation. What intimidated me was the fact that I was quite convinced that Johnny Bower was crazy.

Brian Hayward's one-piece mask from his days in San Jose. One-piece masks are designed to deflect the puck on impact, as opposed to blocking the puck and absorbing the blow, which lessens the overall impact of a puck to the head.

Johnny Bower takes a puck in the face to thwart a
Montreal Canadien scoring chance.

And not just a little bit. Goalies in those days wore no masks, and getting hit in the head was an accepted occupational hazard. I had seen a replay on television of a save Bower had made with his face. The thing about it was that it didn't seem accidental: Bower had his arms pinned behind him in such a manner that he had nothing but his face available to try and block a shot, so that's what he did, willingly.

There are two highlights of my own career that make me think I must have been at least a little crazy to be a goalie. Not as crazy as Johnny Bower mind you, but crazy nonetheless. The first incident happened one night in Winnipeg. My Jets teammates and I were hosting the Calgary Flames, and Calgary was on a 5-on-3 power play.

During our penalty kill, my mask was knocked off my head but play continued on. (They didn't blow the play dead when this happened, as they do in today's NHL.) Inevitably, the puck bounced off a leg and rolled, on edge, directly out in front of the net. Al MacInnis — he of the hardest-slapshot-in-the-game fame — skated in full stride to hammer one of his patented one-timers from 25 feet away. Up on my toes, fully upright and stretching my neck upward as high as I could in order to get my bare face as far away from the ice surface as possible, I watched MacInnis blast the puck over my right shoulder (what seemed like inches then, was, in retrospect, probably more like a couple of feet). The puck bounced off the top of the glass and thankfully bounced out of play, which was a good thing, since my knees would not stop shaking from the only near-death experience of my life. A few days later, one of my coaches commented that I appeared to be flinching on shots in practice, a cardinal sin for goalies. I thought of it more as a survival instinct.

Time would take care of the flinching habit, since after a few days of getting hit by pucks without any significant damage being done, your brain tells you that it's okay to again do what you've been trained to do. Being able to forget quickly has always been a valuable personality trait for any competitive goaltender. Coaches call it the ability to "shake it off." This applies to bad goals, bad games and injuries. The quicker you can forget and move on, the better.

The second moment of my career that made me think twice about my sanity was while I was playing with the Montreal Canadiens. At training camp in 1988, a fresh-faced, 19-year-old kid named Mathieu Schneider ripped the first shot of an early morning practice directly at the middle of my forehead. I was slow to react. It was early into the training camp session, and I was easing into things and getting the cobwebs out. My headgear in those days consisted of what people called the "helmet and cage combination," a style of mask made popular by Russia's Vladislav Tretiak. Unfortunately, my Cooper SK 600 helmet wasn't really up to the task. Unlike today's modern goalie mask that has no flat surfaces on the forehead so as to deflect a puck from any angle and reduce the amount of impact on the goalie, the forehead part of the SK 600 was perfectly flat. Any shot direct to the forehead didn't have to break the helmet to inflict a nasty pressure cut behind the mask. Pressure cuts result when the pressure from the impact actually pops open the skin, forming a jagged cut that looks like a marble has just exploded out of your being, or in this case the middle of my forehead.

Schneider's shot knocked me out cold, and when I regained consciousness after just a few seconds, I could feel blood streaming down both sides of my face. If you have ever suffered a head cut of any type and there was

Hayward wearing his Cooper SK 600 helmet-and-cage style head protection during his time in Montreal.

no mirror readily available, you know that you are left to imagine the extent of the damage by gauging the reactions of people around you. In this case, the first man on the scene was teammate Chris "Knuckles" Nilan, who instantly yelled to the training staff in his South Boston accent, "Somebody call the plastic surgeon or this kid's gonna look like a monster!" Nice. Thirty-two stitches later, the team doctor had finished suturing a star-shaped pressure cut and I was sent home to rest for a few days. I did a fair amount of soul searching in those days immediately following the injury, wondering if the whole pro-goalie thing was really worth it. Maybe it was time to put my business degree to work? But just like my Al MacInnis experience, I quickly forgot about what happened and could not wait to rejoin my team and get back on the ice. I returned to action about four or five days later, with a custom steel half-moon cage protecting my forehead. Whenever I see Mathieu Schneider, I remind him about the incident. He usually just laughs.

The notion that all goaltenders must be crazy to subject themselves to the dangers of the position has been around for some time. Talk to most any NHL forward or defenseman and ask him how he interacts with his goalie on game day and you'll most often get the response, "I stay away from him." We've all heard the term "different breed" applied to goalies when players and coaches are asked to describe what their goalies are like, and to me, "different breed" seems more like a catchphrase for "I have absolutely no clue."

Dana Sinclair, a sports psychologist who works with a number of professional sports franchises, including several NHL teams, dedicates her time to helping athletes overcome whatever emotional hurdles are holding them back from realizing their athletic potential. Of almost equal importance is for her to identify the individual triggers that coaches might be able to exploit to induce better performance. Dana's take on the NHL goalie, even through generalized observations, is quite interesting, as illustrated in the following three points.

1) GOALIES TEND TO BE LOWER ON THE SOCIABILITY SCALE AND SOMEWHAT LESS VERBOSE THAN THE MAJORITY OF THEIR TEAMMATES.

Outside of the shared objective to win games, goalies actually have little in common with the rest of their team — their experience is different from that of forwards and defensemen. Goalies train differently, both on and off the ice. They use visualization as part of their preparation to a much higher degree than their mates. Their gear is completely different. They skate differently. They are looking for completely different things when they sit in on team video sessions. In other words, goalies are completely specialized.

Walk into any NHL locker room after the morning skate and more often than not you will find the starting goalie talking with the other goalie. Goalies also tend to be less social than their teammates because even within their own locker room, they are perceived to be outsiders, and are often treated as such. A former teammate of mine, currently an NHL coach, was not at all impressed when it came to goalies getting vocally involved in team meetings. If you offered up an opinion, he would shout, "Just shut up and stop the puck!" While this attitude has softened in the past decade, there is still an underlying current in the hockey community that goalies should not be offering up advice on what needs to happen on the ice to produce more wins. They have their unique place. Roberto Luongo aside (he's the captain of the Vancouver Canucks), there are very few card-carrying members of the goalies union who are vocal leaders inside their locker rooms.

2) GOALIES ARE "QUIET REASONERS" WHO TEND TO BE VERY INTROSPECTIVE.

This could be attributed to goalies developing their own unique playing style primarily on their own. While there is no question that you can coach basic fundamental techniques to any beginner, those at the top of the goaltending food chain (all NHL goalies) get there because as amateurs, they alone recognize the cause-and-effect relationship between what they do and whether or not they stop the puck or the shot goes into the net. A goalie will see the same shot from a similar spot on the ice thousands of times in practice over the course of any one season, and he uses this repetition to fully develop the techniques that work best for his own unique physical characteristics. If a puck were to be shot from the same spot on the ice against Martin Brodeur, Luongo or Ryan Miller, the manner in which each would stop the puck would look quite different. Each has figured out for himself the exact best way of stopping the puck in most every circumstance. Quiet reasoning has led him to that point.

Most people believe that the goaltender has more pressure on him than any other member of his team. But here is the thing: Goalies (especially the really good ones) don't really see it that way at all. They have spent most of their lifetime preparing for hard-to-stop pucks. It's what they do. They believe wingers, centermen and defensemen all have their jobs to do as well. From the goalies' perspective, the pressure the other position players feel to perform well is equal to the pressure a goalie feels. Goaltending guru François Allaire has an expression he uses when he is pushing his exhausted goalies through repetitive on-ice movement drills. When you've finished your work, he says, "Now that's in your bank." In other words, you've done the hard work and have mastered the technique. Now just go out and play, and let your good practice habits bear fruit. You shouldn't feel any more pressure than anybody else because you've done everything you could to prepare. Just play.

3) GOALIES ARE VERY ANALYTICAL.

This could be viewed as a self-preservation mechanism, as goalies are the last line of defense and blame can always go to the goaltender for virtually every goal scored. And it should. I believe there is almost no such thing as an unstoppable shot. If you disagree with this, just think about all of the amazing "I can't believe he stopped that" saves you've seen on highlight reels.

However, after a goal has been scored, and certainly after the videotape is reviewed, goalies look back at the whole play and can tell when and how every defensive breakdown in front of them occurred. Mostly they keep this information to themselves, but trust me, the goalie in question can tell you which center lost the key faceoff, or which winger failed to get the puck out of the defensive zone, or which defenseman failed to cover the backdoor pass. If you need further evidence of this, check out NHL television broadcasts. Goalies have gravitated to the broadcast booths much the same way catchers dominate baseball telecasts. *Hockey Night in Canada* alone has four former goalies as analysts on their English broadcast roster: Greg Millen, Kelly Hrudey, Kevin Weekes and Glen Healy. As further evidence of the analytical ability of goaltenders, consider the success some former goalies are having at the executive level in the NHL. John Davidson is now the team president of the St. Louis Blues. Jim Rutherford and Ken Holland are both current NHL general managers whose teams have won Stanley Cups in the past five years.

So, are goalies crazy? I would argue, no. The stereotype of the crazy goaltender (social misfit, different breed) that players, coaches and others in the hockey community have perpetuated simply doesn't hold up anymore. Aside from the differences between goaltenders and other position players that arise from the specific demands of the goaltending position, goalies aren't any crazier than a shot-blocking defenseman or a glove-dropping enforcer. They have a role, and they try their best to execute that role dutifully.

I would also argue that today's goaltenders could never be considered crazy on the same level as the goaltenders of the pre-mask days, as goaltending equipment has evolved more than any other athlete's equipment in any sport, from both a protective and functional standpoint. Relative to the era that I played in, and certainly the era that Johnny Bower starred in, you rarely see a goaltender hurt by a shot in today's game. The worry about black eyes, face contusions, broken bones and knocked-out teeth is a thing of the past. Statistics bear this out in that the most common injury among modern-era NHL goaltenders is a torn hip labrum, not a head injury. Hip injuries and groin pulls are hardly occupational hazards that might get you thinking about changing jobs once you've reached the pinnacle of your profession. Add the fact that the goalie-interference rule has significantly reduced the number of in-game collisions, and I would warrant that the position has never been safer.

Men like Johnny Bower, Terry Sawchuk and Jacques Plante certainly put themselves in danger when they were in the line of fire, but today, a goalie is just another great athlete in a sport full of great athletes. The average salary of the 10 highest paid NHL goalies for the 2009–10 season was $6.2 million. Are goalies today still different? Most certainly. But crazy? Crazy like a fox, perhaps.

Photo Credits

Index